W9-AHU-017

The
Supreme Court
vs.
The Constitution

Gerald Walpin

The Supreme Court vs. The Constitution. **Copyright © 2013** Significance Press

All rights reserved.

Printed in the United States of America
First Printing, 2013

ISBN-13: 978-0-9886509-1-6

Significance Press
200 Park Avenue, 26th Floor
New York, NY 10166
www.SignificancePress.com

Cover Design by Jaye Medalia

To The Three Generations of My Love:
My Wonderful Life Partner, My Wife Sheila;
Our Three Children
Amanda, Ned, and Jennifer
and
The Six Children They Produced
Who Provide
Their Grandparents With Great Pleasure

CONTENTS

ACKNOWLEDGMENTS

There are many people whose advice and contribution were invaluable in helping me complete this book.

My wife, Sheila, although – perhaps because – she is not a lawyer, patiently read every word to provide her reaction to whether it was clear, convincing, and free of unnecessary legalese, offered her advice where it was not, and thus further moved the book to be understandable to non-lawyers.

I am forever appreciative of those who read the draft text and provided a "blurb" encapsulating their complimentary comments on my endeavor: General Michael Mukasey, Professor John Yoo, Leonard Leo, Andrew C. McCarthy, Hon. David M. McIntosh, and Professor Lillian BeVier – each of whom provided me a role model in their individual substantial contribution to respect for our Constitution and the rule of law.

Others who were unselfish in giving their time and invaluable critiques included my friends Dean Reuter and Joseph Zuckerman. To them, I am extremely grateful.

Finally, I would be remiss if I did not recognize and thank the indefatigable, able, and always patient people at Significance Press, without whom my conceived idea would likely never have reached this finished book: Robert Dilenschneider (the leader, who never failed to provide thoughtful direction as needed), and his multi-talented staff: Joe Tessitore, Jim Zebora, Bob Berkowitz, Robert Laird, Leo J. Murray, Patrick Malone, Alexis Morley, and Joan Avagliano.

I.

INTRODUCTION

Why did I decide to write this book? Simply because I love this country. I am thus unhappy that various basic principles, values and rules on which this country was established, in the Declaration Of Independence and the Constitution, are being discarded, and replaced by many notions contrary to those our Founding Fathers held sacred.

I believe that most Americans still espouse and support our Founders' principles codified in those two documents, which have structured and protected our country from its birth. Yet, as this book details, within my lifetime, the Supreme Court, tasked with upholding the Constitution, has in fact seriously eroded and altered the rules and principles in those documents as provided by our Founders. This has happened because some justices have substituted their personal view of what the law should be for what the Constitution prescribed and what the law – as enacted by Congress and state legislatures – is.

In a 2011 speech given to the Federal Bar Council at the Waldorf-Astoria Hotel in New York,[1] Supreme Court Justice Samuel Alito referred to various surveys "conducted to see how much the American people know about the Constitution," and the "not too good" results. He opined, "this is to be regretted" because "ordinary citizens should know more *facts* about the Constitution." I am optimistic that the facts in this book concerning the Constitution, and a sampling of misguided Supreme Court decisions – supposedly applying the Constitution, but in fact changing it – will help fulfill Justice Alito's aspiration. This book will thereby enhance Americans' knowledge of how the Constitution is being misused and ignored.

> *"They alter significantly the rules affecting all Americans' security, safety, values and future – essentially your life, liberty and pursuit of happiness."*

My hope is that this book can provide to all Americans, including the overwhelming number who are not lawyers, with a simple, but not simplistic, understanding of what is happening to our Constitution. That knowledge hopefully would induce the reader, together with other awakened countrymen, to take the steps necessary to turn the tide back to the America our Founders envisaged.

Undoubtedly, most Americans obtain some knowledge of actions taken by the president, by Congress, and by the Supreme Court, altering or even discarding previously accepted rules, legal principles and values. That knowledge may be obtained online or from a 30-second report on radio or television or from a newspaper article. None of these sources can be expected to provide the public with a meaningful explanation, understandable to all Americans, of how the action altered our country's direction from what our Founders intended and prescribed. Most Americans quietly continue their lives with little attention to these changes, although they alter significantly the rules affecting all Americans' security, safety, values and future – essentially your life, liberty and pursuit of happiness.

Why such silent acceptance? You would not likely sit idly

by if the bank holding your mortgage suddenly told you that it had altered the provisions of your loan to require you to pay more than what you had agreed, or to add a new restriction on your ability to use your property. Nor would you remain silent if a contract you had signed were unilaterally altered against your interests by the other party.

Yet, this is exactly what has been occurring to the two basic documents that were carefully written by those who gave birth to the United States: The Declaration Of Independence and the United States Constitution. I will provide what I hope will be a better understanding of those documents, and the current status of some of the rules, principles and values that they were intended to protect.

II.

RECENT SPOTLIGHTING OF THE ISSUE OF THE COURT'S DUTY

President Obama spotlighted the issue of the Supreme Court's proper role when, on April 2, 2012, as part of a Rose Garden press conference with two foreign leaders, he interjected a warning to the Supreme Court not to hold unconstitutional his Obamacare law that he considered the highlight of his first term. He labeled the possibility of such a Supreme Court decision as unacceptable "judicial activism," which "would be an unprecedented, extraordinary step of overturning a law that was passed by a strong majority of a democratically elected Congress."[2]

Did this "warning" have the effect of saving the "individual mandate" provision – at the heart of the Obamacare statute – from a Supreme Court declaration that it was unconstitutional? Respected Supreme Court reporter Jan Crawford reported that Chief Justice Roberts "initially sided with the Supreme Court's four conservative justices to strike down the heart of President Obama's health care law ... but later changed his position."[3] It may never be known what caused Justice Roberts' totally unexpected vote, involving his construing the individual mandate penalty as a tax – an interpretation in which no other justice joined. Is it pure coincidence that President Obama voiced his "warning" during the latter portion of the justices' internal deliberations? You can reach your own conclusion.

But, even without establishing any cause and effect between the president's "warning" and the Court's 5-4 vote to leave most of that law in place, the seriousness of its public utterance by a president is without dispute.

It is nothing new in our country for politicians – even presidents – to attack the Supreme Court for being "activists" who usurp the powers of Congress, state legislatures, and even the president, by overruling elected legislators and the president. President Lincoln, in his first inaugural address, warned more generally that "decisions of the Supreme Court," that were within Congress' and the president's jurisdiction, would result in depriving "the people" of their right "to be their own rulers, having, to that extent, practically resigned their government, into the hands of " nine appointed, non-elected justices.[4]

President George W. Bush, Obama's Republican predecessor, also decried judicial activism. Pointing out that the judiciary is "the only branch that is unelected and whose officers serve for life," he called "unfortunate," "a threat to our democracy" and "judicial lawlessness" that "some judges give in to temptation and make law instead of [simply] interpreting."[5]

A layman might look at these attacks on the Supreme

> *"President Lincoln warned that 'decisions of the Supreme Court,' that were within Congress' and the president's jurisdiction, would result in depriving 'the people' of their right 'to be their own rulers, having, to that extent, practically resigned their government, into the hands of' nine appointed, non-elected justices."*

Court by politicians on both sides as indicating that whether the Court is correct depends on whose ox is being gored. Republicans Lincoln and Bush disagreed with the Supreme Court decisions and thus attacked the Court for being improperly "activist." Likewise, Democrat Obama attacked the Court because he saw the possibility that the Court would declare unconstitutional his pet legislation. That might well lead some to conclude that there is no meaning to the term "activist" as applied to judges, and no rules to determine the constitutional limits of judicial power to invalidate what Congress, state legislatures and the president may do. I propose to demonstrate that conclusion is totally wrong; the Constitution in fact sets the limits and defines the courts' powers. The problem is that some justices prefer to impose their personal views as to what the law should be for their limited role to decide whether the law, as enacted or applied by elected representatives, is inconsistent with the Constitution.

> *"The Constitution in fact sets the limits and defines the courts' powers. The problem is that some justices prefer to impose their personal views as to what the law should be..."*

Hence, whether nominees to the Supreme Court will be activist justices imposing their personal views, or believe themselves constrained by the Constitution and what this law is, will be crucial in determining the future direction of this country.

We have recently re-elected Barack Obama to serve four more years as President. Little within the president's power has more impact on the future of this country than his power to nominate new justices of the Supreme Court, who, depending on the age of the nominee, may render decisions for 40, 50 or even more years. At least two Supreme Court vacancies, and possibly as many as four, are likely during President Obama's new term, given the age of the oldest four justices: Ginsburg – 79; Kennedy – 76;

Scalia – 76; Breyer – 74. Two of these justices (Ginsburg and Breyer) are generally considered to be in the Court's activist camp, while Scalia and Kennedy are not. The nomination of another activist justice to replace either Ginsburg or Breyer would do little, if anything, to alter the direction of future Supreme Court rulings. But, if either the Scalia or Kennedy seat were to become vacant during the next four years, the replacement would likely create a majority of five activist justices, with lasting impact on this country.

One last impediment to a nominee's assumption of a Supreme Court seat: consent to the nomination by a majority vote in the Senate (60 percent as a practical matter, due to the Senate's filibuster rule). That vote, following a detailed examination of the nominee's qualifications, character, and, most crucial, views – not on any specific forthcoming case, but on judicial philosophy – provides opportunity for you, as part of the public, to lobby your senators to reject any nominee who will not live by his/her oath to uphold the Constitution and vote in favor of one who will. To do so, you must understand the issues involved and the vast gap between an activist justice and one who is not. I write this book with that objective in mind.

III.

OUR COUNTRY'S FOUNDATION DOCUMENTS: THE DECLARATION OF INDEPENDENCE AND THE CONSTITUTION

To properly evaluate the Court's assigned role in our country, it is essential to have a basic understanding of the two documents that our Founders used to create our country: the Declaration of Independence and the Constitution.

The men who signed the Declaration risked their lives, their families, and all they possessed to give birth to this country. Their immediate objective was the creation of the United States, followed 13 years later by the adoption of the United States Constitution, which was intended to set in concrete – for Americans for all time – the structure, procedures and protections to enable Americans to live by the ideals expressed in the Declaration.

This book seeks to answer the central question of whether we have remained faithful to these sacred documents that our country's courageous Founders gave to us. Unfortunately, particularly in more recent decades, my answer is No. To enable you to reach your own conclusion, it is essential that you fully understand relevant facts concerning both the Declaration of

Independence and the Constitution.

The Declaration of Independence specifies the basic values by which Americans – indeed, all people – have the right to live and which a government must guarantee to its people:

> "... that all men are created equal, that they are endowed by their Creator with certain unalienable rights, that among these are life, liberty and the pursuit of happiness."

In this paragraph, the Declaration also specified the government's role:

> "to secure these rights, governments are instituted among men, deriving their just powers from the consent of the governed."

But it then warns that "whenever" the "government becomes destructive to these ends, it is the right of the people to alter ... it, and to institute new government," one which the people conclude "shall seem most likely to effect their safety and happiness."

These words in the Declaration suggested, as did Justice Alito's more recent words, the importance that Americans understand the Constitution and remain constantly aware of the extent to which those in control of our government have become "destructive" of the Constitution. Only with such understanding can we "alter" the situation to prevent the continued undermining of what our Founders bequeathed to us. Unlike our forefathers, who had to use force to end the British tyranny, modern Americans have the ballot, free speech and a free press to alter what has gone wrong – but only if Americans speak up, organize and act.

That last quoted phrase from the Declaration of Independence is very telling as to what our Founders conceived the work of government: to conduct itself in a manner "most likely" to provide "safety and happiness" to most of the people. The words "most likely" are extremely important in construing the various rights guaranteed in the Constitution and, more specifically, in the Bill of Rights. These two words, "most likely," instruct that "rights" may not always be considered as an absolute right of any one individual, but must, where appropriate, be tempered by what is required "to effect" the "safety and happiness" of all the American people.

Analysis of "safety and happiness" provides further understanding that our Founders recognized the need for balancing the very important aim of providing rights to each individual with the objective of protecting the existence and security of this country, without which no American can enjoy any of the rights guaranteed by the Constitution.

We all can agree on the meaning of "safety": preventing, to the extent reasonably possible, injury and death from domestic criminals and from foreign enemies, and theft and destruction of personal property and homes, while Americans are exercising their rights. Where the rights of any single individual clash with the right of all or many Americans to be safe from domestic criminals and foreign enemies (or, today, foreign/domestic terrorists), can these "rights" to "safety and happiness" be considered absolute? The authors of the Declaration suggest a reasoned balancing, not absolutism, is required by joining together "safety and happiness" – one of which must at times suffer to attain the other – and emphasized the need for reasoned balancing by using the objective of "most likely," in contradistinction to "always" or "must."

"Happiness" is more difficult to define in practical terms. But again, the practical understanding of "happiness" as used in the Declaration demonstrates that a reasoned relative balancing is required. We all know that what makes one person happy may well make another person unhappy. For example, a person who has difficulty sleeping at night might well find happiness in listening to loud music, but that loud music might keep a neighbor

> *"... liberty is limited by the recognition that each of us may have to sacrifice some individual desires, which might make each happier, in order to allow the greater number in our society to attain the happiness in liberty that was promised in the Declaration."*

awake and make him unhappy. Clearly, the authors of the Declaration did not intend to suggest that everything government does must guarantee happiness to every one – an impossibility.

What then was the "pursuit of happiness" phrase intended to convey? As there are no contemporaneous annotations to the text, no one can say with certainty. It may, however, be instructive that Thomas Jefferson, the primary author of the Declaration, was influenced by the writings of John Locke, who, in 1690, had written of the important role of the pursuit of happiness in the existence of "liberty."[6] Locke called that pursuit the "highest perfection of intellectual nature" and "the foundation of liberty." It is thus likely that Jefferson conceived of that phrase as Locke did. Perhaps most relevant to Jefferson's use of the phrase in the Declaration, Locke taught that "real happiness" ... oblige[s]" us "to suspend the satisfaction of our desires in particular cases" for what can create the greatest good for all. And likewise, liberty is limited by the recognition that each of us may have to sacrifice some individual desires, which might make each happier, in order to allow the greater number in our society to attain the happiness in liberty that was promised in the Declaration.

Early on, this view was adopted by the Supreme Court in various rulings that reconcile seemingly absolute freedoms in the Bill of Rights with the needs of society to protect the many from the abuses of the few. For example, the First Amendment prohibits any law from "abridging the freedom of speech." Literally, that would allow anyone to stand up in a crowded theater and yell "fire." But that would create an incident of anarchy, the opposite of rational government intended to be created by the Constitution. Hence, the First Amendment has been interpreted consistent with what the authors intended: The free speech guaranty in the First Amendment does not allow one individual to use his speech right to cause a disturbance of the peace and enjoyment of others, particularly where, for example, the consequence of falsely yelling "fire" in a crowded theater may be a stampede affecting the life and safety of others.[7]

Likewise, in attempting to provide safety to all of its citizens, our government, of necessity, would make some people unhappy. The rapist who, in his warped mind, obtains satisfaction by raping an innocent girl, is going to be unhappy at being caught and incarcerated by the government. Does that mean that, in specifying "safety and happiness" as the objective of government, our country's founders were seeking the impossible? I suggest not so. Notice again that the authors of the Declaration modified their statement of the objective of government by the phrase "most likely." They recognized that government actions cannot please all the people all the time. Rather, they understood that there must always be a balancing of the rights of many against the rights of a few, the safety of most of society against the restrictions of a few.

Let me be clear that this required balancing does not mean that, to make many happy or safe, one or a few individuals can be arbitrarily jailed, enslaved, or otherwise denied the basic freedoms of peaceful conduct, including speech, work, movement, family, etc. Rather, the balancing process places great value on the least restriction of an individual's freedom – the minimum that is essential to ensure the enjoyment of freedom by all others. But yes, jailing, enslavement, and denial of other rights to an individual may be appropriate. Persons who commit crimes are denied liberty by being jailed to provide safety to others. As needed for the defense of all in this country, Americans can be forced to serve years in the military (often looked upon as enslavement). And someone who wishes to express his opinion to others may do so, except if it would unreasonably interfere with the comfort of others, such as by using a loudspeaker in a residential neighborhood at 3 a.m. while people are trying to sleep. Thus, the Founders of our country recognized that "freedom" and "rights" are not always absolute, but require a reasonable reconciliation of an individual's freedom with society's security and safety and other persons' freedom and rights. The Supreme Court itself has recognized the intention of our Founders that "rights" of individuals must be at times adjusted and limited so that "we can have both liberty of expression and an orderly life."[8]

That leads us to the Constitution itself. Thirteen years after the Declaration (and after a failed experiment with the Articles of Confederation – essentially only a treaty among 13 sovereign states), the Constitution was adopted as the document by which this country would live. It put into effect as the law of this land the values and rights so beautifully stated in the Declaration. It also created the procedures to empower the people of this country to choose the government that the people deem most likely to effect their safety and happiness. Thus, the Constitution in 1789 set forth the eternal governing structure and rules determined at the birth of these United States.

> *"Our Constitution is the shield created by the fathers of our country to act in perpetuity to protect all average citizens from the rampage of autocratic, uncontrolled power."*

Without the Constitution, no rights would be sacred. Rather, what the people in power could do would depend on their whim. Without the Constitution, we would run the risk of the total loss of liberty that people in Europe experienced under Hitler, and people in Russia and the Eastern European countries suffered under Stalin. Our Constitution is the shield created by the fathers of our country to act in perpetuity to protect all average citizens from the rampage of autocratic, uncontrolled power.

That is not to say that the Framers of the Constitution did not recognize that future changes might be warranted. But they carefully set forth in the Constitution the procedure required before the Constitution could be changed in any way. Those procedures, contained in Article V of the Constitution, were intentionally made difficult to obtain so as to prevent alteration of constitutional provisions on the emotional or selfish whim of those in power at any given time. We have all seen in very recent years how difficult it is to obtain a 60 percent vote in favor of a new piece of legislation in the U.S. Senate to avoid a filibuster. That 60 percent vote requirement pales in difficulty compared to the votes that the Constitution requires in order to change the Constitution. A constitutional amendment must be first proposed by a vote of two-thirds of both houses of Congress or by a convention called by two-thirds of the state legislatures. Then, if either of these votes is obtained, the proposed amendment must be ratified by three-fourths of the states through their legislatures or conventions in each state.

These enormous hurdles imposed on amending – changing – the original wording and meaning of the Constitution have had the intended effect of keeping changes to a minimum. Excluding the Bill of Rights, found in the first 10 amendments, which further limited the power of government to interfere in the rights of individuals, there have been only 17 amendments to the Constitution in over 220 years – averaging less than one amendment for each 13 years this country has been governed by the Constitution.

The authors of the Constitution did not rest on the difficult amending process in pursuing their objective to protect against future scuttling of the rights, protections and values guaranteed by the document. To protect against any unauthorized assumption of power, which might result in ignoring constitutional limitations, the Constitution established three co-equal branches:

the Executive, meaning the president and his/her appointees; the Legislative, meaning the Congress; and the Judiciary, including the Supreme Court as the highest court. Both the Executive and Legislative branches were subject to political and popular pressures as they were elected for fixed terms and had to receive continuous support from the people in order to remain in office. The Judicial branch, in contrast, was intended to be insulated from that pressure: The judges, once appointed by the president and confirmed by the Senate, were appointed for life.

> *"As few as five justices are the ultimate deciders of whether action taken by the Executive and Legislative branches is or is not allowed by the Constitution."*

All persons serving in each of the three branches are required to take an oath to uphold the Constitution. But the Framers of our Constitution were realists in recognizing that an oath, by itself, was insufficient assurance that our citizens' rights under the Constitution would be protected against any popular, emotional, or political tidal wave. The Framers understood that a watchdog was needed to ensure that those in our government did not ignore the constitutional provisions limiting the power of government and thereby protecting each individual against the government's violation of constitutional protections.

The third branch of government, the Judiciary, was created to be that watchdog to determine whether what the Executive branch or the Legislative branch did was allowed under the provisions of the Constitution. This has ended up giving vast power to the nine justices on the Supreme Court. And since the Supreme Court reaches its rulings in each case by majority vote, as few as five justices – who before becoming a justice were people like you and I – are the ultimate deciders of whether action taken by the Executive and Legislative branches is or is not allowed by the Constitution.

In the later chapters of this book, I discuss specific issues on which a majority of Supreme Court justices have determined that the Constitution requires a different decision today than it did during the previous 150 to 200 years of this country's existence. How is a change in a Supreme Court decision warranted, given that it is not disputed that the Constitution has not changed and the requirement of reaching a reasonable balance between an individual's rights and society's needs has not changed? Yet, as this book will detail, in various subjects crucial to the safety, happiness, health, and values of our people, the Supreme Court's rulings have completely departed from earlier accepted values and rules – the values and rules our country's founders believed that they were protecting and made permanent by our written Constitution.

IV.

ONE QUICK EXAMPLE OF THE COURT'S REWRITING THE CONSTITUTION: FROM GOD AS THE SOURCE OF ALL RIGHTS TO THE BANNING OF GOD

As already noted, The Declaration of Independence specified the basic values guaranteed to all Americans.

The first paragraph of the Declaration of Independence recognized the source of our rights and values that were to be protected by the independent country they created: "the laws of nature and of nature's God." The Founders obviously had no inhibitions or hesitation about acknowledging God as the ultimate source of human rights. The Declaration continued by repeating that it was "the Creator" (God) from whom these rights came, and thus no man or woman could deprive humans of those rights without subverting God's will. And they ended the Declaration by expressing reliance on God to see them and this new country to a successful outcome: "appealing to the Supreme Judge of the world for the rectitude of our intentions" and "with a firm reliance on the protection of Divine Providence."

Even Jefferson, the author of our Declaration Of Independence and one of our country's Founders, and often cited by current opponents of any role of religion in our government, declared the importance of religion to our liberty in his book, *Notes on the State Of Virginia*:

> "[C]an the liberties of a nation be thought secure when we have removed their only firm basis, a conviction in the minds of the people that these liberties are of the gift of God?"[9]

So too, Benjamin Franklin, seldom described as a particularly religious man, addressed the Constitutional Convention on June 28, 1787:

> "The longer that I live, the more convincing proofs I see of this truth – that God governs in the affairs of men. And if a sparrow cannot fall to the ground without his notice, is it probable that an empire can rise without his aid? .... [Unless the delegates recognize this] we shall succeed in this political building no better than the Builders of Babel."[10]

While I will detail in subsequent chapters how the Supreme Court has detoured us away from the words and intent of those documents in crucial areas directly affecting our safety, security, values and liberty, I mention here but one illustrative example.

The Declaration was written while our forefathers were attempting to succeed, against horrible odds, in establishing this country. Its carefully chosen words undeniably prove that the signers felt not only free, but proud, publicly to proclaim their appreciation to and reliance on God.

Recognition of God has remained part of government culture since those early days of our country. Since first convening, both the Senate and House have chosen chaplains and each day's session is opened with a prayer of thanks to God.[11] Presidents did similarly. For example, on June 6, 1944, when our troops invaded France to defeat Nazi Germany, President Franklin D. Roosevelt spoke by radio to the American public in content essentially limited to prayers to God: He asked all Americans "to join with [him] in prayer" to "Almighty God" that our troops receive God's "blessings;" that as to those who "will never return ... embrace them, Father, and receive them, thy heroic servants, into thy kingdom"; and "for those at home ... help us, Almighty God, to rededicate ourselves in renewed faith in thee." President Roosevelt ended with "Thy will be done, Almighty God."[12]

Also, almost midway between our country's reliance on God in the Declaration of Independence and FDR's reliance on God in 1944, during the Civil War, when America faced the threat of being torn apart, this country again publicly acknowledged its dependence on God for its continued existence by proclaiming "In God We Trust" on our money.[13] Indeed, in 1956, that "In God We Trust" became, by statute, our national motto,[14] many years after a paraphrase was repeatedly sung at many ceremonies, including school events, as a line in our national anthem. And more recently in 2006 and 2011, the Senate and the House of Representatives, respectively, reaffirmed "In God We Trust" as our national motto, with the House voting overwhelmingly (396-9) in favor, consistent with polls reporting that 90 percent of the American public agrees.[15]

But despite this overwhelming view of Congress and the American public in support of this public regard for God, can a student today, chosen by a vote of her fellow students to give a non-denominational invocation at her public school football game, include in her remarks a simple short prayer of gratitude to God? The simple, but incredible, answer is no; the Supreme Court has declared it to be unconstitutional.[16]

How can it possibly be unconstitutional for a student at a public school football game merely to paraphrase the Declaration of Independence and our country's motto? The answer is that as few as five persons have so ruled: A majority of the nine members on the Supreme Court have the unreviewable power to decide what the Constitution means. They ruled that such a non-denominational invocation at a public school football game would violate the Bill of Rights mandate of separation of church and state if gratitude to God were spoken in these circumstances.[17] This is but one example of how our Supreme Court has departed from what our Founders intended.

Hopefully, this tip of the iceberg of the slow but sure destruction of the values bequeathed to us by our Founding Fathers will interest you in learning the full record and then doing something to prevent further eradication and erosion of these values.

V.

THE COURTS' PROPER ROLE

The Constitution, as we have already seen, intentionally prescribes a very difficult and burdensome procedure to amend it. Yet, in more recent decades, some people have effected major changes in the protections, rights, and values set forth in the Constitution without complying with the Constitution's very stringent amendment procedure. Knowing that the changes they wish to make could never be approved by the required two-thirds and three-fourths votes prescribed by our Founding Fathers, some people, who seek to alter the protections, rights and values given each of us in the Constitution, have instead relied on the votes of as few as five persons to make those changes: five individuals who have assumed that power because they are justices of the Supreme Court.

You may properly ask: How did our Constitution allow five unelected individuals to assume power effectively to veto what the president, governors, and legislators – all elected by the people – have decided is best for this country? And did the Constitution intend to provide this power to five justices?

We start that analysis by making clear that the

Constitution did delegate to the Supreme Court the duty to decide whether actions taken by legislatures and governmental executives are constitutional. Thus, there can be no doubt that President Obama's assertion, that it would be an "unprecedented, extraordinary" action for the Court to declare unconstitutional a law passed by Congress, was neither factually nor constitutionally true. Even his attorney general, in response to a Federal Appeals Court order to express his view on that Obama assertion, affirmed that the "power of the courts to review the constitutionality of legislation is beyond dispute." [18]

In addition, as a matter of factual history, through 2010, the Supreme Court had ruled at least 165 times that laws passed by Congress were unconstitutional.[19] And, at the same time as Obama made his "unprecedented" assertion, his administration, through its Justice Department, represented in federal court that the Defense of Marriage Act was unconstitutional, even though it was enacted by bipartisan majorities in both Houses (House: 342-67; Senate: 85-14) and signed into law by a Democratic president.[20]

The Constitution[21] itself provides that "the Supreme Law of the Land" includes "[t]his Constitution" and those congressionally-enacted "Laws of the United States" that are "made in Pursuance" of the Constitution – meaning that any enacted law that violates the Constitution is not effective.

The Constitution assigns to the Supreme Court the role of ultimate decider of whether a statute – federal or state – or executive action violates the Constitution. It provides that the "judicial Power of the United States shall be vested in [the] Supreme Court" and that such power "shall extend to all Cases ... arising under this Constitution [or] the Laws of the United States."[22] Any dispute concerning the constitutionality of any law or action clearly fits that description, thus authorizing the Supreme Court to make that decision.

The Federalist Papers, written by three authors of the

Constitution, who then became the most vocal proponents of ratification (Alexander Hamilton, James Madison, and John Jay), confirmed that the Constitution delegated to the Supreme Court the duty to declare statutes unconstitutional if a statute violated the limitations on government power prescribed in the Constitution: The duty "to declare all acts contrary to the manifest tenor of the Constitution void"[23] was assigned to "the tribunal ... to be established under the general [federal] Government"[24] – referring to the Supreme Court.

> *"The Constitution is not an instrument for the government to restrain the people, it is an instrument for the people to restrain the government – lest it come to dominate our lives and interests." -*
> *Patrick Henry*

Having experienced the autocratic conduct by the British government that caused Americans to fight to be free from such conduct, they recognized the need for the Constitution to provide protection from autocratic treatment by the newly-created United States government. Therefore, Americans wanted protection against government infringement of the basic rights enumerated in the Declaration of Independence. Our early great patriot Patrick Henry said it well:

> "The Constitution is not an instrument for the government to restrain the people, it is an instrument for the people to restrain the government – lest it come to dominate our lives and interests."[25]

But Americans insisted on another area of protection, given the nature of the American structure of a federal government with limited powers, and each state government having jurisdiction over its people and state; the Constitution had to protect against the possibility of federal government encroachment upon matters left to each state. James Madison sought to convince Americans that the Constitution protected against an amorphous, ever power-grasping federal government that would overpower state governments, when he wrote that the power of the federal government created under the Constitution "extends to certain enumerated objects only, and leaves to the several states a residuary and inviolable sovereignty over all other objects,"[26] and then subsequently reiterated it:

> "The powers delegated by the proposed Constitution to the federal government are few and defined. Those which are to remain in the State governments are numerous and indefinite."[27]

Indeed, even with the Constitution's authors' repeated assurance that the Constitution protected states from federal encroachment on state rights, and protected individual rights, many people remained uncomfortable that the Constitution sufficiently protected them from an autocratic federal government and from any federal government ability to invade state prerogatives. To alleviate this discomfort, in 1791, the first 10 amendments to the Constitution, which we know as the Bill Of Rights, were adopted.

Most Americans are familiar with the first nine of those amendments, protecting individual Americans from government denial of basic rights, *e.g.,* freedom of speech and religion, requirement of search warrants, and no compelled self-incrimination. The Tenth Amendment, unlike the other nine, was adopted to ensure against the federal government expanding its powers into areas that were supposed to be left to the states, and thereby made explicit what the Constitution's authors stated was intended by the Constitution:

> "The powers not delegated to the United States by the Constitution, nor prohibited by it to the States, are reserved to the States respectively, or to the people."

In simple language – although those words themselves seem quite clear – it mandated that, unless the Constitution specifically granted the federal government the power to exercise power over, or interfere with, a facet of Americans' lives and activities, the federal government could not Constitutionally exercise such power. Even Justice William O. Douglas, one of the most liberal justices to sit on the Court, recognized that "[o]ur national government is one of delegated powers alone," and that all power not delegated "rests with the States."[28]

This constitutional protection against an ever power-grasping federal government – inherent in the original Constitution and emphasized even more explicitly in the Tenth Amendment – has given birth to many of the cases requiring the Supreme Court to determine the constitutionality of statutes and executive action.

Early on, in 1803, the Supreme Court itself affirmed that the Constitution required it to decide whether a law enacted by Congress violates the Constitution, and, if so, declare the statute unconstitutional: "It is emphatically the province and duty of the Judicial Department to say what the law is. ..... [T]he Constitution is superior to any ordinary act of the Legislature," meaning that "the Constitution, and not such ordinary act, must govern the case to which they apply."[29]

Hence, the issue is not whether Supreme Court justices have the right and duty to invalidate unconstitutional statutes, enacted by federal and state legislatures, and acts by government officials. Rather, the issue is what governs their decisions on constitutionality. Do they base their decisions on the words of the Constitution, the meaning of those words, and the intent of those who wrote and enacted those words? The only other alternative is that the justices do not decide on the basis of what the Constitution says, but on their personal views as to whether they personally approve or disapprove of the legislation or official's acts being attacked as unconstitutional. If the Constitution has any continuing meaning and controlling impact, the answer must be the former, not the latter.

We abhor when, in other countries, judges act as political tools, rather than abiding by their constitution. For example, the Nicaraguan constitution, as does the United States Constitution, forbids any individual from serving as president for more than two consecutive terms. That provision, on its face, would appear, to any fair reader, to have barred Nicaragua's two-term President Ortega from seeking reelection. To evade this constitutional provision, Ortega successfully induced that country's Supreme Court to overrule that provision, finding it to be a violation of human rights. Few would dispute that those judges were activist judges, improperly rendering that decision to favor their personal political allegiance to Ortega, rather than following their oath to enforce the constitution.[30]

That is an easy example of activist judges ignoring and violating the constitution. But how do we apply that example to our Supreme Court justices? When are our Supreme Court justices, in holding legislative or executive acts to be unconstitutional, merely performing their duty to decide whether such acts are consistent with the Constitution? When, on the other hand, are they striking down such an act because they personally disagree with the act of the legislature or of the president, although nothing in the Constitution or in prior decisions of the Court demonstrates that it is contrary to the Constitution?

The proper role of judges was early described by Sir William Blackstone, the most renowned 18th century legal scholar, and author of *Commentaries On The Laws Of England*, which became the basic textbook for American lawyers, in view of the fact that United States' law springs from English common law. He prescribed that, to avoid being an activist judge – to him, an improper role for judges – a judge must construe the words and "intentions at the time when" the provision was enacted.[31]

American Supreme Court Justice Oliver Wendell Holmes – recognized by all as one of our greatest justices – similarly instructed that a judge must interpret a provision based on "what those words would mean in the mouth of a normal speaker of English, *using them in the circumstances in which they were used.*"[32] He explicitly warned against activist judges, whom he described as judges who "undertake to renovate the law" as "that is not their province."[33] Words being construed by the Court must be read in "a sense most common to the common understanding *at the time of its adoption.*"[34] That meant to him that a judge's role was not simply to "tak[e] the words and a dictionary, but by considering their origin …."[35]

> *"I have an abiding idea that if the Framers had wanted to let judges write the Constitution on any day-to-day beliefs of theirs, they would have said so instead of so carefully defining their grants and prohibitions in a written constitution."*
> -Justice Hugo Black

Holmes' application of these principles to specific cases shows that he decided constitutionality on the basis of the meaning of the words enacted at the time of enactment, not on the basis of Holmes' personal views or what was then politically preferable. Thus, he held a tax constitutional under the Fourteenth Amendment because those "methods of taxation … were well known when that Amendment was adopted"[36] – meaning that, whatever might be popular judgment at the time of his decision, the existence of the tax when the Fourteenth Amendment was enacted made it logical that the amendment was not intended to void it. In another case, he further described how a legislative act should be considered:

> "I think the proper course is to recognize that a State Legislature can do whatever it sees fit to do unless it is

restrained by some express prohibition in the Constitution of the United States or of the State, and that Courts should be careful not to extend such prohibitions beyond their obvious meaning by reading into them conceptions of public policy that the particular Court may happen to entertain."[37]

He summarized that the deciding factor for any judge should be "does the decision represent what the lawmaking power [meaning, in the case of Constitutional issues, the authors of the Constitution] must be taken to want?"[38] In the end, he wrote, a judge's role is "to see the game is played according to the rules whether [the judge] like[s] them or not."[39] The basic rule, he specified, is that "[w]hen we know what the source of the law has said that it shall be, our authority is at an end."[40]

Another highly respected justice, Hugo Black, similarly opined:

"I have an abiding idea that if the Framers had wanted to let judges write the Constitution on any day-to-day beliefs of theirs, they would have said so instead of so carefully defining their grants and prohibitions in a written constitution. .... Should I do so, I feel that we are deciding what the Constitution is, not from what it says, but what we think it would have been wise for the Framers to put in it. That to me would be 'judicial activism' at its worst."[41]

I am certain that some readers will raise their eyebrows at the suggestion that justices are required to subrogate their personal, even political, views to what the words of the Constitution required. After all, these readers would correctly point out that Supreme Court appointments are made by the president, an intensely-political position, and confirmed by the Senate, also composed of intensely-political members elected following a very political campaign. And some readers would point to examples of intensely political Senate confirmation hearings that resulted in a Senate vote denying confirmation to a Supreme Court nominee whose personal views were rejected by a Senate majority.[42]

But that the nomination is made by the president and must be confirmed by the Senate – two political branches of our government, created by the Constitution – does not mean that, once a Supreme Court Justice is confirmed and assumes a court seat, that justice remains a political animal. Indeed, the Constitution was written to insulate each justice from political domination. The president and each senator has a fixed term, requiring them to return to the political arena – a re-election for a first-term president and each senator – in order to retain the office. In contrast, justices are appointed for life. As our Constitution's authors explained, "the judiciary remains distinct from both the legislative and executive" – the two political branches – with "permanency in office," in the form of life tenure, contributing "so much to its fairness and independence."[43]

Even recent history has shown that justices, once appointed, do not, in their votes on the Court, necessarily remain loyal to the political and social views of the president who made the appointment. Two of the most liberal justices on the Court, Earl Warren and William Brennan – the two leaders of the Warren Court in announcing many of the most liberal decisions in history – were appointed by conservative Republican President Dwight D. Eisenhower, who later publicly acknowledged their repeated rejection of his views, by describing their nominations as his two "biggest mistakes as President."[44] Likewise, conservative Republican President Gerald Ford appointed John Paul Stevens, and conservative Republican President George H. W. Bush appointed David Souter – both of whom, once appointed for life, frequently voted against conservative tenets.

Historically, voting contrary to the presumed political loyalty to the appointing president was not unique to appointments by Republicans. For example, Justice Byron White, although appointed by liberal Democrat John F. Kennedy, dissented from many liberal iconic Court decisions, including the legalization of abortion in *Roe v. Wade*,[45] and the creation by the Court of a required warning to defendants in *Miranda v. Arizona*.[46] Another "disappointing" Democratic nomination was Hugo Black, appointed by President Franklin D. Roosevelt, who, after a number of years on the Court, voted contrary to liberal positions on "civil rights protests, poll taxes, anti-birth control laws and electronic eavesdropping."[47]

Exemplifying how justices, who believed themselves duty-bound to follow the Constitution rather than their personal views – and therefore no longer a political loyalist once appointed to the Court – Justice Holmes voted for the position of an appellant even though he personally viewed that appellant to hold "a creed which I believe to be the creed of ignorance and immaturity."[48] This same requirement, for justices to sublimate their personal views to what the Constitution says and requires, was repeated by the Court in 1935:

> "Even should we consider the act unwise and prejudicial to both public and private interest, if it be fairly within delegate power, our obligation is to sustain it. On the other hand, though we should think the measure embodies a valuable social plan and be in entire sympathy with its purpose and intended results, if the provisions go beyond the boundaries of constitutional power we must so declare."[49]

Let's consider the view in favor of "activist" judges who believe – in contrast with Justice Holmes' view and the above-quoted Court ruling – that they may rule on constitutionality based on their personal judgment of contemporary values, instead of based on the words in the Constitution and what was accepted and intended at the time the constitutional provision was enacted.

I have already provided the example of the wrong imposed by activist judges in Nicaragua. Unfortunately, America has experienced similar wrong. Here are two examples of decisions by activist justices, which most, today, would agree were unacceptable.

In 1791, the Fifth Amendment was added to the Constitution to provide, as relevant here, that "no person shall be ... deprived of life, liberty, or property, without due process of law." Yet, in 1857, the Supreme Court, in an opinion written by then Chief Justice Roger Brooke Taney, ruled that a black man, being of an "inferior class of beings," "had no rights which the white man was bound to respect."[50] It thus declared unconstitutional the congressional statute, known as the Missouri Compromise, barring slavery in specified (northern) portions of the territories and states derived from the Louisiana Purchase. While Taney attempted to dress his decision in asserting that he was merely applying the founders' view of blacks as slaves, he was actually basing his decision on his personal bias as a staunch supporter of slavery. His decision was widely condemned by opponents of slavery as an activist justices' ruling, which usurped for those justices the power that the Constitution had given to Congress, and which Congress had exercised. In contrast to Taney's unacceptable basis for his decision, one of the two dissenters noted that he "prefer[red] the lights of Madison, Hamilton and Jay," the authors of the Federalist Papers who explained the meaning of the Constitution, "as a means of construing the Constitution,"[51] not Taney's personal bias.

The second example is the 1896 Supreme Court opinion supposedly applying the Fourteenth Amendment. That amendment has very clear language: "No State shall ... enforce any law which shall abridge the privileges ... of citizens of the United States; ... nor deny to any person within its jurisdiction the equal protection of the laws." Despite this language, Louisiana arrested Homer Plessy, who was 7/8ths Caucasian and 1/8th black, for violating the state law that reserved specified railroad coaches for whites only, thereby denying to blacks the right or privilege, afforded to whites, to sit in those coaches. He appealed to the Supreme Court from his conviction. Seven justices, while admitting that the "object of the amendment was undoubtedly to enforce the absolute equality of the two races before the law," [52] held that, as long as separate accommodations are equal, a state may deny blacks access to a white-only coach.

As recognized years later, when the Supreme Court overturned this decision in the school segregation cases,[53] the *Plessy* decision did not reflect adherence to the Constitution; clearly it reflected the personal preference of activist justices who, like much of public opinion at that time, preferred to have blacks kept separate from whites.

Some activist advocates support their position by arguing that the Constitution must be considered a living document that the Court must apply to events and activities never envisaged by the authors of the Constitution. That is a straw man, because no one disagrees with that view. But that does not mean that justices should ignore the words of the Constitution and the intent of the Framers when applying it to modern changes in our society. For Thus, we know that airplanes and automobiles did not exist when the Constitution was enacted. But that does not mean that the justices should ignore the words and intent of the Constitution when deciding a constitutional issue as applied to current operation of airplanes and automobiles. Rather, it requires the justices to determine the meaning of the words and intent of the Constitution and apply that meaning to societal innovations. Thus, if any state today were to create segregated airplanes within its borders, that there were no airplanes when the Fourteenth Amendment was adopted would be irrelevant. Rather, the Court would look to the words and purpose of the Fourteenth Amendment and hold that denial of equal rights to blacks is prohibited on any mode of transportation, whether a train or later-invented airplane.

As the authors and proponents of the Constitution

explained, unless the American people amended the Constitution to change it, "the established form" in the Constitution's original wording "is binding," and is what the justices are duty bound to enforce.[54]   Even Jefferson, who was not himself a Federalist proponent nor author of the Constitution, recognized that the words of the Constitution, not the personal views of justices, were binding: He rejected "confidence in man" [*i.e.,* the view of five justices] because, we have "limited constitutions to bind down those we are obliged to trust with power," and therefore all are bound "down from mischief by the chains of the Constitution."[55]

Similarly, one does not have to be a lawyer to recognize the importance of what the Framers of the Constitution said, as to the meaning of the Constitution, when a court, over 200 years later, is deciding the meaning of that language. Neither the words in the Constitution nor what the Framers explicitly said those words were intended to mean can mutate over time. They are what they are and remain the same. They therefore are binding on every justice who honors his/her oath to uphold the Constitution.

Recognizing the validity of this reasoning, some judicial-activist advocates[56] propose a supposed "compromise" under which they agree that the intent of the Constitution's authors controls, but only if the words used in the Constitution to express that intent by themselves make the intent apparent; where the Constitution's authors employed an evaluative standard, they would disregard the authors' intent on the meaning of that standard in favor of later justices' opinion of what they believe is a "better" current meaning in view of changed circumstances.

Exemplifying this proposed "compromise," Yale Law School Professor Jack Balkin compares various excerpts from the Constitution; as they all present the same issue, I will discuss two of his examples: the provision fixing "the age of thirty five years" as the minimum age for eligibility to be president,[57] as contrasted with the prohibition against "cruel and unusual punishments."[58] Balkin argues that the Constitution's authors made their intent clear in specifying 35 years,[59] while their use of the evaluative words "cruel and unusual" was "a standard or a principle" that is not a clear specification of what the Founders intended to be prohibited in the future.[60] Therefore, according to this "compromise," the Founders' intent controls in perpetuity as to the meaning of the 35-year minimum provision, but the "cruel and unusual" phrase should be interpreted by subsequent justices based on their opinion of changed circumstances, disregarding what the Founders intended by this phrase.

> *"It is insulting to our Founding Fathers – and, most important, false – to suggest that they chose words in the Constitution that did not reflect what they intended thereby to mandate."*

This is a simplistic proposal that does not withstand analysis. It provides no consistency. If, as Professor Balkin agrees, the intent of the Constitution's authors should control, their intent should control as to all words and phrases, not solely where the intent pops out automatically from the words themselves. Judges and juries, in deciding life-or-death issues, determine intent based on the acts and statements prior to and surrounding the act in question, as, for example, whether the defendant on trial for murder intended to kill the victim. This same judicial method to determine intent is much easier and more certain in determining our Founders' intent as, unlike criminals, there never was any attempt to hide that intent.

It is insulting to our Founding Fathers – and, most important, false – to suggest that they chose words in the Constitution that did not reflect what they intended thereby to mandate. In fact, the Constitutional Convention deliberations establish that our Founding Fathers carefully chose all words in the Constitution to express exactly what they intended to be the rules governing our country.

Let's analyze those two examples from the Constitution that Professor Balkin used, in his "compromise," to determine if changed circumstances or original intent should control their meaning today. I agree that, by the words themselves that they placed in the Constitution, our Founders made clear that they intended to make age 35 the minimum age of a president. For this reason, Professor Balkin agrees that the intent of the Constitution's authors controls this meaning in the Constitution, to the exclusion of changed circumstances. But, hold up. If changed circumstances should ever trump the authors' intent, why shouldn't changed circumstances control in applying this provision where it is obvious that our Founders based the 35-year provision on the circumstances at that time, and would not likely have used the same minimum age if today's changed circumstances had then existed? In 1787, life expectancy in our country was less than 40 years.[61] Our Constitution's authors had to have written this provision to choose a minimum age that, in that era, combined as much experience-time as possible with being young enough to increase the likelihood of living to serve the full term. Indeed, America's first two choices as president – Washington at age 57 and Adams at age 61[62] – indicated that our Founders, most of whom participated in those choices, preferred someone substantially older than 35. In fact, we did not elect a president who was even under 50 until 1960[63] – almost two centuries after the provision was included in the Constitution.

Today, as compared to 1787, life expectancy has doubled to 78½ years,[64] and we have elected (or reelected) a candidate as old as 73, who then completed his term in office.[65] Would our Founders have wanted the 35-year minimum if the life expectancy had then been 78½ years? Probably not. But because the words used by the writers of the Constitution, in fixing the 35-year minimum age, had a meaning that they intended, no one suggests that their intent should be disregarded in favor of the changed circumstances that would, today, certainly allow for an older age-eligibility in order to ensure greater experience while still retaining probability of not dying in office.

No reason exists why the intent of our Constitution's authors should not similarly govern as to the meaning of every other provision in the Constitution. As with all constitutional provisions, the Founders' intent in choosing the phrase "cruel and unusual punishments" is clear. They purposely chose that phrase, "cruel and unusual punishments," because it had a specific meaning that they intended to import into the Constitution. As detailed later in this book (Chapter IX), these words in the Eighth Amendment were copied from the English Declaration Of Rights of 1689, originally written to protect Englishmen from the horribly uncivilized ("cruel and unusual") punishments decreed by the Stuart Kings during the Bloody Assizes. Those punishments were the likes of drawing and quartering, burning of women, beheading and disemboweling. England – and America by statute before and during the adoption of the Eighth Amendment – affirmed that other punishments like the death penalty and life sentences remained acceptable as not "cruel and unusual." It is thus a false and defamatory allegation to make against our country's founders that they did not know specifically what they intended to prohibit – and what they intended to allow – by the prohibition against "cruel and unusual punishments," and that they did not leave a record of their intent.

Certainly, the Constitution's authors could have substituted a voluminous enumeration of prohibited and acceptable punishments for the terse phrase "cruel and unusual punishments." But they found it unnecessary to burden the otherwise short Constitution with what is more reasonably found in a criminal code statute, written to be consistent with the framework set forth in the Constitution. In fact, the Congress created under the then-new Constitution promptly had no difficulty in writing that statutory criminal code based on what Congress easily understood was intended by this phrase – specifically then implementing that phrase by authorizing the death penalty and various terms of imprisonment, including a life sentence. The reason that our Founders did not believe that they had to weight down the Constitution with the equivalent of a criminal code was because they knew that it was beyond dispute that they were accepting the specific punishments allowed and disallowed under that phrase, "cruel and unusual punishments," in England, in the American colonies, and then in the states before the Eighth Amendment was adopted. Thus, our Founders' intent in the meaning of that phrase is indisputable. That intent included allowing, for example, the death penalty. Overriding that clear intent, some justices today (see Chapter IX) have concluded that the death penalty should no longer be constitutional because they suddenly decided that a death sentence, long held not to be "cruel and unusual," had somehow mutated over time to become prohibited as "cruel and unusual."

No one suggests that justices could change our Founders' intent to raise the 35-year eligibility for the presidency merely because of undisputed changed circumstances. All recognize that, to make that change, a constitutional amendment would be required. There is no rational basis for five justices to reject what our Founders intended by any other provision in the Constitution, and thus substitute a different meaning based on contemporary justices' view of what is better due to their personal opinion of what changed circumstances should require. The Constitution provides the sole means for such change: an amendment.

A good historical example that an amendment is required to override the intent of a constitutional provision, despite changed circumstances, is the Nineteenth Amendment, ratified in 1920. That amendment gave women the right to vote. In 1868, over 50 years before, the Fourteenth Amendment had been added to the Constitution, to grant to "all persons born or naturalized in the United States" all "privileges and immunities" of any other citizen, and not deny "the equal protection of the laws." Certainly, it would have been easy to decide that women were included in "all persons" and that the right to vote was a "privilege" not to be denied to women in the equal protection of all laws.

Also, between 1868 and 1920, circumstances had changed regarding women's "place" in the United States to support equal rights for women. In the early 1800s, generally husbands legally could exercise total authority over their wives, and married women could not retain their own wages, control their own property, or, if they sought a divorce, obtain custody of their children. Circumstances had changed before 1920: Women had been accepted in different careers;[66] starting in 1869, 15 territories and states granted the vote to women, and, in 1916, a woman was elected to Congress from Montana.[67] If changed circumstances ever would lead the courts to interpret a constitutional provision in accordance with what was then the popular view and direction, there would have been no need to wait until 1920 for a constitutional amendment to give women the vote. Indeed, lawsuits, as early as 1871 seeking a ruling that the Fourteenth Amendment granted the vote to women were rejected (without reaching the Supreme Court).[68]

But such an application of the Fourteenth Amendment to women's suffrage would have ignored the intent of the amendment's authors and those who voted to ratify it. As the Supreme Court held only four years after the ratification of that amendment – such a short time thereafter, causing the Court to note that the amendment's "history is fresh within the memory of us all ... free from doubt"[69] – the "prevailing purpose" of the amendment was "the protection of [each former black slave] from the oppressions of those who had formerly exercised unlimited dominion over him."[70] As the intent in enacting the Fourteenth Amendment was limited to protecting the rights of blacks, and not anyone else, that intent was regarded as controlling. Following that reasoning, and despite a popular cause and changed circumstances, it was apparent that nothing less than a constitutional amendment was required to afford the vote to women.

To summarize: Sworn to uphold the Constitution, the Supreme Court justices, by definition, should be limited to the words of the Constitution, and helped in understanding the meaning of those words by the evidence left by the authors of the Constitution as to what they meant by the words they chose. That means that a justice abides by his/her oath to uphold the Constitution by either (i) striking down a law inconsistent with the words and intent of the Constitution, or (ii) upholding the constitutionality of a law that does not violate the words or intent of the Constitution, both without regard to the justice's personal view of the legislation. In contrast, a justice is an activist when substituting his/her judgment as to what should be the law, by (i) striking down legislation that is supported by prior Court rulings and is not contrary to the words and intent of the Constitution, or (ii) creating new law that is not required by or violates the words and intent of the Constitution.

The justices of the Supreme Court also are supposed to be strongly – and appropriately – guided by the legal rule called *stare decisis* (pronounced starey decisis, to rhyme with "precise" with an "iss" at the end). That literally means "to stand by that which is decided," practically translated as adhering to prior relevant decisions of the Supreme Court interpreting the Constitution. This guiding *stare decisis* principle recognizes that prior decisions should not lightly be overridden; easily rejecting and overruling prior decisions would make a mockery of the Supreme Court as an institution, and strongly suggest this country is governed by the rule of the individuals who just happen to be on the Supreme Court when a decision is rendered, rather than by the rule of law which is the motto of this country's judicial system. As Justice John Marshall Harlan so well put it half a century ago, "[it] certainly has never been a postulate of judicial power that mere altered disposition, or subsequent membership on the Court, is sufficient warrant for overturning a deliberately decided rule of

Constitutional law."[71]

It is accepted that the principle of *stare decisis*, which is binding on all courts, is not absolute; it does not preclude an infrequent exception to acting consistently with earlier decisions – but only in the most extreme situation where the prior decision was totally and obviously wrong. Most important, that exception does not depend upon the personal feelings or political leanings of the overruling justices. Rather, rejection of a prior Court ruling is appropriate only where the overruled justices had clearly acted contrary to the letter of the law they were bound to uphold and apply. Recently, the Supreme Court explained this exception as follows: "Our precedent is to be respected unless the most convincing of reasons demonstrates that adherence to it puts us on a course that is sure error."[72]

A good example of when the *stare decisis* doctrine does not require blind adherence to an earlier decision is the previously discussed 1896 decision in *Plessy v. Ferguson*,[73] that held constitutional a Louisiana statute requiring African-Americans to ride in a railroad car separate from those for whites. Because that decision could not be reconciled with the express wording of the Constitution (in the Fourteenth Amendment) that "No State shall make or enforce any law which shall abridge the privileges ... of citizens of the United States ... nor deny to any person ... the equal protection of the laws,"[74] the Supreme Court, in the 1954 school segregation case,[75] unanimously overruled that earlier *Plessy* decision.

Hence, the Constitution, together with the rule of *stare decisis*, created a structure and procedure that should bind justices to decide cases based on what the Constitution required and, absent clear error of a prior decision, on how earlier decisions of that Court had construed the words of the Constitution. The authors of the Constitution wrote that this is exactly what they intended:

"To avoid an arbitrary discretion in the courts, it is

indispensable that they should be bound down by strict rules and precedents, which serve to define and point out their duty in every particular case ....”[76]

And they instructed that justices may not “substitute their own pleasure to the constitutional intentions of the legislature ....”[77]

Although that was the intention of the Constitution, the obvious, but uncorrectable, glitch is that the Constitution creates no body to oversee and ensure that Supreme Court justices abide by their oath to uphold the Constitution. It is this absence of any control over a justice’s decisions, once nominated and confirmed by the Senate, that has allowed some justices to render decisions not in accord with the Constitution. Yes, all justices must take the oath of office to “support and defend the Constitution,” which should cause all justices to abide by the Constitution in reaching decisions. But, as already shown and with further examples in subsequent chapters, too many justices disregard their oath and render opinions based on their personal political and social views, rather than abiding by the Constitution. This reality makes the president’s choice of a nominee to sit on the Supreme Court, and the Senate’s confirmation vote, so crucially important. It also makes essential the public’s involvement in the process, to communicate to both the president and senators strong objections to any nominee who does not recognize that a justice’s oath means making decisions based on the words and original intent of the Constitution.

On occasions, justices who vote to create a new constitutional right – contrary to anything our Founding Fathers envisaged – will pay lip service to the importance of the text of the Constitution and then ignore it to put into law their own view as to what the law should be. For example, in a decision prohibiting the death penalty for any 17-year-old, despite commission of a planned horrible murder[78] (details in example No. 11, Chapter IX), the Court majority wrote:

"the Constitution … sets forth, and rests upon, innovative principles original to the American Experience, such as federalism; a proven balance in political mechanisms through separation of powers; … and broad provisions to secure individual freedom and preserve human dignity. These doctrines and guarantees are central to the American experience and *remain essential to our present-day self-definition and national identity.*"[79]

Having paid lip service to the Constitution as written, the Court majority proceeded to rule in favor of a new constitutional right not found in the words of the Constitution. Moreover, only 15 years before, the Supreme Court had expressly rejected it as a constitutional right. So much for both the words of the Constitution and for the rule of *stare decisis*. They were cast aside as being in the way of what that Court majority personally believed *should be* the law, even though legislatures had decided to the contrary.

On other occasions, various justices have been unabashedly proud to substitute their own personal views of what society needs today for what the Constitution's words would require. Prof. Mark Tushnet, in his book, "A Court Divided,"[80] relates an anecdote that he attributes to Justice William Brennan, one of the leading liberal justices from 1956 to 1990, that dramatically portrays the view that what is in the Constitution is not as important in reaching a ruling as compared to what a Court majority of five justices decide they would prefer that the law *should be*: "Each year Brennan asked his law clerks to name the most important rule in constitutional law." I assume some clerks provided the very logical response of "the words of the Constitution," which Brennan would have summarily rejected. After they failed to provide the answer Brennan was looking for, Brennan gave them the answer: "'This,' he said, holding up one hand with his [five] fingers spread, 'is the most important rule in constitutional law.' Brennan knew that it took five votes to do anything, and, he may have thought, with five votes you can do anything."

> *"Justices Brennan and Stevens exemplify those justices who tell us that their decisions are not driven by what the Constitution says, nor by what the authors of the Constitution intended, but by what individual justices believe is the best result."*

The words and meaning of the Constitution are thus totally rewritten when that view of a justice's uncontrolled power is combined with Brennan's expressed judicial philosophy: While he says that he "look[s] to the history of the [constitutional provision at the] time of framing and to the intervening history of interpretation, ... the ultimate question [to him] must be, what do the words of the text mean in our time"; not in the "meaning it might have had in a world that is dead and gone," but how it can be adapted "to cope with current problems and current needs."[81]

Another justice, who does not feel constrained to follow the Framers' view of the Constitution and prior rulings of the Court, is Justice John Paul Stevens, who openly boasted that "our understanding of the Constitution does change from time to time."[82]

Putting it into plain English, Justices Brennan and Stevens exemplify those justices who tell us that their decisions are not driven by what the Constitution says, nor by what the authors of the Constitution intended, but by what individual justices believe is the best result. Add three more justices who vote based on their policy views, not controlled by the words of the Constitution, and you have a runaway Court, whose rulings reflect not what the Constitution says, but what the justices want the law to be.

That is not consistent with the "rule of law" that is the

bedrock of our judicial system; it converts it into the unacceptable rule of the men and women who happen to be on the Supreme Court at the time. And it rejects the time-honored instruction of the first Chief Justice of the Supreme Court, John Marshall, that, in construing constitutional provisions, "we have no need to go beyond the plain obvious meaning of these words in these provisions of the Constitution."[83] Justice Hugo Black, in 1967, also strongly disagreed with the Brennan view. Black rejected the idea that the role of the Court was "to rewrite the [constitutional provision] in order 'to bring it into harmony with the times' and thus reach a result that many people believe to be desirable;" for him, abiding by his oath to uphold the Constitution, "the language of [the constitutional provision] is the crucial place to look in construing a written document such as our Constitution."[84]

> *"Justice Antonin Scalia perhaps phrased it best when he asked this question: 'By what conceivable warrant can nine lawyers presume to be the authoritative conscience of the nation?'"*

There is no provision in the Constitution or the Bill of Rights that delegated to five justices (or even all nine) the right to impose their own personal views as to what is or is not constitutional. And, as already quoted, the Framers expressly instructed that justices may not do so. Justice Antonin Scalia perhaps phrased it best when he asked this question: "By what conceivable warrant can nine lawyers presume to be the authoritative conscience of the nation?"[85] Very recently, Justice Anthony Kennedy similarly decried allowing major policies in our democracy to depend "on what nine unrelated people from a narrow legal background have to say."[86] These statements are particularly correct, given that certain justices many times have substituted their personal views for the decision of state legislatures, which are the direct representatives of the people, and in situations in which polls show that Americans generally also reject the justices' view. Yet, some justices have assumed that power, contrary to the expressed intention of the framers of the Constitution. As they explained in the Federalist Papers, it would be the legislatures that "are more immediately the confidential guardians of the rights and liberties of the people," while the judges "are too far removed from the people to share much in their" intentions and beliefs.[87]

A binding written Constitution and the *stare decisis* rule were supposed to create a consistency of and continuity in Supreme Court decisions. This is the hallmark of the rule of law as contrasted with the rule of men. Yet, the only consistency in many crucial Supreme Court decisions is that they appear to represent the personal views of a majority of the justices as to what is politically correct and acceptable to them – often by one vote more than the dissenting justices. How else can one explain those justices' decisions in which the asserted reasoning in one case is contradicted by their decision in another case? For example: the justices' assertion that a minor under the age of 18 is mature enough to decide to have an abortion without parental consent (chapter VIII), but, because of "a lack of maturity" which results in "impetuous and ill-considered actions and decisions," the same minor may not be subject to the death penalty for the most horrible murder (chapter IX). The only possible thread of consistency between these totally opposite assertions as to the maturity of a minor under 18 is that which was necessary to support their politically correct results to overrule legislatures, because these justices personally favored abortions and opposed the death penalty.

Justices, whose decision is based on their own view as to what the law should be, rather than what the law is, unfortunately have a much greater adverse impact on our judicial system than that limited to the single case wrongly decided. If these justices proclaim their right to ignore the meaning and intent of the Constitution and ignore precedents, it legitimates earlier and subsequent decisions by justices who had a contrary view of what is best for society. For example, recall the *Plessy* decision that upheld the prohibition against African-Americans having the same right as whites to choose the railroad car in which to ride. At the time of that decision, in 1896, most of society looked upon blacks as inferior beings who should not be allowed to mix with whites. Thus, although this denial to blacks of the whites' privilege to choose the car in which to ride was a literal violation of the Fourteenth Amendment prohibition against abridging privileges of blacks, the Supreme Court then approved that abridgment because a majority of justices believed it fit within their view of societal needs. Effectively, they ruled that the Constitution be damned in favor of what they thought the law should be.

That 19th century disregard of what the Constitution said was by justices who would be categorized as conservative. In more modern times, it has been primarily justices classified as liberal who are violating their oath to uphold the Constitution. But, as already recognized, it is important to reiterate that the "activist" advocate is not limited to either liberal or conservative or Republican or Democrat. Neither being liberal nor conservative carries with it a license to ignore or rewrite the Constitution. Historically, the tendency to want to void statutes or executive actions is most found in proponents of the party not in power. (Whether one party or the other is more likely to resist implementing that desire, and abide by the principles that Justice Holmes followed, I leave to each of my readers.)

The bottom line is that judges who decide cases on the basis of their personal views are making policy as to what they personally believe the law should be, instead of being bound by their constitutional oath to decide what the law is and to apply it. These justices, by making the law rather than applying the law written by our Founders, are acting contrary to what the

Constitution mandated; the Constitution assigned the responsibility of making policy to the legislative and executive branches, not to the courts. In assuming the legislature's area of responsibility, these Supreme Court justices violate and ignore their Court's own prior ruling that "[W]e leave debatable issues as respects business, economic and social affairs to legislative decision."[88] And again, 11 years later in 1963, in a decision supported by eight of the nine justices (with the single dissenting justice not disagreeing on this point), the Supreme Court reiterated that it is required to abide by "the original constitutional proposition that courts do not substitute their social and economic beliefs for the judgment of legislative bodies, who were elected to pass laws."[89]

In the following chapters, I have chosen several important areas of constitutional law decisions of the Supreme Court, directly relevant to the safety, security, morals and health of our country and our people – basic needs of all citizens – and discuss how a simple majority of the Supreme Court justices have ignored and rewritten the Constitution to promulgate rules not in the Constitution, obviously contrary to values held by our country's founders, and often at odds with earlier Supreme Court rulings. The specific rulings of the Supreme Court discussed are: Miranda warnings (chapter VI); exclusion of truthful physical evidence of guilt due to innocent errors by a policeman (chapter VII); abortion (chapter VIII); death penalty (chapter IX & X); holding some prison sentences unconstitutional (chapter XI); pornography (chapter XII); debasing societal morality (chapter XIII); and usurping congressional power to order federal funds to be used to pay for lawsuits to attack laws enacted by Congress (chapter XIV).

I recognize that most people, including you and I, have personal, often strong, opinions on each of these subjects, as, for example, should abortions be illegal or left to the personal choice of each individual; should the death penalty be authorized or not. While, on some of these subjects, I present my own analysis on the merits, this book does not question the right of Americans to decide that abortion should be legal or illegal, or that the death penalty should be outlawed or should be allowed. Americans in this democracy have the right to make these determinations through constitutional amendments, if the Constitution, by its words and intent of its authors, already rules on the issue, or otherwise by actions by state legislatures or Congress – depending on whether the Constitution places the issue within state or federal jurisdiction. Rather, this book disputes that these and other similar issues may be decided for millions of Americans by five justices, thereby ignoring what is in the Constitution, or overruling contrary decisions by our elected legislatures. Our Founders never intended to give such untrammeled power to five persons who happen to compose a Supreme Court majority, or, in fact, to all nine, even if they were unanimous. Yet, as you will see in future chapters, justices have assumed that power.

VI.

MIRANDA:
SUPREME COURT INVENTION OF NEW
"CONSTITUTIONAL RIGHT," ALLOWING THE
GUILTY TO GO FREE

It has long been recognized by the Supreme Court that "the primary function of government ... is to render security to its subjects. And any mischief menacing that security demands a remedy commensurate with the evil."[90]   In simple language, that means that our governments, local, state and federal, have the responsibility to protect the life and property of all people from criminals by, where appropriate, jailing those who, the evidence establishes, have committed crimes endangering people, such as murder, rape, armed robbery, etc.

Has our Supreme Court in the last half-century derailed our governments from thus protecting us?   You decide, after reading these following examples and facts:

    –   The defendant and the deceased were seen quarreling, following which a shot was fired, killing the deceased.   Hours later, the police arrested the defendant in his boardinghouse room, and asked him if he owned a gun. The defendant responded affirmatively.   Asked where it was, he directed the police to the washing machine, where it was found. Ballistic tests established that gun fired the fatal shot. A jury convicted the defendant of murder. Yet, without questioning his guilt, the Supreme Court reversed the conviction, and freed the defendant, based on a Supreme Court ruling unrelated to his guilt.[91]

- A Brooklyn housewife freely confessed to taping the mouth of her four-year-old son and beating him to death with a broomstick. Based on a Supreme Court ruling, unrelated to her guilt, the trial court set her free.[92]

- The defendant freely confessed to killing his wife and five small children by stabbing them more than 100 times. Yet, based on a Supreme Court ruling, unrelated to his guilt, the trial court set him free.[93]

- A young girl disappeared from her apartment. The defendant, who lived in the same building, disappeared at the same time, and then was found and arrested in an adjoining state. A policeman, bearing a warrant for his arrest, drove to that adjoining state and started driving the defendant back. In chatting, the policeman commented that the parents of the girl were most troubled that, if she had been murdered, she had not received a Christian burial. This single comment caused the defendant to give the policeman directions to the place in which he had placed the body, and the body was thus found. Yet, based on a Supreme Court ruling, unrelated to his guilt, the trial court set him free.[94]

In most of these cases, unquestionably reliable objective evidence corroborated the defendants' admissions of guilt. Only if guilty could the defendant direct the policeman to the gun that was scientifically shown to be the murder weapon. Similarly, only if guilty could the defendant have directed the policeman to where he had buried the murdered girl. In each of these cases – and they are merely examples of many more – a murderer was returned to society instead of being put away so as to protect other innocent individuals.

The Supreme Court case, binding each of these trial judges to release a clearly guilty murderer, was one decision: *Miranda v. Arizona*[95] – a 1966 ruling that, by a slim 5 to 4 vote majority, changed the law and criminal justice rules after more than 150 years to the contrary. In *Miranda,* the Court, for the first time in its long history of considering the admissibility of a defendant's confession or other statement, held that no statements given by a defendant while in custody – no matter that it was voluntarily given – may be admitted in evidence unless the defendant had been advised (i) of his right to remain silent; (ii) that any statement he does make may be used against him; (iii) that, if he does not wish to be interviewed by the police, and he so states, the police must halt any questioning; (iv) of his right to have an attorney present while interviewed; and (v) if he does not have the financial means to retain an attorney, of his right to have an attorney appointed.

> *"Indeed, the five-justice Miranda majority expressly admitted that 'the Constitution does not require any specific code of procedure for protecting the privilege against self-incrimination during custodial interrogation.'"*

Scrutinize our Constitution as microscopically as you can, you will not find any provisions containing this standard as required for the admissibility in evidence of a defendant's self-incriminating statement. The Fifth Amendment's language concerning that subject is clear and simple: "No person ... shall be *compelled* in any criminal case to be a witness against himself."[96] It does not say, as the *Miranda* ruling mandated, that no defendant in custody may be *permitted* voluntarily to provide evidence against himself unless first given this specified five-part instruction. Indeed, the five-justice *Miranda* majority expressly admitted that "the Constitution does not require any specific code of procedure for protecting the privilege against self-incrimination during custodial interrogation."[97] Even years after the *Miranda* ruling, the Supreme Court reiterated that, what it described as the "prophylactic Miranda warnings ... are *not themselves rights that are protected by the Constitution* but are instead measures to insure that the right against compulsory self-incrimination is protected."[98]

Unexplained was the authority of these five justices to mandate this new code of procedure if "the Constitution does not require any specific code of procedure." After all, procedures to implement constitutional requirements are ordinarily enacted by legislatures, not the Court. Indeed, the Constitution delegates to Congress, not the Court, the power to "make all laws which shall be necessary and proper for carrying into execution ... all ... powers vested by this Constitution in the Government of the United States,"[99] which include the power vested in our courts over the "Trial of all Crimes."[100] Some defenders of the *Miranda* rule assert Supreme Court power to set procedural rules for the federal courts, in the absence of any statute on the subject. While true, that power over **federal** courts would not have permitted the Supreme Court to rule, as it did, that the *Miranda* rule applied to all states. A procedure that, as the Court stated, is not mandated by the Constitution, cannot be forced upon states. The Tenth Amendment to the Constitution, adopted as part of the Bill Of Rights, together with the Fifth Amendment's ban on compelled self-incrimination, limits the Supreme Court's authority over state procedures by prescribing that "[t]he powers not delegated to the United States by the Constitution ... are reserved to the States respectively ...." Nothing in the Constitution gives to the Court the power to direct non-constitutionally-required law enforcement procedures for each state.

Years later, a subsequently-appointed Supreme Court justice, who, while supporting the requirement of *Miranda* warnings, candidly admitted that, if not required by the Constitution, "the Court ... must regard the holding in the Miranda case itself, as well as all of the federal jurisprudence that has evolved from that decision, as nothing more than an illegitimate exercise of raw judicial power."[101] Rarely is there such a clear record of exercise of unconstitutional power by the Court as here: The *Miranda* majority admitted that the rule it mandated was not required by the Constitution and a later supporting justice admitted that, without a basis in the Constitution, the Court was grabbing power it did not have.

Not only is there no basis in the Constitution for the *Miranda* decision, it violated the *stare decisis* rule that, as already discussed, the Court is ordinarily duty bound to follow to not overrule its prior rulings on the same subject. No question existed on prior rulings on this subject: For almost two centuries, in applying the constitutional provision against compelled self-incrimination, the Supreme Court had rejected mandating any specific procedure to govern admissibility of a defendant's confession or statement. For example, a unanimous Supreme Court in 1884 explained:

> "The admissibility of [an admission or statement of a defendant] so largely depends upon the special circumstances connected with the confession that it is difficult, if not impossible, to formulate a rule that will comprehend all cases. [T]he courts have wisely foreborne to mark with absolute precision the limits of admission and preclusion."[102]

Many Supreme Court decisions in the Court's first century and a half rejected establishing any specific conditions precedent to admissibility of a defendant's confession, as long as the facts establish that it was voluntary. For example, a unanimous 19th century opinion written by the strong civil rights supporter, Justice John Marshall Harlan,[103] held properly admissible a confession made by a prisoner in custody, despite the absence of any *Miranda*-type warnings.[104] The Court then enunciated the following standard and procedure – at odds with the subsequent *Miranda* decision – to determine admissibility: "confinement or imprisonment is not in itself sufficient to justify the exclusion of a confession, if it appears to have been voluntary and was not obtained by putting the prisoner in fear or by promises."[105] As to the effect of being in custody when the confession was given, the Court explained that it was simply only one of the circumstances to be considered in determining from all the circumstances "whether the confession was voluntarily made, or was extorted by threats or violence, or made under the influence of fear."[106]

"Until the Miranda decision, when the five justices outvoted their four colleagues, the Supreme Court many times reiterated that a confession obtained while the defendant was in custody was admissible, without any specific required procedures, as long as the evidence showed that it was freely given and not induced by fear or threats."

Just three months later, in 1896, the Supreme Court considered an appeal in which the defendant sought to reverse his conviction on the ground that he had not been given warnings before he confessed while in custody: The interrogator "did not tell [the prisoner] that he had a right to answer or not as he chose, or advise him of his rights, or tell him he had a right to be represented by counsel."[107] The Supreme Court unanimously held the confession admissible, despite the absence of such *Miranda*-type warnings, in view of the "evidence of its voluntary character, the absence of any threat, compulsion, or inducement, or assertion or indication of fear ...."[108]

Until the *Miranda* decision, about 70 years later, when the five justices outvoted their four colleagues, the Supreme Court many times reiterated that a confession obtained while the defendant was in custody was admissible, without any specific required procedures, as long as the evidence showed that it was freely given and not induced by fear or threats.[109] The facts in some of the cases before the Supreme Court, in which the Court rejected fixing *Miranda*-type conditions precedent, demonstrate the Supreme Court's position until *Miranda*: A Fifth Amendment violation does not occur unless the evaluation of all relevant circumstances – not just the absence of warnings to the prisoner – establishes a coerced confession.

For example, in 1941, the Court upheld the admissibility of a confession in a capital conviction, despite the prisoner's detention for two days, denial of an opportunity to consult counsel, and being assaulted – all held to be illegal acts by the police. "But illegal acts ... committed in the course of obtaining a confession ... do not furnish an answer to the constitutional question we must decide," which is whether the confession was "voluntary, that is, not the result of inducements, promises, threats, violence, or any form of coercion."[110] I present this, what I consider to be a factually extreme case in which the confession was held admissible, not because the reader, or even this author, necessarily would have reached the same jury conclusion that the confession was voluntarily provided. But it demonstrates the Supreme Court's many-times-reiterated ruling that admission of a confession depends on a judge or jury determination, after considering all circumstances surrounding the confession, whether it had been voluntarily given, or coerced involuntarily. It is no different from the ultimate jury decision whether a defendant is guilty of the crime charged: The jury considers all relevant evidence, not any mechanical rule, in determining whether the defendant is guilty or not guilty. Many bystanders may disagree, but it is the jury that decides on what conclusion is reached from the evidence.

The facts of one other case are of interest in understanding the Supreme Court's long-time doctrine on admissibility of confessions. In *Crooker v. California*,[111] the defendant, while in custody for 14 hours before providing his confession, had been denied his request to call an attorney.[112] The Court concluded that "no violation of constitutional right had occurred"[113] by admitting the confession, because, considering all the evidence, a conclusion that it was voluntarily given was warranted. Among the evidence was that the defendant was a college graduate and had attended first year of law school where he had studied criminal law.[114] Those circumstances evidenced that he was not likely to be bamboozled into an involuntary confession, particularly as his criminal law studies guaranteed that he knew that he had a right to remain silent and have an attorney before he answered any questions. This is, I suggest, a totally logical decision rendered eight years before the *Miranda* ruling, but which, under the *Miranda* rule, would have resulted in freeing an obviously guilty defendant.

Thus, the *Miranda* ruling is neither required by the Constitution nor consistent with the Court's earlier decisions rejecting any need for warnings before recognizing the evidentiary value of a confession. Amazingly, almost 20 years after the *Miranda* ruling, a six-justice majority opinion in 1985, authored by Justice Sandra Day O'Connor, voiced views that appeared to contradict the reasoning behind *Miranda*: "The failure of police to administer Miranda warnings does not mean that the statements received have actually been coerced," and "when the admission is not coerced, little justification exists for permitting the highly probative evidence of a voluntary confession to be irretrievably lost to the factfinder."[115] But that recognition of the reality that the admissibility of confessions should rest on whether or not it was coerced, and not on the giving of specified warnings, did not last.

The Court quickly returned to requiring the *Miranda* warnings.

All of this establishes that the Supreme Court ignored the constitutional prohibition against the Court's power to legislate a criminal justice procedure not required by the Constitution nor enacted by Congress or state legislatures. While thus irrelevant to the Court's usurpation of power in requiring the *Miranda* warnings, let's go one step further and determine the value of these warnings: Does the *Miranda* ruling assist law enforcement authorities in protecting the life and liberty of law-abiding persons from criminals who seek to murder, rape, maim or steal property from them? I will show that the answer is clearly not. Indeed, I have never heard any proponent of the *Miranda* seriously so claim. Rather, any fair-minded evaluator must conclude that it hinders law enforcement authorities in their effort to rid our streets of such criminals.

I could rest, in answering that question, by pointing to the number of clearly guilty criminals who have been let free to repeat their crimes against other innocent people, examples of whom were set forth at the beginning of this chapter. I add another ironic example. After Miranda was finally released from prison and paroled in 1972, he was, at the age of 34, stabbed to death in a bar fight. The man suspected as the murderer invoked his *Miranda* rights and refused to talk with the police. He was released and never charged.[116] Would he have walked the streets if the police had been permitted to continue interrogating him, instead of stopping at this opening juncture? We will never know. However, what is certain is that further interrogation of that suspect could not have hurt, and may have assisted, the police's endeavor to convict the killer.

But let's not rest with the many examples of guilty persons released to society to be able to commit the same type of crimes against other innocent persons. Let's do a thorough logical analysis of the impact of the *Miranda* rules.

The analysis must start with the value to law enforcement

of obtaining a confession to be presented to a jury, which will decide whether the defendant should be returned to the streets or convicted. There is no doubt that a defendant's own statement, admitting guilt or inculpating facts, is very effective evidence for a prosecutor. Almost a century before *Miranda*, a unanimous Supreme Court extolled the value of confessions in law enforcement, as, "among the most effectual proofs in the law, ... and constitutes the strongest evidence against the party making it."[117] Even the Supreme Court in *Miranda* recognized its value: "the admissions or confessions of the prisoner ... have always ranked high in the scale of incriminating evidence."[118]

Given this admitted value of confessions to law enforcement, why then create procedural burdens to the police's ability to obtain them? The five justices who authored the *Miranda* ruling had the temerity to claim that their *Miranda* "decision is not intended to hamper the traditional function of police officers in investigating crime."[119] Yet, in each of the two following decades, the Supreme Court candidly admitted that "[j]urists and scholars uniformly have recognized that the exclusionary rule imposes a substantial cost on the societal interest in law enforcement by its proscription of what is concededly relevant evidence."[120]

Moreover, as a former prosecutor, I know how ludicrous the *Miranda* justices' assertion is that their ruling does not hamper police investigations. Without the intervention of a defense counsel, a good police officer or prosecutor very often has the ability to convince a suspect, just by talking with him, that it is in his best interests to come clean.

What happens when the police must invite in a defense counsel? Based on my experience both as a prosecutor in seeing what defense counsel advise their clients, and subsequently as a defense counsel advising my own clients, any competent defense counsel will immediately, on being retained, instruct his client to invoke his Fifth Amendment right to say nothing to the police. It would be malpractice for a lawyer to throw his client into police interrogation, certainly at least until defense counsel has reviewed all the facts, determined if, despite the inculpatory facts, there might be a way to obtain an acquittal, and even then, not permit the client to talk to the police until an attempt is made to make a deal with the prosecutor. This reality is not just my opinion, but is recognized by most experienced litigators. Indeed, Supreme Court Justice Robert H. Jackson, a former U.S. Attorney General and prosecutor, wrote in one of his opinions: "Any lawyer worth his salt will tell the suspect in no uncertain terms to make no statement to police under any circumstances."[121]

The five justices who enunciated the *Miranda* opinion wrote, contrary to Justice Jackson's practical knowledge, that "it can be assumed" the lawyer for a suspect who, in fact, is innocent "would advise his client to talk freely to police in order to clear himself."[122]   They provide no factual basis for this surprising assertion that most experienced criminal lawyers would describe as inviting malpractice liability. Why? Every lawyer knows that it is common that even a guilty client will insist on his/her innocence, making it unacceptable practice for a lawyer to accept an assertion of innocence until completing independent fact-finding, including a careful cross-examination of the client. And even when so convinced, a good lawyer will not simply have his client jump into the police interrogation chamber, but will first obtain what is called a "Queen-for-a-day" agreement with the prosecutor, providing that, if prosecution still occurs, what the client told the police would not be used against the client in the prosecutor's affirmative case.

Not only is the *Miranda* majority therefore wrong concerning their conclusion that the *Miranda* warnings would not inhibit innocent suspects from submitting themselves to police interrogation, but the subject is totally irrelevant. The objection to the *Miranda* ruling is not that innocent suspects will be found guilty because they did not subject themselves to police questioning. Rather, it is that guilty persons, who are thus threats to our society, will not be convicted because police are deprived of their ability to interrogate them without a lawyer, who will instruct the client to remain silent and object to any interview.

The five justices who voted for the *Miranda* opinion apparently recognized that the prime objection to it is that it would deny law enforcement authorities a most important tool in successfully prosecuting criminals. They thus defensively assert, without any supporting basis or even rationale, that "our decision does not in any way preclude police from carrying out their traditional investigatory functions."[123] This defensive, self-serving assertion is inconsistent with many years of Supreme Court jurisprudence. Only eight years before the *Miranda* ruling, the Supreme Court explained that a "doctrine" to "preclude police questioning ... until the accused was afforded opportunity to call his attorney" – what became a major component of the *Miranda* ruling – "would have a ... devastating effect on enforcement of criminal law."[124] Why? Because, as already quoted, the Supreme Court had, before *Miranda,* proclaimed that a confession has "always ranked high in the scale of incriminating evidence" and "constituted the strongest evidence against" the defendant.

Perhaps the strongest indication that the *Miranda* rules would hamstring law enforcement is in the virtual nationwide unanimity in opposition to them by law enforcement officials. Briefs opposing these new rules were submitted to the Supreme Court by the U.S. Attorney General, who is the top federal law enforcement official, by the attorneys general of 30 states and of Puerto Rico and the U.S. Virgin Islands, and by the National District Attorneys Association, representing all city and county district attorneys.[125] How many law enforcement officials submitted a brief favoring *Miranda*-type rules? None. Moreover, legal literature since *Miranda* documents that "thousands of violent criminals escape justice each year as a direct result of *Miranda*."[126] And, most compelling, the Supreme Court itself, after about 18 years of experience under the *Miranda* rules, recognized "the cost to society in terms of fewer convictions of guilty suspects."[127]

Thus, only the blind would deny that the *Miranda* rule hinders law enforcement. I grant that is not the end of the evaluation, because, if the *Miranda* rules provided needed protection of innocent people from an improper conviction, they may still have been of value. That's how the Supreme Court explained its acceptance of fewer convictions of guilty suspects: "That cost [of letting guilty persons go free] would simply have to be borne in the interest of enlarged protection for the Fifth Amendment privilege."[128] That leaves the question, however, of whether the *Miranda* rules meaningfully protect innocent persons from being compelled to make untruthful confessions.

Do the *Miranda* rules in fact protect against compelled untruthful confessions any more than the 175-year-old pre-*Miranda* accepted judicial procedure for implementing the Fifth Amendment's prohibition against coerced confessions? Before *Miranda*, as already shown, a jury was not permitted to consider a confession if the evidence did not establish that it was voluntarily given, without any compulsion, mistreatment, or promised reward. Often, the defendant would claim that mistreatment by the police forced him to confess. In such cases, the policemen would testify to the contrary, and the judge or jury had to determine who was telling the truth: the defendant or the police. If the defendant's testimony was accepted, the confession would be excluded; if the police testimony was accepted, the jury could consider the confession as evidence.

Defenders of *Miranda* argue that it was needed to protect innocent defendants because policemen would lie and deny any coercion was imposed to elicit the confession. I have no doubt there are some policemen, as there are persons in all professions, who would lie, by falsely denying that brutal or coercive conduct led to inducing the confession. But that does not mean that the *Miranda* warnings would protect the innocent defendant. As a practical matter, the policeman who would engage in brutal conduct to obtain a confession, and lie that he had not, would not hesitate to testify falsely that he had timely furnished *Miranda* warnings. Thus, if protection against lying was the *Miranda* purpose, it could not be successful.

Unfortunately, while it does not protect against lying, the *Miranda* warnings' requirement has another related, but adverse, impact against convicting guilty defendants. That is due to the reality that the *Miranda* rules penalize the honest policeman, who would not engage in brutal conduct to obtain a confession. That policeman also would not lie by claiming to have given *Miranda* warnings when they had not been given. The result: The freeing of a guilty defendant because the policeman was honest. What is the benefit from a rule that frees a guilty defendant who voluntarily confessed to a policeman just because the policeman honestly admits that he had neglected to inform the defendant that he did not have to confess?

The *Miranda* rule thus runs counter to law enforcement and societal needs. Why should society entreat a defendant not to confess? As already noted, the Fifth Amendment – which the five *Miranda* justices purported to be implementing – does not proscribe or even demean confession evidence; it only prohibits "compelled" confessions.

In 1884, a unanimous Supreme Court, with great clairvoyance, warned against over-protecting defendants by imposing unnecessary conditions on admissibility of confessions: "Justice and common sense have too frequently been sacrificed at the shrine of mercy."[129] Yet, a bare majority of five in *Miranda*, less than 100 years later, ignored that wise advice, as if a prior unanimous Court had never written it.

The interesting question is why. Why did these five justices overrule all of these precedents; why did they prescribe a specific litany for admissibility of confessions when the Court had many times before expressly said the Constitution required no such

> *"These five justices sought to use this issue, of the non-admissibility of confessions without the advice of counsel, as a means of social engineering of our society in a manner they personally believed would be a better society, by equalizing the poor and the rich."*

procedure; why did they suddenly mandate that, although a confession had not been compelled but voluntarily furnished, it must be excluded if the policeman had not first uttered their newly prescribed litany? The answers to each of these "why" questions are not easily found in the majority's opinion. But I suggest a possible answer: that these five justices sought to use this issue, of the non-admissibility of confessions without the advice of counsel, as a means of social engineering of our society in a manner they personally believed would be a better society, by equalizing the poor and the rich. At one point in the *Miranda* opinion, the majority asserts that, without their *Miranda* rules, the rules on admissibility of confessions "would discriminate against the defendant who does not know his rights."[130]

And who are those supposedly discriminated-against defendants? According to these five justices, they are not those "'defendant[s] whose sophistication or status'" may make them know they shouldn't talk to the police[131] – *i.e.*, the rich and educated. Thus, these five justices seek to create class equality by frustrating law enforcement's ability to obtain and use confessions: Because the rich most often have lawyers who will advise them not to cooperate with law enforcement, the poor must be placed on an equal footing to be instructed not to cooperate. This may be these five justices' opinion of good social engineering, but it is nowhere mandated in the Constitution. Rather, the Constitution delegates to Congress such social-engineering decisions, if Congress believes it good for America, which Congress has clearly demonstrated it does not.

Congress' reaction to the *Miranda* decision was an overwhelming and prompt rejection. Two years after Miranda was decided, Congress enacted a statute (18 U.S.C. §3501) to overrule the *Miranda* decision. This new statute directed that a defendant's confession is admissible in a criminal prosecution as long as the jury finds that, considering all surrounding circumstances, it was voluntarily given, even though no *Miranda*-type warnings had preceded it. This statute thus codified what had been the many Supreme Court holdings before the *Miranda* decision. For example, the Supreme Court had held in 1941 that, even though a defendant had given confessions after being improperly held without access to counsel for a lengthy period, his confessions were admissible as long as the jury was instructed "'that the confessions must be utterly disregarded unless they were voluntary, that is, not the results of inducements, promises, threats, violence, or any form of coercion'."[132] The statute also reflected the Supreme Court's statement in 1943 that the "civilized conduct of criminal trials cannot be confined within mechanical rules" but "must rely on the learning, good sense, fairness and courage of federal trial juries."[133]

In fact, Congress codified in section 3501 what the Supreme Court specified, only three years before *Miranda,* to be the correct procedure to use concerning the admissibility of confessions. In that earlier 1963 case, the defendant had been held for an "approximately 16-hour period between … his arrest and the making and signing of the written confession," and his requests "to allow him to call an attorney" were repeatedly rejected with the response that "he would not be allowed to call unless and until he 'cooperated' with the police and gave them a written and signed confession."[134] The Court reaffirmed that failure to provide the type of warnings later required by its *Miranda* decision does not automatically make a confession inadmissible. Rather, "'the true test of admissibility is that the confession is made freely, voluntarily and without compulsion or inducement of any sort'."[135]

It went on to specify the instructions that the jury should receive on how it should determine voluntariness and therefore whether it should consider the confessions as evidence: It must consider "as relevant on the issue of voluntariness of the confession the fact that a defendant ... is not cautioned that he may remain silent, that he is not warned that his answers may be used against him, or that he is not advised that he is entitled to counsel."[136] This is exactly what Congress prescribed in enacting section 3501.

As already noted, in the years following *Miranda*, the Supreme Court several times reiterated that the prescribed warnings "are not themselves rights that are protected by the Constitution but are instead measures to insure that the right against compulsory self-incrimination is protected."[137] The category "measures" was used as a synonym for "procedures." The Supreme Court had many times previously ruled that the Court had "the power to judicially create and enforce non-constitutional rules of procedure and evidence for the federal courts ... only in the absence of a relevant act of Congress."[138] Thus, while the absence of a statute, at the time the Court decided *Miranda*, may arguably have authorized the Court's promulgation of the procedure for Federal courts (but not for state courts as well), once Congress enacted §3501, it should have been held to supersede the *Miranda*-directed procedure. Therefore, by following the Supreme Court's own prior pronouncements, it should have been a slam-dunk that the Court would uphold section 3501, and direct all trial courts to follow the procedure Congress specified in that statute.

Indeed, the Supreme Court admitted, in considering the validity of §3501, that "the power to judicially create and enforce non-constitutional 'rules of procedure and evidence for the federal courts exists only in the absence of a relevant act of Congress.'"[139] Section 3501 was such an act of Congress setting forth rules of procedure and evidence for the federal courts. Yet, the Court declined to follow its own rulings and properly hold that Congress had trumped and eliminated the *Miranda* warnings, thereby undoing the Supreme Court's social engineering. To avoid that result, when the constitutionality of section 3501 came before it, suddenly the Supreme Court determined that its *Miranda* rules were constitutionally required,[140] ignoring all of its prior rulings to the contrary. The Supreme Court thereby demonstrated how far it would go to insist on its dominance over Congress in pursuing its agenda of assuming powers not granted by the Constitution, and "legislating" through Court decisions on matters that the Constitution left to the legislatures. It was a blatant assumption of power by the Supreme Court, thereby revising the Constitution, not enforcing it as written.

> *"Suddenly the Supreme Court determined that its Miranda rules were constitutionally required, ignoring all of its prior rulings to the contrary."*

One noteworthy postscript to that decision: Chief Justice Rehnquist wrote the opinion invalidating §3501, and Justice Kennedy concurred, creating a 7-2 vote. Both justices would be considered unlikely to have voted for the *Miranda* opinion if they had then been on the Court when it was decided. Unlike the justices who voted for the *Miranda* opinion who ignored *stare decisis*, Justice Rehnquist wrote that "[w]hether or not we would agree with Miranda's reasoning and the resulting rules, were we addressing the issue in the first instance, the principles of stare decisis weighs heavily against overruling it now." *Id.* at 443. Thus, *Miranda* warnings became the law when a majority of five justices ignored *stare decisis* of 150 years of rulings to the contrary – many unanimous – but it remained the law because responsible justices, who likely disagreed with the *Miranda* ruling, felt themselves bound by *stare decisis* from the *Miranda* decision only 34 years before. Hardly a rational result.

It may be hard to believe, but four justices have recently tried to extend the *Miranda* rule to exclude a defendant's statement even when he was given the prescribed warnings and never said that he wanted to halt questioning. In 2010, a defendant, convicted of first–degree murder, appealed to the Supreme Court, claiming that his statements to the police were admitted in violation of *Miranda*.[141] The defendant did not assert that his statements were compelled or that the police engaged in any threats, force, or inducements. Nor did he dispute that he received the full *Miranda* warnings; indeed, at the police request, he himself had read aloud the portion of the warnings of his "right to decide at any time ... to use your right to remain silent and ... to talk with a lawyer."[142] During the 2¾ hours of questioning following the warnings, the defendant said very little, in addition to "yeah," "no," or "I don't know" to non-substantive questions.[143] But then, when asked a series of questions on his belief in God, ending with "Do you pray to God to forgive you for shooting that boy down," he answered "yes."[144] While this was not the sole evidence of the defendant's guilt – a second shooting victim who survived also testified[145] – its receipt in evidence was the basis for the appeal to the Supreme Court.

The Court's bare majority of five ruled that, since the defendant had been fully advised of his rights, was not compelled to make his admission, and never invoked his right to halt questioning, his admission complied with *Miranda* and thus was properly received in evidence. Four justices, however, dissented, contending that the defendant's statement should have been excluded "[e]ven when warnings had been administered and [the] suspect has not affirmatively invoked his rights," and he "made inculpatory statements after Miranda warnings were given and understood."[146] According to these dissenters, a suspect's overall silence, even though interrupted by some responses, should be construed "as an invocation of the right to remain silent."[147] Can you imagine any greater example of Orwellian doublespeak: Silence is speaking.

If one more anti-law enforcement justice is appointed, the

result will be totally handcuffing the police instead of the criminals. Supporters of *Miranda* extolled it as a clear unambiguous rule. The dissenters here admitted that their extension of *Miranda* "does not provide police with a bright-line rule."[148] They do not – and cannot – instruct the police how long a period of silence must be to be construed as an invocation of the right to remain silent, so that the police would know that they have to cease their questioning. The result of such a ruling, if supported by one more justice, would be more uncertainty and caution by police in performing their duties. It would effectively limit police from seeking facts from a suspect who ponders his decision whether to respond. The bottom line of that result, barring more volunteered, un-coerced admissions, would only protect more criminals from being convicted. That, from a Supreme Court thereby legislating its belief as to what the law should be, despite Congress having already legislated otherwise, and nothing in the Constitution supporting the Court's conclusion.

VII.

SUPREME COURT REWRITES CONSTITUTION TO EXCLUDE RELIABLE AND BEST PHYSICAL EVIDENCE OF GUILT

We have seen in the preceding chapter that the Supreme Court, in its *Miranda* decision, created an exclusionary rule to exclude from evidence a defendant's confession even though no basis existed to find that it was obtained by coercion, fraudulent inducement or intimidation. The supposed rationale came down to a speculative possibility, without evidence, that the confession *might* be coerced and thus not truthful.

Not even such a speculative possibility can exist as to hard physical evidence of guilt that police may have uncovered: a dead body, a revolver that tests establish was used in the murder, illicit drugs, counterfeit money, stolen jewelry, burglary tools, etc. This type of hard evidence, if connected to the defendant by being in defendant's possession or bearing defendant's fingerprints, is independent and extremely convincing evidence of guilt. The probative value and reliability of such evidence does not depend on whether the police officers, in finding and seizing that evidence, did or did not first obtain a search or arrest warrant from a judge or magistrate. Nor can the probative value of such evidence be speculated away on the possibility that this evidence would not have been there if a warrant had first been sought.

Consider these actual cases and decide for yourself whether the evidence should have been admitted and the conviction affirmed:

A. An undercover police officer, who had previously been in defendant Mincey's apartment and made arrangements to return to buy heroin from him, returned with other policemen and a county attorney. As they entered, Mincey fired a volley of shots, killing the undercover police officer. Mincey was convicted of murder, assault and narcotics offenses. Among the evidence used to convict him was evidence gathered in the apartment by homicide detectives who arrived within 10 minutes of the shooting, and continued the search for four days, without a warrant. The evidence was overwhelming in support of guilt. The Supreme Court recognized that, if any of the policemen who had been present at the time of the shooting had immediately started to perform the search, the emergency situation created by the shooting would have validated the warrantless search. But, in compliance with a local Police Department directive that prohibited police officers from investigating incidents in which they are involved, those policemen, because they had been present when shot at, allowed the homicide detectives who arrived at the scene within 10 minutes to do the search.[149]

B. Powell was convicted in state court of murder in shooting a store manager's wife, on evidence that included (i) his possession of a revolver seized by police when he was arrested without a warrant on a vagrancy charge 10 hours after the murder, and (ii) expert testimony that the seized gun had killed the victim.[150]

C. Rice was convicted of murder of a policeman who had been lured to a location where a suitcase full of explosives detonated when the policeman examined it. Police obtained a warrant to search Rice's residence, where they discovered dynamite, blasting caps and other materials used in constructing explosive devices. When Rice, who was not at his residence, surrendered, his clothes tested positive for dynamite particles.[151]

D. The murder victim was a chambermaid in the hotel who disappeared after she went to her sixth-floor assignment immediately after reporting to work at 9 a.m. Her clothes and partially eaten lunch were found on that floor. She was not located during an initial search by hotel residents and management, nor on a subsequent police search. Mitchell, in his room, denied seeing her, and the police, glancing at the room while talking to Mitchell, did not see anything suspicious. Later that day, after Mitchell had gone out, police opened Mitchell's room door with a passkey, noticed a reddish-brown stain on various items, and then opened the closet door where they found the chambermaid's body.[152]

Following are the court decisions on admissibility of the seized evidence in each of these cases:

A. The Supreme Court reversed the Arizona Supreme Court's ruling upholding admissibility of the evidence, and ordered a new trial with the evidence from the search excluded.

B. The Supreme Court held that, because the officer lacked probable cause to arrest Powell, this seized evidence would have had to be excluded if the defendant had made a motion to exclude at trial.

C. The Supreme Court held that the search was invalid because of insufficient basis in the supporting affidavit, and thus, a correct decision at the trial would have been to exclude the evidence.

D. The New York Court Of Appeals, clearly attempting to abide by binding Fourth Amendment rulings by the Supreme Court, and yet motivated not to release a defendant obviously guilty of murder, felt compelled to engage in the most disingenuous reasoning to allow this evidence. It relied on the exception to requiring a warrant when "the protection of human life or property in imminent danger [is] the motivation for the search rather than the desire to apprehend a suspect or gather evidence for use in a criminal proceeding."[153]   Objectively considered, the facts strongly negated that the police had any real hope, and thus motive, to find the chambermaid alive.   The partially eaten lunch suggested an interruption; she could not have voluntarily left without her clothes; the reddish-brown stain around the room suggested foul play; the chambermaid had been missing in this limited area for a number of hours; and no sound came from the closet to which the detectives were self-directed by finding the blood-color stains in the room. If these judges were forced to abide by Supreme Court rulings, they would have had to admit that the detectives should have first obtained a search warrant before using a passkey to enter defendant's room and search the closet. But, to keep a murderer out of society, these judges were forced to engage in a charade to find this police activity was still trying to save the chambermaid's life. The Supreme Court rulings, discussed in detail below, did not allow for the honest ruling that, whatever technical error the detectives made in not first seeking a search warrant, the evidence found – including the chambermaid's body in his closet – was so reliable and so overwhelmingly establishing of guilt, that the murder conviction must be affirmed. Wouldn't that honest reasoning have been a better path to have allowed that court to follow?

The New York Court Of Appeals was not permitted to make that honest and correct ruling because a majority of Supreme Court justices has created an exclusionary rule that excludes such unquestionably valid and important evidence of guilt. In creating this exclusionary rule, these justices did not even question the reliability of the seized evidence. Instead they looked solely to certain procedural technicalities: Did the seizing police officers first obtain a search or arrest warrant or have an emergency need to enter the premises or arrest the defendant? If the answer is in the negative, the evidence must be excluded.

Moreover, the justices have extended this judge-created rule to create a further evidence bar that might properly be

> *"One does not have to be a lawyer, and certainly not a justice, to be able to read the Fourth Amendment, which has only 54 words, and conclude that nothing in the Fourth Amendment provides that evidence obtained without a warrant must be excluded."*

described as taking the ridiculous to the absurd: Even where the evidence was seized after the police officer, following the procedural rules, had sought and obtained a warrant from a judge or magistrate, but a later reviewing court determined that the judge erred by issuing the warrant without a sufficient basis, the exclusionary rule would still be applied to exclude the evidence.

In excluding all such credible evidence, these justices assert that they are thereby enforcing the Fourth Amendment. One does not have to be a lawyer, and certainly not a justice, to be able to read the Fourth Amendment, which has only 54 words, and conclude that nothing in the Fourth Amendment provides that evidence obtained without a warrant must be excluded. Indeed, the Fourth Amendment does not even require a warrant for police to perform a search or seize evidence. Rather, it provides only that, for a search and seizure to be lawful, it must not be "unreasonable," and that *if* a warrant is obtained, it must be based "upon probable cause" and "particularly describ[e] the place to be searched, and the persons or things to be seized."

Further, all historical evidence establishes that our Framers and more than a century of Supreme Court rulings rejected the exclusionary rule which 20th century justices suddenly imposed to exclude such valid evidence of guilt.

The language used in the Fourth Amendment followed closely the phraseology used in certain state constitutions, one of which was New Hampshire's,[154] enacted in 1784, seven years before ratification of the Fourth Amendment. The Supreme Court of New Hampshire recognized that the language was not "intended to restrain the legislature from authorizing [police action] without warrant, but to guard against abuse of warrants after issuance by Magistrates."[155]

Supreme Court Justice Joseph Story, the recognized and respected Constitutional scholar, authored *Commentaries on the United States Constitution*, first published in 1833, which is still frequently cited in construing our Constitution. Justice Story held in an 1822 decision that "the right of using evidence does not depend, nor ... has ever been supposed to depend, upon the lawfulness or unlawfulness of the mode, by which it is obtained. .... [T]he evidence is admissible on charges of the highest crimes, even though it may have been obtained by the highest crimes, ... or any other forcible and illegal means."[156]

As late as 1904, a unanimous Supreme Court reaffirmed Justice Story's ruling, to hold that, although evidence used against a defendant may have been "'unlawfully obtained, this is no valid objection to their admissibility if they are pertinent to the issue.' [C]ourts do not stop to inquire as to the means by which the evidence was obtained."[157] The famed civil libertarian Justice Benjamin Cardozo, while he was sitting on the New York Court of Appeals, explained why he agreed with this ruling:

> "A room is searched against the law, and the body of a murdered man is found. If the place of discovery may not be proved, the other circumstances may be insufficient to connect the defendant with the crime. The privacy of the home has been infringed and the murderer goes free. .... We may not subject society to these dangers."[158]

Justice Cardozo then succinctly explained his rejection of the exclusionary rule: It is contrary to reason and the enforcement of justice that the "criminal is to go free because the constable has blundered."[159] It is difficult to comprehend anyone disagreeing with this practical logic.

Yet, in 1914, the Supreme Court suddenly found that the

Fourth Amendment required the prosecutor to return and not use as evidence anything seized without what the justices determined to be strict compliance with that amendment.[160]

But on what basis did they declare that the exclusionary rule was a requisite of strict compliance with the Fourth Amendment? It certainly does not appear in the words of that amendment. Indeed, the justices later admitted that the exclusionary rule, barring use of such evidence in prosecutions, "was not derived from the explicit requirements of the Fourth Amendment; it was not based on legislation," but was solely "a matter of judicial implication."[161] To put it in simple terms, the Supreme Court admitted that its exclusionary rule was not created by the authors of the Constitution or amendments, and was not legislated by Congress, but was mandated by the judgment of a majority of Supreme Court justices as what they believed our Founding Fathers and our Congress should have provided, but did not.

Amazingly, the Supreme Court decision that first imposed the exclusionary rule on our courts asserted that its purpose was to "perpetuat[e] ... principles of humanity and civil liberty which had been secured in the mother country ..., so as to implant them in our institutions."[162] These justices, however, knew and thus ignored that England had never adopted an exclusionary rule to enforce the civil liberty principles copied into the Fourth Amendment.[163]

Examining the Court's reasoning in creating this exclusionary rule makes the decision even more mystifying and fallacious.

First, these justices sought to justify the exclusionary rule, and requiring return of such evidence to the defendant, on the ground that, if the evidence could "be seized and held and used in evidence against a citizen accused of an offense, the protection of the 4th Amendment ... is of no value, and, so far as those thus placed are concerned, might as well be stricken from the

Constitution."[164] But that is demonstrably not true. As the Supreme Court long before recognized, the Fourth Amendment was designed "to punish wrongful invasion of the home of the citizen or the unwarranted seizure of his papers and property," by disciplinary action against the policeman/violator or holding him personally liable.[165] Similarly, 35 years after announcing this exclusionary rule, a Supreme Court majority declared that the Fourth Amendment was sufficiently enforced on violation by state officials, by remanding victims of state official's illegal searches "to the remedies of private action and such protection as the internal discipline of the police."[166]

> *"No Supreme Court justice has ever disputed the obvious: that 'the rule of exclusion,' of unquestionable evidence establishing guilt, 'results in the escape of guilty persons.'"*

Congress expressly provided the statutory remedy to punish the police violator: Any police officer or any other government official who, "under color of any law," deprives "any person" of "any rights ... protected by the Constitution ... shall be fined ... or imprisoned not more than one year or both."[167] An example of the effective use of this statute to punish law enforcement officials who violate the Fourth Amendment is the conviction and imprisonment of a Georgia sheriff for depriving a defendant of his Fourth Amendment rights,[168] with the Court specifying that the "purpose of the statute was ... to furnish the means of ... vindication" of any violated constitutional right.[169]

No Supreme Court justice has ever disputed the obvious: that "the rule of exclusion," of unquestionable evidence establishing guilt, "results in the escape of guilty persons."[170] That is because "the physical evidence sought to be excluded is typically reliable and often the most probative information bearing on the guilt or innocence of the defendant," and "often this evidence alone establishes beyond any shadow of a doubt that the defendant is guilty'."[171]

Then what is the supposed benefit from excluding such convincing evidence of guilt and freeing criminals to return to society to be free to commit additional crimes against innocent people? The 20th century Supreme Court explanation for the exclusionary rule was that it was necessary to deter other law enforcement officials from violating the Fourth Amendment: "Its purpose is to deter – to compel respect for the constitutional guaranty in the only effectively available way – by removing the incentive to disregard it."[172]

There are many obvious flaws in relying on any deterrence effect from excluding from evidence the results of a search and seizure that failed to comply with the Fourth Amendment. First, there can be no or very little deterrence impact when the act supposedly being deterred is not intentional, but the result of negligent misjudgment. Take automobile accidents as an example. No one wants to be responsible for an automobile accident. The imposition of liability for the results of an accident that a driver negligently caused adds no deterrence against being involved in an accident that no driver wants. The same is true as to almost all search and seizures by law enforcement officials: The law enforcement official performing the search and seizure has no interest in spinning his wheels in performing a search that will be held invalid with the results excluded from use at trial.

Many searches that have been invalidated involved a policeman who provides an affidavit of probable cause to a judge or magistrate who concludes that the search warrant should be issued and does so. If the judge had said that more evidence was needed, the policeman could have added additional basis to his affidavit. If a later court rules that the affidavit was insufficient probable cause, and thereby excludes the seized evidence, it is not even the policeman who was negligent – it was the issuing judge. Excluding such evidence cannot result in deterring any subsequent search warrant being issued, like this now-invalidated one, on the good-faith belief of both the police officer and judge that the affidavit supplied sufficient cause.

Likewise, it can have no deterrent effect on any police officer who performs a search without obtaining a warrant where he holds the good faith belief that emergent circumstances warrant the search, knowing that it is his responsibility to do so in emergent circumstances, as the courts have upheld. The realistic bottom line is that no police officer is intentionally going to perform a search that he knows will be held invalid. That, despite this almost 100-year history of the courts' exclusion of evidence due to a policeman's mistake, many police searches continue to be held invalid, establishes that the exclusionary rule has had no deterrent effect.

I am not the only person who has reached this conclusion that the exclusionary rule has had no deterrent effect. As already discussed, it was first in 1914 that the Supreme Court imposed its exclusionary rule. It was only in 1961 – almost 50 years later – that the Supreme Court decided that the Fourteenth Amendment – which also says nothing about any exclusionary rule – required all states to exclude evidence obtained in a search that failed to meet Fourth Amendment specifications.[173] Thus, for almost 50 years after the Supreme Court imposed its exclusionary rule on criminal prosecutions in the federal courts, it allowed state courts to use search evidence that would have been excluded in federal criminal cases. During that period, in which each state could decide for itself whether an exclusionary rule should be imposed, about two-thirds of the states rejected the exclusionary rule and allowed the evidence where the search was held to be illegal.[174] This division among the states created a perfect test on whether the imposition of an exclusionary rule in fact reduced the number of searches that violated the Fourth Amendment. The Supreme Court reported the results of that comparison: "There is no reliable evidence ... that inhabitants of those states which exclude the evidence suffer less from lawless searches and seizures than those of states that admit it."[175] As late as 1960, even the five justices upholding the exclusionary rule admitted that they could not "show that the inhabitants of states which follow the exclusionary rule suffer less from lawless searches and seizures than do those of states which admit evidence unlawfully obtained."[176] The best that two of the most adamant supporters of the exclusionary rule, Justices Brennan and Marshall, could say about its deterrence value was that it was "guesswork about deterrence."[177]

Faced with this proof that deterrence does not support the creation of the exclusionary rule, some justices retreat to the claim that the exclusionary rule is necessary to maintain "respect for" our criminal justice system.[178] What basis is offered to support that claim, other than these justices' say-so? Do they really believe that from 1791, when the Fourth Amendment became effective, until 1914, when a majority of justices suddenly imposed the exclusionary rule on the federal courts, our criminal justice system had no integrity? Not even exponents of the exclusionary rule have so defamed our country's first 123 years. To reach that conclusion, one would also have to hold that the criminal justice systems in all of the British Commonwealth, including the United Kingdom, Canada and Australia – recognized bastions of due process and from whom we drew our Bill Of Rights – have no integrity, as none of those jurisdictions has imposed an exclusionary rule.[179] Even the European Court of Human Rights held in 2000 that England's allowing use of improperly seized evidence did not deny a convicted defendant a fair trial.[180]

Finally, other decisions by the Supreme Court demonstrate that even it recognizes that the exclusionary rule is not required by the Constitution, and that, therefore, evidence seized in a search inconsistent with Fourth Amendment requirements is not *per se* excluded from use in court. If the Constitution barred such evidence, it could never be used in any judicial proceedings. But, to the contrary, the Supreme Court has held that, as long as the evidence is not offered as affirmative evidence in a criminal trial against the defendant, it is admissible. Thus, the Supreme Court has held that such evidence may be introduced by the government (i) in grand jury proceedings, (ii) in opposing a *habeas corpus* proceeding brought by the defendant after a conviction, (iii) to impeach a defendant, even in the criminal trial against the defendant who has testified contrary to the facts established by the "illegal" search,[181] and (iv) in civil proceedings even when commenced by the government.[182] Also, (v) the testimony of a witness, who is located only because of information obtained in an "illegal" search, was allowed over the objection that it rewards the government for the "illegal" search.[183] Finally, (vi) the Supreme Court rejected the application of any exclusionary rule to bar "illegal" search evidence from parole revocation hearings,[184] and (vii) from deportation proceedings.[185]

Allowing the introduction of evidence seized in a supposedly illegal search in these many types of cases is inconsistent with excluding the evidence in a criminal case – either admission of such evidence is not allowed by the Constitution, or it is allowed. How did the Supreme Court explain why it rejected the exclusionary rule in, for example, civil deportation proceedings, but applies it in criminal proceedings? Supposedly, it was based on "weigh[ing] the likely social benefits of excluding unlawfully seized evidence against the likely costs."[186] The Court found that "application of the exclusionary rule in [deportation proceedings] would compel the courts to release from custody persons who would then immediately resume their commission of a crime through their continuing, unlawful presence in this country."[187]

Can you believe this topsy-turvy thinking? I do not excuse illegal immigrants for their violation of U.S. law by entering illegally and staying in this country. But it is obvious that the adverse effect on our society and innocent people in the deportation-proceeding context is non-existent when compared with a rapist, murderer or robber who is set free because the exclusionary rule is applied to prevent introduction of evidence obtained in an "illegal" search, thus preventing a conviction. Most illegal immigrants, particularly such as those arrested in the case in which the Supreme Court held that the exclusionary rule should not be applied in deportation hearings, are peaceful working people, arrested at their place of employment, whose only crime is trying to remain in this country. The defendant who commits a rape, murder or robbery not only has already harmed innocent persons, but, due to the very high recidivism rate of such criminals,[188] is very likely to repeat such crimes against other innocent people. Thus, according to this reasoning by a majority of justices, the consequence of allowing a peaceful, working, illegal immigrant to remain in this country is too high a price for society to pay to apply the exclusionary rule, but allowing a rapist, murderer or robber to return to his criminal activities is not too high a price for application of the exclusionary rule. That makes no sense.

One other reality puts the icing on the cake that the exclusionary rule simply does not work. The greatest injury from an illegal search befalls the innocent person who has committed no crime, and suddenly has the police bursting into his or her home and disrupting all personal belongings without a warrant or without any justification. The Supreme Court has admitted that the "wrong condemned by the Amendment is 'fully accomplished' by the unlawful search itself, ... and the exclusionary rule is neither intended nor able to 'cure the invasion ... which he has already suffered.'"[189]

So let's get back to the Fourth Amendment and its wording, which, as already discussed, does not mandate or even mention any exclusion of reliable evidence obtained in violation of any Fourth Amendment provision. The Fourth Amendment specifies that its purpose is to protect the "right of the people to be secure in their persons, houses, papers and effects." I recognize that it continues with the words "against unreasonable searches and seizures." But no one seriously would deny that the reason our country was formed included the protection by our government of the overall "right of the people to be secure in their persons [and] houses." Indeed, our government was created to fulfill the promise of our Declaration of Independence to all Americans that our "new Government" would "effect their Safety and Happiness." The right to be secure and safe in one's home, and thus any person's safety and happiness, is more threatened by releasing back into circulation a murderer or rapist or assaulter of innocent persons than by a police officer who negligently fails to meet all the conditions of the Fourth Amendment. In worldly reality, what person would rather be murdered or raped than be the object of a law enforcement search that failed to obtain a warrant?

A unanimous 1927 Supreme Court opinion said it well: "A criminal prosecution is more than a game in which the government may be checkmated and the game lost merely because its officers have not played according to rule."[190] Somehow a majority of justices ignored their own stated lesson by rewriting the Constitution to require public safety be checkmated in favor of a technicality not mandated by either the Constitution or any legislative act.

> *"The right to be secure and safe in one's home, and thus any person's safety and happiness, is more threatened by releasing back into circulation a murderer or rapist or assaulter of innocent persons than by a police officer who negligently fails to meet all the conditions of the Fourth Amendment."*

VIII.

FORCING LEGALIZED ABORTION ON ALL STATES - SEVEN JUSTICES REJECTED PRECEDENT AND STATES' RIGHTS

It was only about four decades ago that the Supreme Court, by its decision in *Roe v. Wade*,[191] declared state statutes prohibiting abortions to be unconstitutional, thereby altering a long history to the contrary.

The *Roe* decision remains an emotional and divisive issue in our country. Justice Harry Blackmun, writing for seven out of the nine members of the Court, recognized the nuclear impact their decision would have on our society and values by acknowledging "the sensitive and emotional nature of the abortion controversy, and of the deep and seemingly absolute convictions that the subject inspires," influenced by one's "philosophy, one's experiences ... one's religious training, one's attitude towards life and family and their values, and the moral standards one establishes and seeks to observe."[192]

Given this recognition of great differences in our society on the issue, one would think that the Court would not interfere with the judgment of state legislatures, and would declare abortion a constitutional right only if they found in the Constitution an express protection of a right to an abortion. Of course, there is no such provision in the Constitution. Instead, the *Roe* Court relied on a two-step assertion: that the Constitution guaranties an individual's right of privacy, and that privacy right encompasses a woman's right to an abortion. But neither of those "rights" – privacy or abortion – is even mentioned in the Constitution, although, as already discussed, other specific rights are expressly enumerated in the Bill of Rights.

The public debate over this decision unfortunately has primarily rested on the irrelevant issue of whether abortion should be legal. In actuality, those who oppose the Supreme Court legalization of abortions recognize the right of the people in any state to allow abortions, even on demand. This determination is left by the Constitution to a decision by each state, through the elected state legislature or referendum of the people. The Constitution did not delegate to nine justices the power to decide what should be lawful in the areas of safety, health, morality, and social and physical well-being in each state, and thereby overrule the judgment of the state legislatures; rather, such decisions were reserved for the states.

> "*The Roe Court relied on a two-step assertion: that the Constitution guaranties an individual's right of privacy, and that privacy right encompasses a woman's right to an abortion. But neither of those 'rights' – privacy or abortion – is even mentioned in the Constitution...*"

Significantly, even Justice Ruth Bader Ginsburg (whom, despite my disagreement with many of her views, I salute as extremely intelligent and a wonderful human being), known as a champion of women's rights, recently criticized the *Roe v. Wade* decision, as having "moved too far, too fast," to reach a result with which she agreed, but that should have been left to a decision "legislature by legislature," not "by unelected judges."[193]

No Provision In The Constitution Or Bill Of Rights
Of A Right Of Privacy Or Abortion

The Constitution, as originally adopted, contained no guaranties of rights to individuals. It was that void in the Constitution that caused the early adoption of the Bill of Rights – the first ten amendments to the Constitution – pursuant to which certain specified rights of each individual were expressly protected, but only against federal government interference, as the Bill of Rights was not applicable to state action. Let's revisit what is included in the Bill Of Rights:

First Amendment: freedom of "religion," "speech," "press," "assembly" and "to petition the Government";

Second Amendment: "to keep and bear arms";

Third Amendment: to prevent compulsory quartering of a soldier in one's home;

Fourth Amendment: "against unreasonable searches and seizures" of "persons" and "houses";

Fifth Amendment: requirement of grand jury indictment to charge a felony crime, prohibition of double jeopardy, and against being "compelled in any criminal case to be a witness against himself" (self-incrimination), and guaranty of "due process" before "life, liberty, or property" is taken;

Sixth Amendment: guaranty in criminal cases of "a speedy and public trial" and other procedural protections;

Seventh Amendment: right to jury trial in civil cases;

Eighth Amendment: prohibits "excessive bail," "excessive fines," and "cruel and unusual punishments";

The Ninth and Tenth Amendments do not protect any specific rights, but instead provide rules to interpret and apply the Constitution. The Ninth Amendment guaranties that any rights that Americans had in 1791, when the Bill of Rights was enacted, remain rights of the people, even though such rights are not specifically mentioned in the Constitution as amended. The Tenth Amendment provides that all powers that the Constitution does not delegate to the federal government, nor prohibit to the states, remain powers of the states (or of the people).

Thus, the Bill of Rights provides great specificity of those individual rights that it was guarantying. There is no mention of any "Right Of Privacy" as a general right, or of abortion as a specific right. Hence, pursuant to the Ninth and Tenth Amendments, unless a right to abortion existed in 1791 – which it did not – the power to decide whether abortion should be allowed or prohibited is left to each state.

How did the *Roe* Court reach its conclusion that state statutes that prohibited or meaningfully restricted abortions were unconstitutional as a violation of an unspecified component of the unexpressed right of privacy? Let's analyze both essentials of the decision: that the Constitution creates a right of privacy, and that the privacy right embraces a right to abortion, and see what support each has. That

> *"The seven justices who voted to strike down the many state laws against abortion ignored the words of the Constitution and multiple legal principles previously enunciated by the Supreme Court, and by hook or by crook reached the conclusion that they personally preferred."*

analysis demonstrates that the seven justices who voted to strike down the many state laws against abortion ignored the words of the Constitution and multiple legal principles previously enunciated by the Supreme Court, and by hook or by crook reached the conclusion that they personally preferred, thereby overriding the contrary decisions of elected state legislatures.

Very early in the life of our country, the still-revered fourth Chief Justice of the Supreme Court, John Marshall, in an opinion for the Court, wrote a simple explanation of how we should determine if the Constitution was intended to protect a particular right: While "the spirit of an instrument, especially of a constitution, is to be respected not less than its letter, yet the spirit is to be collected chiefly from its words."[194] As we have seen, there are no words in the Bill of Rights that speak of either a right of privacy or a right to an abortion.

> "The authors of our Bill of Rights did not intend to protect an all-encompassing right of privacy. If they had, they would have specified privacy as one of the rights protected in the Bill of Rights."

Significantly, while the Bill of Rights does not mention either privacy or abortion as a protected right, among the rights it does enumerate are several guaranties against carefully delineated invasion of privacy: the right not to have the privacy of one's home violated by compulsory quartering soldiers in the home (Third Amendment); the right not to have the privacy of one's home, property, and body violated by any unreasonable search and seizure (Fourth Amendment); and the right not to have the privacy of one's mind violated by being compelled to testify against oneself (Fifth Amendment). Two conclusions are inescapable from this careful and limited specification of rights against specified invasions of privacy:

First, the authors of our Bill of Rights did not intend to protect an all-encompassing right of privacy. If they had, they would have specified privacy as one of the rights protected in the Bill of Rights and would not have needed to specify the three rights that they did because they would have been covered within a general right to privacy. It is logical to conclude from the express inclusion of certain specific rights of privacy that the authors did not intend to create others (such as an abortion right). Courts uniformly accept that reasoning in construing the meaning of any controlling law: "A frequently stated principle of statutory construction is that when legislation expressly provides a particular remedy or remedies, courts should not expand the coverage ... to subsume other remedies."[195] In simple terms, because the authors of our Bill of Rights expressly guaranteed specific rights involved in the protection of an individual's privacy, they excluded others, and courts are not permitted to expand the Bill of Rights to add other specific rights or a general right of privacy.

Second, if the authors of our Bill of Rights intended that a right to abortion be protected, they would have said so, just as they specified the protected rights in the Second, Fourth and Fifth Amendments.

Yet, the majority in the Supreme Court violated that bedrock rule of construction, in holding that state statutes which prohibited or strictly regulated abortions were unconstitutional as an unspecified component of an unexpressed right of privacy.

The Justices Who Found A Right Of Privacy In The Constitution Can't Even Agree Where In The Constitution It Is Found

So where in the Constitution did the seven justices purport to find that all-encompassing right of privacy? Believe it or not, they admit that justices who believe such right exists do not agree on the provision of the Constitution that is the source of this asserted right. Over the years, as the *Roe* majority recognized, the Court has cited six different constitutional provisions as the possible source of that freedom: "[i]n various contexts, the Court or individual Justices have indeed found at least the roots of that right" – note, not that right itself, but the "roots" of that right, whatever that means – "in the First Amendment, in the Fourth and Fifth Amendments, in the penumbras of the Bill of Rights, in the Ninth Amendment, or in the concept of liberty guaranteed by the first section of the Fourteenth Amendment."[196] Let's examine each of those supposed sources.

Right Of Privacy Not Found In Any Of The Cited Parts Of The Bill Of Rights

The First Amendment protects Americans from any law restricting freedom of religion, press, or assembly and the right to petition the government. In guarantying free exercise of religion, perhaps it can be stated that the First Amendment guaranties the right of privacy in practicing one's religion. But it is illogical to infer from freedom of religion an all-encompassing right of privacy, when, if a right of privacy had been intended, the authors could have easily included it with the other rights expressly specified. Moreover, none of the other specified rights in the First Amendment in any way involves privacy; indeed, they suggest the antithesis of privacy by protecting one's right freely to communicate to others. Thus, no basis exists to find a general right of privacy in the First Amendment.

The Fourth and Fifth Amendments protect specific, carefully delineated, rights that may be said to involve the privacy of individuals against search of one's home and person without warrant, and against self-incrimination. Again, there is no logical basis to conclude that those protections also create a general right of privacy. Wording that specifies what is covered cannot rationally be construed to cover other unspecified items, because, if the drafter intended to include other items, he would have expressly mentioned them as well.

As to "the penumbras of the Bill of Rights," all that "penumbra" means is a right "guaranteed by implication."[197] Hence, this phrase is an acknowledgement that no right of privacy is in fact found in the Constitution. To say that it is implied ignores the illogic of finding a right of privacy in the Bill Of Rights, which, although carefully explicit as to those rights being protected, does not specify any right of privacy.

Relying on the Ninth Amendment demonstrates the

bankruptcy of the *Roe* decision's finding a right of privacy that is then used to uphold a newly found constitutional right to choose abortion. The Ninth Amendment states that the "enumeration in the Constitution, of certain rights, shall not be construed to deny or disparage others retained by the people." Thus, for a right to be protected by this amendment, it had to be a right that was already possessed by the people. But, at the time of our country's founding and for almost two centuries thereafter, abortion was not a right, and it was, from early in the life of our country, in fact a crime in most states.[198] And the first mention by the Supreme Court of a general right of privacy came close to two centuries after our Constitution's adoption.

The *Roe* Court ignored the meaning of the Ninth Amendment. Why did the authors of our Bill of Rights include the Ninth Amendment, which, unlike the First through the Eighth Amendments, contains no specific right? Because they recognized the logical, accepted rule of construction that the specification of certain rights in those first eight amendments would warrant the conclusion that no other rights existed. The Framers, therefore, expressly provided that their "enumeration ... of certain rights, shall not be construed to deny ... others" to the extent that they then existed. But the converse is also true: Because the right of privacy did not then exist, the enumeration of certain rights in the Bill of Rights meant that a right of privacy (and a right to abortion) was not created by the Bill of Rights. The Court, in its rush to validate abortions, never even tried to resolve this defect in its reasoning.

The Last Possible Source: The Fourteenth Amendment

The last possible source mentioned by the *Roe* Court for finding the unsaid right of privacy, and the one on which the *Roe* Court ends up relying to hold that state statutes prohibiting abortions are unconstitutional, is "in the liberty guaranteed by the first section of the Fourteenth Amendment." That supposed location as the source of a right to privacy requires scrutiny of the cases the *Roe* Court cited[199] as previously finding a right of privacy, and then the Fourteenth Amendment itself.

The cases on which Roe relies do not support a general right of privacy

The earliest decision cited, an 1891 Supreme Court ruling, refused to compel "a woman to lay bare [her] body or to submit it to the touch of a stranger without lawful authority."[200] The Court in that decision described that conduct as "an assault, and a trespass,"[201] but never used the phrase right of privacy. It did not need to because it was akin to an unreasonable search and seizure of that woman's person, expressly prohibited by the Fourth Amendment. Other cases that the *Roe* Court cites as having previously recognized a constitutionally protected right of privacy in fact also relate to a specific constitutional amendment: the First Amendment right to read books of a person's choosing, even pornography,[202] and to give a lecture;[203] the right of association, which "is a form of expression of opinion" protected by the First Amendment," particularly in marriage;[204] the Fourth Amendment right to be free from search and seizure without a warrant;[205] and the right of a teacher to teach and a student to learn, akin to the freedom of speech expressly protected by the First Amendment, which are rights "long freely enjoyed."[206]

None of these cases, relied on by the Supreme Court for purportedly holding the right to an abortion to be constitutionally protected, points to any specific constitutional provision as creating a general right of privacy, separate from the specific privacy protected in the identified amendments. And in fact, two of these cases contain language that actually negates any constitutional (general) right of privacy.

In 1923, the Supreme Court enumerated "rights long freely enjoyed," and therefore considered as protected by the Fourteenth

Amendment: "the right of the individual to contract, to engage in any of the common occupations of life, to acquire useful knowledge, to marry, establish a home and bring up children, to worship God according to the dictates of his own conscience, and generally to enjoy those privileges long recognized at common law as essential to the orderly pursuit of happiness by free men."[207] Significantly, the right to an abortion was not included – clearly because it could not have been called a "right long enjoyed," or even a right then enjoyed, given that, at the time of that Supreme Court decision, an abortion was considered a criminal act.

Even more telling – but ignored by the Supreme Court majority in *Roe* – is the **rejection** by the Supreme Court of a general right of privacy, in a 1967 decision[208] – six years before the *Roe* decision. While that decision concerned the Fourth Amendment, it applies equally to the Fourteenth Amendment, which was enacted to impose on the states the same restrictions against violation of rights that the first 10 amendments applied against the federal government. The Supreme Court in that 1967 decision held that "the Fourth Amendment cannot be translated into a general 'right of privacy,'" but can only be applied "against certain kinds of governmental intrusion." The opinion then continued to make clear that the protections against privacy intrusions are limited to the specific rights in each of the Bill of Rights:

> "The First Amendment ... imposes limitations upon governmental abridgement of 'freedom to associate and privacy in one's associations. [citation omitted]. The Third Amendment's prohibition against the unconsented peacetime quartering of soldiers protects another aspect of privacy from governmental intrusion. To some extent, the Fifth Amendment too 'reflects the Constitution's concern for ... the right of each individual to a private enclave where he may lead a private life.'" [209]

Then, this coup de grace against the *Roe* majority's reliance on a general right of privacy:

> "Virtually every governmental action interferes with privacy to some degree. The question is whether that interference violates a command of the United States Constitution."[210]

As we have already shown, and as the *Roe* Court admitted, there is no such command in the Constitution for a right of privacy or a right to an abortion. Only six years before its *Roe* decision, the Supreme Court explained: The "protection of a person's *general* right to privacy – his right to be left alone by other people – is like the protection of his property and of his very life, left largely to the law of the individual states."[211] When it came to its abortion decision, the Supreme Court ignored and violated its own admonition – it not only failed to leave the protection of the (general) right of privacy to the states, but in fact preempted and overruled the decision of nearly all state legislatures, which had affirmatively prohibited abortions.

> *" When it came to its abortion decision, the Supreme Court ignored and violated its own admonition – it not only failed to leave the protection of the (general) right of privacy to the states, but in fact preempted and overruled the decision of nearly all state legislatures, which had affirmatively prohibited abortions."*

Not only does this "right of privacy" not appear in the Constitution, and those who somehow find it in the Constitution do not agree where it is found, but several Supreme Court justices, even apart from the 1967 decision quoted above, have expressly rejected that a general constitutional right of privacy exists. For example, Justice Hugo Black wrote that there is no "constitutional provision or provisions forbidding any law ever to be passed which might abridge the 'privacy' of individuals"; there are only "guarantees in certain specific constitutional provisions which are designed in part to protect privacy in *certain times and places with respect to certain activities*," as, for example, the "Fourth Amendment's guarantee against 'unreasonable searches and seizure.'"[212]

The history and purpose of the Fourteenth Amendment rejects any right of privacy

As previously shown, the Fourteenth Amendment was added to the Constitution in 1868, following the Civil War, to ensure that southern states – primarily those that had joined the Confederacy – not be permitted to deny African-Americans their constitutional rights. The Supreme Court, in 1872, explained that the sole purpose of that amendment was "the freedom of the slave race, the security and firm establishment of that freedom, and the protection of the newly-made freeman and citizen from the oppression of those who had formerly exercised unlimited dominion over him."[213]

The Supreme Court, almost a century later, reaffirmed the limited purpose of the Fourteenth Amendment to protect African-Americans: The "clear and central purpose of the Fourteenth Amendment was to eliminate all official state sources of invidious discrimination in the States" against blacks.[214] As the Supreme Court, in a more recent decision,[215] related: "Senator Jacob Howard, who spoke on behalf of the Joint Committee on Reconstruction and sponsored the Amendment in the Senate, stated that the Amendment, addressed to protecting African-Americans, protected all of 'the personal rights guarantied and secured by the first eight amendments of the Constitution;'"[216] and Representative John Bingham, the principal author of the first part of the amendment, limited the amendment to "arm[ing] the

Congress with the power to enforce the bill of rights as it stands in the Constitution today."[217]

Hence, its purpose was to protect blacks by applying to the states the restrictions against violating rights already in the Constitution and its amendments. Indeed, the Supreme Court, in initially construing the Fourteenth Amendment shortly after its adoption, expressly held that it was not "intended to bring within the power of [the federal courts] the entire domain of civil rights heretofore belonging to the States."[218] The Fourteenth Amendment was, in fact, to continue the power of each state to regulate "civil rights – [defined as] the rights of person and property – essential to the perfect working of our complex form of government."[219] It further defined those civil rights as "protection by the [state] government, with the right to acquire and possess property of every kind, and to pursue and obtain happiness and safety, subject, nevertheless, to such restraints as the [state] government may prescribe for the general good of the whole."[220] Prohibition of abortion, enacted in most states, fits within the power of the states, which the Supreme Court there upheld.

The Court also expressly rejected the idea that "this court [is] a perpetual censor upon all legislation of the States, on the civil rights of their own citizens, with authority to nullify such as it did not approve as consistent with those rights, as they existed at the time of the adoption of this amendment."[221] The Court went on to describe that invasion of state prerogatives as never "intended by the Congress which proposed these amendments, nor by the legislatures which ratified them."[222] And, in a much later case, the Supreme Court, in an opinion written by the very liberal Justice William O. Douglas, referred to "the moral, social, … and physical wellbeing of the community" as matters left to state "legislative judgment."[223]

For that reason, the Court in 1873 stated: "We doubt very much whether any action by a State not directed by way of discrimination against the negroes as a class, or on account of their race, will ever come within the purview of this provision. It is so clearly a provision for that race and that emergency that a strong case would be necessary for its application to any other."[224]

Thus, in total contradiction of these earlier Supreme Court decisions, the *Roe* majority acted as a "censor upon ... legislation of the States, ... to nullify" the anti-abortion statutes "it did not approve,"[225] and thereby imposed on the states a new civil right to have an abortion even though the Court had previously acknowledged such a decision must be left to the states.

And, in doing so, it simply ignored its prior ruling, already noted, that an interference with privacy is not unconstitutional unless it "violates a command of the United States Constitution"[226] – none exists on privacy in general or abortion specifically.

Further manipulation of the words of the Fourteenth Amendment to reach its pro-abortion result

To reach its desired end, in addition to contradicting or ignoring its prior rulings, the *Roe* majority had to redefine and expand the term "due process of law," as used in the Fourteenth Amendment (no state shall "deprive any person of life, liberty, or property, without due process of law"). The identical "due process" language, in the Fifth Amendment, adopted in 1791, had never before been interpreted to create a general right of privacy. Hence, if the Court had remained true to its own precedents, it would never have voided state abortion laws on the basis that the Constitution created a general right of privacy. The Court, in its rush to legalize abortions, did not even try to explain how the same language in two different amendments could have two different meanings.

Avoiding those prior rulings, the Court instead sought to fit the right to privacy and a right to an abortion into a new definition of "liberty," which the Fourteenth Amendment expressly protected from state denial. But in doing so, the *Roe* majority ignored years of its opinions that had defined the "liberty" interest in the Amendment in a manner that excluded the privacy/abortion right.

The Supreme Court has variously described with different words – but, in reality, the same or similar substance – the test to determine when a state statute causes an impermissible violation of an individual's liberty interest. In 1905, the Court said that a state statute is unconstitutional only if the statute is "beyond all question, a plain, palpable invasion of rights secured by the fundamental law."[227] Shortly thereafter, the Court similarly limited state action that violates the Fourteenth Amendment to action that violates "immutable principles of justice which inhere in the very idea of free government which no member of the Union may disregard."[228]

Since then, the Supreme Court reaffirmed the limited test of unconstitutionality under the Fourteenth Amendment's Due Process Clause. If a state statute infringes "rights long freely enjoyed,"[229] it would violate the Fourteenth Amendment. Another way that Supreme Court phrased it is that, to be unconstitutional, the rights, being restricted by state statute, must be "so rooted in the traditions and conscience of our people as to be ranked as fundamental."[230] Further, "[i]n determining which rights are fundamental, judges ... must look to the traditions and collective conscience of our people to determine whether a principle is so rooted there ... as to be ranked as fundamental.'" The "inquiry is whether a right involved 'is of such a character that it cannot be denied without violating those fundamental principles of liberty and justice which lie at the base of all our civil and political institutions.'"[231] Six years before its *Roe* decision, the Supreme Court repeated that, for a state statute to be unconstitutional, the freedom being restricted must be a "fundamental" one, meaning that it must have "long been recognized as one of the vital personal rights essential to the orderly pursuit of happiness by free men."[232] And, in 1968, only five years before the *Roe* decision, the Supreme

Court said that only those state statutes that restricted a right which no "civilized society could be imagined that would not accord" it, would violate the Fourteenth Amendment.[233]

How could a right to abortion meet these tests? Can anyone with a straight face seriously contend that the right to an abortion had been "long freely enjoyed," and "long recognized as one of the vital personal rights essential to free men," or was "so rooted in the traditions and conscience of our people" as to be considered fundamental," and that without the right to an abortion, no free government or civilized society can exist?

Let's look at the facts.

Current public rejection of abortions

Before we look at history, it is helpful to check the contemporary conscience of the American people, as it is likely that people today are less receptive to what to some seem today like moral codes than they were in the past. Yet, a May 2012 Gallup poll found that 51 percent of Americans called abortion "morally wrong" as against only 38 percent who said it was acceptable.[234] An even more recent Marist poll, in December 2012, increased to 58 percent the number who view abortions as "morally wrong," 83 percent support significant restrictions on abortions, and only 11 percent support abortions as a free choice at any time.[235] Note that neither poll limited its polling to judges and politically-correct elite, but sampled a cross-section of Americans who made it clear that, even today, they reject abortions as contrary to their conscience and belief as to what is right.

An even clearer overwhelming public view that an unborn baby should not be killed but allowed to live was dramatically seen when pollsters avoided asking technical legal questions as to a right to abortion, and instead focused on the unborn baby. A 2001 Gallup/CNN/USA Today poll framed the question: "Suppose for a moment that a violent crime is committed against a pregnant woman and the unborn child is harmed or killed. Do you think that the criminal should or should not face additional charges for harming the unborn child as well as the woman?" 93% of the responders said "should," with only 5% responding negatively.[236]

Given the large number of Americans, living in a free society, who believe that abortion is morally wrong, and that it is a separate crime to kill an unborn baby, it is impossible to conclude that a free and civilized society cannot exist without legalized abortions – one of the requisite findings previously specified by the Court to hold unconstitutional a state statute under the Fourteenth Amendment.

Historical rejection of abortions

American history reflects an almost unanimous rejection of abortions. It is most relevant to start with our state statutes as they are enacted by state legislatures that are elected by the people of each state, and therefore most closely reflect the "traditions and collective conscience of our people."[237] Beginning in the first half of the 19th century, most states enacted laws criminalizing abortions.[238] Even the majority opinion in *Roe* conceded that the criminal statutes "under attack here are typical of those that have been in effect in many states for approximately a century."[239] The Texas criminal statute, which was the specific anti-abortion statute held unconstitutional in *Roe*, was enacted in 1854 – more than 100 years before the *Roe* decision, and only about eight years after Texas became a state. The Supreme Court noted that the Texas statute "has remained substantially unchanged to the present time."[240]

In fact, up to the time of the *Roe* decision, states "had [placed] restrictions on abortions for at least a century."[241] "By the end of the 1950's, a large majority of the jurisdictions banned abortions, however and whenever performed"; the only "exceptions" were "Alabama and the District of Columbia ... in permitting abortions, but solely to save the life of the mother."[242]

In light of this history and modern public sentiment, the conclusion is compelled that a right to have an abortion is not rooted in the traditions and conscience of the American people – one of the prerequisites previously fixed by the Supreme Court for holding a state statute unconstitutional under the Due Process Clause. Even though the Supreme Court had earlier observed that the "clearest and most objective evidence of contemporary values is the legislation enacted by the country's legislatures,"[243] the *Roe* Court substituted the personal views of seven justices for the decisions made by legislatures and for the undisputed conscience of Americans.

> "*A right to have an abortion is not rooted in the traditions and conscience of the American people – one of the prerequisites previously fixed by the Supreme Court for holding a state statute unconstitutional under the Due Process Clause.*"

Another interesting relevant fact is that at least 18 states and the federal government have enacted statutes making it a crime for someone to kill an unborn child in the womb of a woman during the first trimester.[244] This is completely at odds with the *Roe* decision. The Supreme Court ruled that it is unconstitutional to prevent the destruction of the "potential life" in a womb through an abortion; yet, anyone other than the woman carrying that life may be criminally prosecuted in states and in federal territory for destroying the very same "potential life."

We can go much further in looking back in American history and in the common law that America's founders brought to these shores and is still considered as part of the foundation of our jurisprudence. As the *Roe* opinion conceded, the "Hippocratic Oath ... the famous Oath that has stood so long as the ethical guide of the medical profession," forbade doctors from giving "to a woman an abortive remedy."[245]

The majority opinion in *Roe* reflects contradictory sources describing the legal status of abortions in common law England. It notes that the recognized expert of that time, Henry of Bracton, "writing early in the 13th Century [*"On The Laws and Customs of England"*], thought it homicide."[246] Referring to other sources, it concludes that an abortion before the 16th to 18th week of pregnancy (at which point the fetus is described as "quick") "was not an indictable offense,"[247] while abortions during the remainder of the pregnancy was a crime, but "a lesser offense" than homicide.[248] In any case, England made clear where it stood by criminalizing abortions in 1803: Abortion was declared a capital crime (authorizing a death sentence) if it involved a quick fetus, and otherwise lesser penalties.[249]

American medical professionals have, for most of their existence, opposed the use of abortions on a woman's choice. For example, the medical profession, through the American Medical Association, as early as 1859 expressed support for the Hippocratic Oath's rejection of abortions, and, thereby, the state statutes prohibiting abortions. The AMA then "deplored abortion and its frequency," and protested "against such unwarrantable destruction of **human life**."[250] In 1871, the AMA reiterated its view that any abortion was "unlawful and unprofessional" unless with the concurrence "of at least one respectable consulting physician, and then always with a view to the **safety of the child**."[251]

In contrast to resting an abortion simply on the woman's choice, the AMA went so far as to call "the attention of the clergy of all denominations to the perverted views of morality entertained by a large class of females – aye, and men also, on this important question."[252] More than a century of the AMA's total rejection of abortions was modified only in 1967, when it reiterated its "opposition to induced abortion," but provided very limited exceptions for the health or life of the mother, a child with incapacitating physical deformity or mental deficiency, or rape or incest. Even these exceptions were carefully limited by the requirement that such abortion could occur only with the concurrence of two physicians of "recognized professional competence."[253]

Our medical profession and our state legislatures for over a century thus make clear that the rooted "traditions and collective conscience of our people" are against abortions, not in favor of abortions. Hence, under the test of unconstitutionality of state statutes fixed by the Court, abortion statutes should have been held constitutional by the Supreme Court.

To legalize abortions, the Roe Court violated all of its prior rulings

Let's summarize by comparing the undisputed long-time anti-abortion history with the standards fixed by the Supreme Court for determining the constitutionality of a state restriction of what is asserted to be a right. Abortion cannot be considered to be a "fundamental" right or part of our "fundamental law" given that it was prohibited in England, from which we received our heritage, prohibited in the United States for most of our country's history, and considered improper by doctors, who set the medical ethical and professional standards. Similarly, abortion is not a "right long freely enjoyed," nor is it essential to any civilized society, or part of the traditions and collective conscience of our people. The *Roe* Court ran roughshod over each of these standards in validating abortions.

The States that ratified the 14th Amendment were opposed to legalizing abortions

One other undisputed fact further undermines the Court's finding that the Fourteenth Amendment made state abortion restrictions unconstitutional. The Court significantly never suggests that the authors of that amendment, or the congressmen, senators, and state legislatures that voted to enact the Fourteenth

Amendment, intended thereby to grant women free choice on abortion.

Indeed, the facts are diametrically to the contrary. All those responsible for enacting the Fourteenth Amendment would be rolling over in their graves at such a thought. When the Fourteenth Amendment was finally adopted, "there were at least 36 laws enacted by state or territorial legislatures limiting abortion"[254] – 36 out of 37 states then in the union. It belies belief that this overwhelming number of states – the same states whose votes were required to enact the Fourteenth Amendment – ever contemplated or intended that their enactment of the Fourteenth Amendment would void the anti-abortion statutes for which they voted and which remained the law of their respective state for over 100 years. Yet, the Supreme Court, in addition to ignoring the legal standard it itself had fixed, turned on its head the clear intent of the authors of the Fourteenth Amendment by making unconstitutional the generally-existing and long-standing state statutes which rejected abortions.

It is helpful to consider what the Supreme Court did in another case, not concerning abortion, also requiring a decision whether a rule, followed in a majority of the states, violated the Due Process Clause of the Fourteenth Amendment. There, the Court upheld the decisions of a majority of states, because "[w]e cannot brush aside [their] experience."[255] But on abortion, without explaining the difference, the Court swept away two centuries of state experience and judgment.

The Roe Court violated the Supreme Court's rule against usurping the jurisdiction of state legislatures

We are thus compelled to re-ask the question: On what proper legal foundation did the Supreme Court ignore its own standards and disregard the intent of the drafters and enactors of the Fourteenth Amendment to hold the many state statutes prohibiting abortions to be unconstitutional?

The answer is none. In fact, the seven justices who declared abortion restrictions to be unconstitutional violated another of the Supreme Court's basic rules, namely, that the wisdom of legislation is left to the legislature; the courts "do not sit as a super-legislature to determine the wisdom, need, and propriety of laws that touch ... social conditions."[256] The Supreme Court "has more than once recognized as a fundamental principle that 'persons and property are subjected to all kinds of restraints'" imposed by the legislature to further "the safety, health, peace, good order, and morals of the community'" as to "which the legislature is primarily the judge."[257] Recall that, at the beginning of the *Roe* decision, the Court observed that one's views on abortion depends on "one's attitude towards life and family, and their values, and ... moral standards."[258]

> *"On what proper legal foundation did the Supreme Court ignore its own standards and disregard the intent of the drafters and enactors of the Fourteenth Amendment to hold the many state statutes prohibiting abortions to be unconstitutional? The answer is none."*

If, as the Court wrote, these are matters as to "which the legislature is primarily the judge,"[259] why did the Court overrule the legislatures' determination to adopt statutory restraints on abortions? State legislatures evaluated and weighed what they believed the impact of abortions was on the health, both physical and moral, of society, and on the protection of potential life. The Supreme Court agreed that it was the responsibility of the states, through their legislatures, to protect those "interests in safeguarding health, in maintaining medical standards, and in protecting potential life."[260] Further, the *Roe* Court even expressly recognized the "important state interests" in governing this subject,[261] but it rejected the long-standing judgment of the many state legislatures that abortion should be banned. The majority thereby substituted the judgment of seven appointed individuals counter to centuries of law and tradition (and even counter to current popular views).

The Roe Court acts as a legislature in deciding when life begins

The seven justices comprising the majority in *Roe* dictated in their decision that, for purposes of abortion, each pregnancy is broken into three distinct terms, with essentially no restrictions on abortions in the first trimester, minor restrictions in the next period, and more restrictions in the last. Of course, these justices cite nothing in the Constitution to support this detailed breakdown of abortion availability. These justices were doing what legislatures are required to do: evaluate pros and cons and prescribe rules that they believe are most fair, most protective of society and most efficient. That duty is not the duty of a justice, who is sworn to uphold the law as it is written in the Constitution and in statutes that are not inconsistent with the Constitution. Yet, in *Roe*, these justices supplanted the legislatures and prescribed their personal view as to what the law should be, thereby overriding what the law is, and constituting the Court as a super-legislature – exactly what the Supreme Court only eight years before had said the Court should not do.[262]

> " *Their decision in Roe is based on those justices' personal opinion as to when life begins in the womb.* "

Their decision in *Roe* is based on those justices' personal opinion as to when life begins in the womb. Those justices concede that their decision would have had to be diametrically opposite, and would have allowed states to continue to bar abortions, if the "fetus is a 'person' within the language and meaning of the Fourteenth Amendment"; in that case, "the fetus' right to life would then be guaranteed by the [Fourteenth] Amendment."[263] The justices admitted that the Constitution did not give them any assistance in defining when a potential life becomes a "person" because "the Constitution does not define 'person' in so many words."[264] Clearly then, this ruling on when life begins was not constitutionally-based, but rested on the personal preferences of those seven justices.

Nor was it required by relevant medical and biological facts. Long before the end of the first trimester, during which, the Supreme Court ruled, a woman has the unrestricted choice to have an abortion, what is inside the womb is not simply a mass of nothing. Rather, the embryo has most of the components of life that exist when birth occurs. Its heart is beating between two and four weeks after conception, and the brain is generating brain waves after seven weeks. By the second month – which is when most abortions occur – the arms, legs, fingers, toes, ears, nose, mouth, muscles, organs and bones are either formed or far on the way and therefore very visible.[265]

So how do these justices reach their conclusion that the potential life is not a "person" in the first trimester? They claim to base it on what they say is the fact that, "throughout the major portion of the 19th century," prevailing "legal abortion practices were freer than they are today."[266] The factual basis for that assertion, even if relevant, is not provided. As discussed above, England had, by statute, in the first few years of the 19th century, made abortion a crime. The Court does not cite any state in which abortions were lawful during the 19th century. As shown above, on the date the Fourteenth Amendment became law in 1868 – the most relevant date, if any date is relevant to when the potential life becomes a "person," because the Court was interpreting the Fourteenth Amendment ratified in 1868 – the overwhelming number of states prohibited abortions. The most expert and relevant view at the time was that expressed by the medical profession in 1859, and remained outstanding while the Fourteenth Amendment was being debated and adopted. The American Medical Association then "deplored abortion," and criticized the "wide-spread ignorance" inherent in the belief "that the foetus is not alive until after the period of quickening."[267] This AMA view was reaffirmed in 1871, again referring to the fetus as "human life."[268]

There is, thus, no constitutional basis for the *Roe* majority's assessment of when life begins, and no medical professional support, contemporaneous to the enactment of the Fourteenth Amendment, for their conclusion. That is enough to conclude that these justices improperly assumed the role of a super-legislature, overruling the legislative findings and judgments made by an overwhelming number of state legislatures.

While, therefore, unnecessary to showing the unsupportable nature of the ruling, I also suggest that nearly everyone's – including each justice's – personal experience belies what they wrote in the *Roe* opinion as to when life begins. Each expectant mother and father considers this question in a very practical way – without delving into legal authorities or jargon. This usually occurs as soon as the future parents realize that conception has occurred. Has anyone ever heard the future mother express the wonder of what was occurring inside her body as "I'm carrying a 'fetus' or an 'embryo'"? Or when a loving husband pats the slowly rounding stomach of his wife, does he ever refer to what is inside as a "fetus" or "embryo?" Or when the first internal "kick" is felt, does anyone say that the "fetus" or the "embryo" was kicking? The honest answer clearly is no, because, in each of these instances, the proud parents-to-be invariably refer to "our child" or "our baby." That is the reality, which the Court ignored.

It is interesting that, when the Massachusetts legislature enacted a law concerning abortions,[269] it realistically referred to the pregnant woman as the "mother" in the statute, not the future or potential mother, but simply the "mother." As a woman is a "mother" only to a child, it logically follows that the Massachusetts legislature recognized that a child existed within the mother.

Rev. Jesse Jackson said it well in 1977[270] (years before he chose to run for president and decided he could not win without a 180-degree turnabout). Effectively describing abortions as "black genocide," he explained that proponents of abortion attempt to "dehumaniz[e]" abortions "through the rhetoric used to describe it" by "not call[ing] it killing or murder," or "aborting a baby," both accurate descriptions, "because that would imply something human," and instead "talk about aborting the fetus," which sounds less than human. He properly posed the question, "what kind of a society will we have" and "what happens to the ... moral fabric of a nation ... that accepts the aborting of the life of a baby without a pang of conscience?"

> *"What kind of a society will we have (and) what happens to the ... moral fabric of a nation ... that accepts the aborting of the life of a baby without a pang of conscience?" - The Rev. Jesse Jackson, 1977*

The Roe Court's attempt to explain its ruling

The *Roe* Court tried to explain why, in 1973, abortions suddenly became a constitutional right when, up to then, abortions had been criminal for a very long period. The explanation did not come easy because the *Roe* Court had to admit that each state had an important state interest in health and medical standards involved in an abortion, including the state's "duty in protecting prenatal life."[271]

But, as if finding the rabbit in the hat, the Supreme Court found that the state right to regulate health and medical matters inherent in abortions was limited to "a late stage of pregnancy."[272]

Where in the Constitution does it say that a state's right to regulate a health matter within its state is allowed only during certain periods? It doesn't. The seven justices on the Supreme Court made it up in order to impose on all states the **legislative** views these justices thought should supplant the absolute prohibition legislation enacted in each state by the elected legislators. Isn't this action – converting the Supreme Court into a super-legislature for all states, determining what the legislation should be – contrary to the Supreme Court's own directive that legislation should be left to the legislatures?

The *Roe* Court's attempt to answer this question only further demonstrates the runaway nature of this decision. The issue of abortion, the Court admitted, is entirely "different from" those prior cases in which the Court found that the Constitution provided a right of privacy, such as cases involving "marital intimacy, or bedroom possession of obscene material, or marriage, or procreation, or education" – all fitting within the "fundamental" rights standard previously fixed by the Supreme Court. Hence, the Court also admitted, "it is reasonable and appropriate for a State to decide" that a state may restrict abortions because an interest other than the woman's privacy, "that of the health of the mother or that of potential life, becomes significantly involved," and overrides the woman's choice of abortion. But, here again, the Court limits this state right to "some point in time" during the pregnancy,[273] when nothing in the Constitution converts a constitutional right into not a constitutional right based on any lapse of time. And again, the Court offers no explanation of why setting the parameters of when a statutory restriction applies is not a legislative matter, and thus outside of the Supreme Court's jurisdiction.

Indeed, the only rationalization it offers for its decision is that times have changed since the state statutes prohibiting abortions were adopted in the 19th century. According to these seven justices, "[w]hen most criminal abortion laws were first enacted, the procedure was a hazardous one for the woman," while today "[m]odern medical techniques have altered this situation."[274] But they also concede that, even today, abortion is "not without risk," making it a serious judgment call. That sort of judgment call is ordinarily left to the state legislatures, not the Supreme Court. Significantly, the Court follows this discussion with reference to "important state interests" involved. And the Court also admits that, "as long as at least potential life is involved," each state also "may assert interests beyond the protection of the woman alone."[275] Call it a baby, a fetus or an embryo, how does someone conclude that a "potential life" does not exist within a pregnant woman which is, as the Court agreed, subject to state protection? There is – and can be – no logical answer from the Supreme Court.

No one doubts that each state rightfully should consider the need to protect the woman who is pregnant. But, as the Court said in *Roe*, there are "interests" to be protected by the states "beyond the protection of the woman alone."[276] It has always been the rule, made clear by the Supreme Court over many years, that it is the state legislature, not the federal courts, which evaluates competing societal interests and reaches the legislative conclusion – unless a constitutional right is being violated.

The supposed changes in conditions involving abortions, on which the *Roe* Court relies for changing the law of the land, do not meet the test that the Supreme Court itself prescribed for allowing a change in the interpretation of the Fourteenth Amendment so as to make unconstitutional previously permitted state action. "The Fourteenth Amendment, itself a historical product, did not destroy history for the States.... If a thing [*e.g.,* prohibiting abortion] had been practiced for two hundred years by common consent, it will need a strong case for the Fourteenth Amendment to affect it ..."[277] The Court recognized that what "may at a given time be deemed ... [among] the essentials of fundamental rights," and therefore protected by the Fourteenth Amendment, may change, but only if several identified "elements" demonstrate an alteration is required.

Let's look at those elements fixed by the Supreme Court, but which the *Roe* Court ignored, to determine if they support the *Roe* decision to change two centuries of law in this country:

– Have the restrictions on abortion that "free people have found consistent with the enjoyment of freedom for centuries" been "discredited" by current popular views?[278] No, as the very current poll data, quoted above, indicates, a greater number of Americans oppose a right to abortion than favor it.

– Is there a "long history of" restrictions on abortion "continually ... applied ... through those very years when the rights of individuals to be free from peremptory official invasion received increasing legislative and judicial protection?"[279] Yes, as discussed above, at the time the Supreme Court declared abortion prohibitions to be unconstitutional, an overwhelming majority of states had retained long-standing state statutes restricting abortions.

– Is there a "new body of knowledge [that] displaces previous premises of action" and "important modification in the circumstances or the structure of society which calls for a disregard of so much history?"[280] No, the only purported new body of knowledge or other relevant changes mentioned by the *Roe Court* was that the medical risks from abortion had been reduced, but not eliminated. It hardly displaces previous premises of state action that considered not only the physical health of the pregnant woman, but also the future life of the baby, the mental health of the woman, and the morality of society. All of these remain unchanged, and, at least, must be regarded as factors for the legislatures to consider.

– Is there the "need to maintain basic, minimal standards ... to prevent ... that pervasive breakdown in the fiber of a people?"[281] Yes, certainly the states, by continuing the anti-abortion statutes, and the people, as shown by the poll discussed above, believe there is a need to continue the anti-abortion laws. The Supreme Court provided no evidence to the contrary.

The public relations slogan of "I can do what I want with my body"

The pro-choice or pro-legal-abortion view often comes down to "individuals have unlimited autonomy with respect to their own reproductive systems,"[282] or, in simpler language, "I can do what I want with my body."

A nice slogan created for public relations purposes, but without legal, logical, or practical validity. The argument, of a "right of every freeman to care for his own body and health in such way as to him seems best," was expressly rejected by the Supreme Court early in the 20th century.[283] As the well-respected Justice John Marshall Harlan explained, there is no "absolute right in each person to be, at all times and in all circumstances, wholly freed from restraint." Rather, it is a "fundamental principle that 'persons ... are subjected to all kinds of restraints and burdens,'" as shall be determined by the state legislature, on which "the legislature is primarily the judge," to be "'essential on the safety, health, peace, good order and morals of the community.'"[284] Justice Harlan observed that, absent the legislature's violation of a right "secured by the fundamental law,"[285] the Supreme Court should not interfere with the state legislature's judgment. He further explained that "[i]n a free country, where the government is by the people, through their chosen representatives, practical legislation admits of no other standard of action, for what the people believe is for the common welfare must be accepted as tending to promote the common welfare, whether it does in fact or not."[286]

The Supreme Court in *Roe* ran roughshod over this long enunciated rule. The Court did not even seriously try to explain how the legislature's view – indeed not just one state legislature but an overwhelming number of all state legislatures that have long voted to restrict abortions – should be overridden and rejected by the preference of seven individuals who happen to be justices of the Supreme Court. Seven justices overruled these many legislatures on legislation which the legislatures judged was needed to further the health and morality of the community, and which clearly does not involve denial of a long-held contrary fundamental right.

In the case *Jacobson v. Commonwealth Of Massachusetts,*[287] on which Justice Harlan wrote the Court's opinion, the plaintiff had claimed that vaccinations, which were required by the state statute under attack, could harm his health, life and mental well-being, and presented evidence of past injurious vaccination effects, just as the *Roe* plaintiffs presented evidence of deleterious effects in the past from not being allowed a lawful abortion. Justice Harlan quickly rejected the idea that evaluation of such evidence was within the Court's jurisdiction, holding that it would be improper to have "the court and jury to go over the whole ground gone over by the legislature when it enacted the statute."[288] That ruling was silently ignored by the seven justices in *Roe.*

The popular cry of "it's my body to do with as I please" has been roundly rejected in matters unrelated to abortion. Motorcyclists, despite some very vocal objections, are required to wear a helmet while riding; car drivers and passengers are required to harness themselves in a safety belt; persons in the privacy of their home are not permitted to inject themselves with heroin or to commit suicide; individuals, even in emails typed in the privacy of the home, may not share child pornography with anyone else, including a family member or friend, etc. The restraints on what an individual may want to do with his or her body are too numerous to list, but they all have one link in common: the state or local legislature determined that the restraint furthers society's interest in health, welfare, and/or morality. The legislature evaluates the pros and cons, balances what the legislature determines is in society's best interests against the individual's interest to be free of the restraint, and votes on behalf of the state's citizens to enact the restraint believed appropriate. And the courts do not – and should not – interfere because that is the area the Constitution leaves to the legislatures, unless – only if – the restraint deprives people of a fundamental right or a right without which liberty cannot exist. Abortion does not fit into those exceptions.

Considering fundamental rights, no one – until the abortion controversy – really ever questioned the fundamental right of a parent to supervise and determine the upbringing of a minor child. A child commits an infraction in school and the parent is called. A child gets in trouble and the parent is called. A child runs away and the parents have the right to seek government help in finding and returning the child. A school nurse believes that the child in school should have a simple aspirin, but may not give it to the child without calling and obtaining the parents' approval.[289] This respect for the parents' role in "child rearing" has been given constitutionally-protected status, because "it is deeply rooted in this Nation's history," and is premised on the objective to "inculcate and pass down many of our most cherished values, moral and cultural."[290]

But let's look at the "upside-down" rule the *Roe* Court created. Suppose a child, as young as 11 years,[291] seeks an abortion. The Supreme Court has previously wisely recognized that "a lack of maturity and an underdeveloped sense of responsibility are found in youth," often resulting "in impetuous and ill-considered actions and decisions."[292] Consistent with that Supreme Court determination, all but one of the 50 states "prohibit[] those under 18 from ... marrying without parental consent."[293] It would thus seem to follow that the very serious decision by a minor to have an abortion should also call for parental involvement. But no; in the rush to ensure abortions for all, the *Roe* Court ignored all these previous rulings, to hold that a child must be allowed to choose an abortion without the consent – and even over the opposition – of the parents. Indeed, in certain circumstances,[294] the abortion must proceed without even notice to the parents. The Supreme Court has thus cut off the relationship between parent and child on this important decision that dramatically can affect the child's future.[295]

No one can deny the damage this does to the parents' ability to help determine the child's upbringing, direction and moral principles. But that important fundamental parental right has been diluted – in fact, drowned – in the emotional tidal wave of allowing each woman, even an 11-year-old, to decide to have an abortion. Who overrode the wisdom that it is clearly not wise for society to deprive parents of their normal right to decide matters for minor children? The answer is that seven justices decided that abortion is the future mother's prerogative, even if that future mother is only 11 years of age.

Ironically, while courts have thus elevated the right to an abortion over parental rights, the *Roe v. Wade* decision, as a practical matter, enabled parents to overrule a child's decision to choose life for her baby, and instead force an abortion – a compulsion less easy if abortions had remained illegal. Here are two actual fact situations where *Roe v. Wade* disabled a young woman from being able to do what she wanted with her body:[296]

> A minor, in a hospital drug program, became pregnant and wanted to have her baby. The parents, however, told her she could not come home with the baby and, through the hospital medical director, informed their daughter that they would abandon her if she did not have an abortion. She had the abortion.

> A minor became pregnant by a boy of another race. Although she wanted to have the baby, her single-

parent mother, who did not want such a bi-racial child in the house, pressured her to have an abortion, and she did.

So much for the slogan that *Roe v. Wade* protected a young woman's right to do what she wants with her body.

Violation of the constitutional rights of men

While the *Roe* decision supposedly protected the woman's rights, it totally disregards the other party involved in the conception of a potential living being: the father. The last I heard it was an undisputed biological axiom that creating a baby requires two to tango: a man's provision of sperm which fertilizes the woman's supplied egg. Yet, according to the Supreme Court, the interest of the man – even one within a longtime marriage or other long-time relationship – in seeing the birth of his child is of no moment, eradicated simply by the woman's desire for an abortion.[297] Amazingly, the Court so ruled even after recognizing "that the decision whether to undergo or forego an abortion may have profound effects on the future of any marriage, effects that are both physical and mental, and possibly deleterious."[298]

How does that result safeguard the recognized liberty interest that a man has in protecting the life of his offspring? It does not; it simply destroys it. How is it consistent with the Fourteenth Amendment's guaranty of due process before depriving any person of life, liberty or property, that the simple say-so of his partner in conception destroys all of his right to enjoy the life of the child he had conceived with the woman? Apparently neither the life of the child nor the wishes of the father require due process to extinguish. It is ironic, and sad, that the last sentence of the section of the Fourteenth Amendment, on which the Supreme Court relied to uphold the woman's right to an abortion, also mandates against denial "to any person … the equal protection of the laws." What is it but a denial to the man, equally responsible with the woman for causing the conception, of the same rights and protections afforded to the woman?

Moreover, the Supreme Court had previously ruled that "procreation" is a "fundamental" right, involving "one of the basic civil rights of man."[299] That decision was in the context of holding unconstitutional an Oklahoma statute authorizing sterilization of criminals with three felonies involving moral turpitude. Granted, this sterilization statute did not limit the destructive effect to a single child as an abortion directly imposes; but an abortion does kill the one exercise of procreation that is involved – something that any man or woman conception partner, who desired the life, would never freely accept. In that regard, the man who doesn't want the abortion, is, as the Supreme Court explained in the sterilization case, "forever deprived of a basic liberty"[300] – the life of the child he partnered in conceiving.

The overly simplistic response to this point is that it is the woman, not the man, who has to spend nine months with the baby in her body. Society (and Mother Nature) imposes different responsibilities on the putative mother and father. Thus, it is not all one-sided after birth. Remember, the father has, among other responsibilities, at least 18 years of responsibility for financial support.

Recently, the State of Kansas dramatically emphasized the financial responsibility that is imposed on a man who provides the sperm that, when added to a woman's egg, creates a baby. In 2009, William Marotta had responded affirmatively to an ad on Craigslist for a sperm donor to allow one partner of a lesbian couple to have a child.[301] In the following year, shortly after the birth of the child, the lesbian couple separated, with the mother, who had been inseminated and had borne the child, apparently now partnering with a man. After an interval, the other part of the lesbian couple suffered what was called a "significant illness," that prevented her from continuing to work and, therefore, she became unable to continue financial support for the child. The couple then, in July 2012, applied to the state for support for the child, resulting, by September 2012, in Kansas taxpayers already paying over $6,000.

The Kansas Department for Children and Families then did what the law required of it – to take steps to obtain, for the taxpayers, reimbursement of the amounts already expended and to impose continuing liability on the person responsible for the birth of the child: It demanded the name of the father and, on the receipt of the identity of the sperm donor, it commenced a proceeding to obtain financial support from that father. Within a few months, Marotta already had spent several thousand dollars in legal fees in attempting to defeat the state's case against him and expects that amount to increase substantially in the ongoing case.

Marotta points to a written agreement that he had with the lesbian couple under which he relinquished all parental rights, including financial responsibility. Whether that has any legal effect on the rights of the child to support from the man who caused her to be born, and on the state's taxpayers who, without a responsible father, would pay for much of the child's necessary expenses, is highly questionable, and will be decided by Kansas courts. One fact that may have some impact on the court's legal ruling is the report that, during the child's three-year life, Marotta was not totally separated from and disinterested in the baby, but was "occasionally" "updated" on the baby's "well-being," and may have had some, albeit "little[,] contact" with the child.

Whatever the final outcome, this case certainly spotlights the burdens imposed on the male whose sperm resulted in conception, demonstrating that the future father should not be ignored when the life of that fertilized egg is being considered.

The Roe decision would permit racial discrimination

Consider the following hypothetical and decide for yourself whether the Supreme Court's legalization of abortion on a woman's demand is consistent with the no-racial-discrimination reason for which the Fourteenth Amendment was adopted: Assume that the woman is white, but the father is African-American. The woman, holding unfortunate cultural views, mistakenly declares that she does not want a half-black child because, she announces, having a black child would "force upon [her] a distressful life and future," with probability of "psychological harm" and "distress ... associated with the unwanted child," and "the problem of bringing a" black "child into a family already unable, psychologically and otherwise" to accept a black child into the family. All these quotes come from the Court's *Roe v. Wade* opinion explaining why a woman should not be forced to have a child she does not want.[302] Yet, wouldn't it be ironic that the Fourteenth Amendment, enacted because of the need to prevent discrimination against African-Americans, would thus be used to prevent a black man from having his child live merely because he is black? That is the effect of the *Roe* decision.

While this is a very reasonable hypothetical, the actual fact situation, described above, of a young woman, pregnant by a boy of a different race, who was forced to have an abortion over her desire to keep her baby because of parental pressure against a bi-racial grandchild, dramatically demonstrates how *Roe v. Wade* has enabled racial prejudice.

Roe is a repeat of the now-rejected Supreme Court mistakes of 1905

This *Roe v. Wade* decision, written by the supposedly "liberal" majority of the Supreme Court, reminds us of the now-rejected decisions by the "conservative" majority of the Court in the first part of the 20th century, epitomized by the 5-4 decision which held unconstitutional a New York statute that limited the number of hours bakers could be compelled to work to 10 hours a day.[303] Today, that type of statute is recognized as appropriate state regulation of working conditions. Yet, in 1905, it was declared unconstitutional under the Fourteenth Amendment, because it was an "illegal interference with the rights of individuals" to decide to contract for long hours."[304]   Justice Oliver Wendell Holmes, dissenting from that decision, criticized the decision as substituting the justices' personal beliefs for state legislators' determinations: "neither the 14th Amendment ... nor any other amendment was designed to interfere with the power of the state, sometime termed its police power, to prescribe regulations to promote the health, peace, morals, education, and good order of the people."[305]

Years later, in the 1930s, the Supreme Court changed sides, and adopted as correct Justice Holmes's dissent. Yet, in *Roe,* the Court again rejected Justice Holmes's position, in order to read into the Constitution a right to an abortion, because, to use the words of the conservative majority in 1905, it was an "illegal interference with the rights of" women to decide to have an abortion. Thus, in *Roe,* the Supreme Court adopted the same reasoning that the Supreme Court had used to declare unconstitutional the state statute regulating the number of work hours in order to declare unconstitutional the state statutes regulating abortions. But with these critical differences: The Fourteenth Amendment expressly provided that it was designed to protect against deprivation of "property" without due process. The freedom to contract to work long hours in the 1905 Supreme Court decision was a property right, expressly protected by the Fourteenth Amendment. As previously discussed, there is no mention in the Fourteenth Amendment of either a right to privacy or a right to an abortion. Thus, to the extent that there is virtual unanimity – and there is – that state statutes restricting hours to be worked are constitutional, the logic of that ruling should apply even more clearly to state statutes restricting abortions.

But instead, this Supreme Court decided otherwise, contrary to all constitutional provisions, its own prior rulings, and the expressed view of the state legislators and the people of most states. The personally-held – what they thought were politically-correct – views of some of the justices trumped clear and rock-solid judicial principles.

Conclusion

These facts underscore one of the critical popular misconceptions of the *Roe v. Wade* case. That is, contrary to what was said in massive public demonstrations and carefully framed publicity, the case was not about pro-choice versus pro-life. Yes, of course, those who supported the Court's ultimate decision did seek a ruling that abortions could not be prohibited. But, those who disagreed with the Court's result had **not** sought a declaration by the Supreme Court that abortions were and should be illegal. Rather, what they had asked the Court to do was to abide by the long-time principle that the Constitution left this issue to the good judgment of each state. If a state were to legalize abortion, that would be the prerogative of that legislature; and if any legislature retained laws prohibiting abortion, that also was the prerogative of the state legislature. During the six years preceding the *Roe* decision, legislatures in 18 states had in fact enacted legislation amending their abortion laws to make them less restrictive.[306] States thereby exercised their constitutionally delegated powers to enact laws on health, marriage and morality, which cover abortion. The Constitution did not include these subjects within congressional power.[307] Thus, pursuant to the Tenth Amendment, which "reserved to the States" all "powers not delegated to the United States by the Constitution," the Constitution reaffirmed that power over abortion was to be left to the states.

> *"As to abortion, the Supreme Court has usurped to itself what the Constitution mandated was a power 'not delegated to the United States.'"*

As to abortion, the Supreme Court has usurped to itself

what the Constitution mandated was a power "not delegated to the United States." The Court departed from its past rulings and told the public and all state legislatures that seven justices of the Supreme Court, not the state legislatures elected by the people, know better what is best for the people of all the states. Neither justice nor the best interests of all Americans were furthered by this judicial revision of our Constitution.

IX.

FIVE JUSTICES REVISE THE CONSTITUTION, OVERRULE LEGISLATURES, JURIES, TRIAL JUDGES, AND PRIOR SUPREME COURT RULINGS TO BAR THE DEATH PENALTY

From the beginning of this country, starting with the transportation of English law to these shores, the law, as enacted by state legislatures and by Congress, uniformly authorized the death penalty for the most heinous and injurious crimes. Our forebears determined that this ultimate penalty was essential to protect the life and person of others. For centuries, starting in England and continuing in this country – until very recently – all courts had upheld the death penalty as an appropriate authorized penalty. Yet, suddenly in 1972, five justices of the Supreme Court started their attack on the death penalty, contrary to that history. Let's look at the facts behind this recent 180-degree change.

Our country's birth certificate, the Declaration of Independence, proclaimed that "Governments are instituted" to protect the rights of all law-abiding persons to "Life, Liberty, and the Pursuit of Happiness." It makes the government responsible for "effect[ing] their Safety and Happiness."

The preamble to our country's Constitution highlighted its

purpose to "insure domestic Tranquility" – meaning the ability to live without fear of harm to one's life, body and property. The proponents of our Constitution agreed that the peoples' "safety" is the government's "first" purpose.[308] The Constitution implemented this objective by authorizing Congress to "provide for ... the general welfare of the United States," and to "make all laws ... for carrying into execution the foregoing powers."[309]

In our country, criminal laws are enacted by Congress, but also by state and local governments. The Constitution specified certain provisions that Congress must include in the federal criminal laws: "To provide for the Punishment of counterfeiting the Securities and Coin of the United States," and "To define and punish Piracies and Felonies committed on the high seas and Offenses against the Law of Nations."[310]

> *"The Supreme Court has violated its own rule as to the supremacy of the legislature in determining the punishment for a crime."*

It is significant that the Constitution did not simply say that it shall be a crime to counterfeit government securities and coin or to engage in piracy. It carefully delineated that Congress – not the president and not the courts – had the responsibility to provide for the punishment for those offenses. Because this delegation to Congress of the power to prescribe punishment for crimes is so clear, our Supreme Court more than a century ago affirmed that it had no power to overrule any legislature's judgment in fixing the penalty for crimes. For example: "The function of the legislature [in fixing the punishment for a crime] is primary, its exercise fortified by right and legality, and is not to be interfered with ... by any judicial conception of its wisdom or propriety."[311] As we shall see, the Supreme Court has violated its own rule as to the supremacy of the legislature in determining the punishment for a crime, by, in practice, deciding that the personal views of five individual justices overrule the sentencing judgment of the legislature.

As we consider the Supreme Court's recent decisions on the death penalty, we must recall that the Constitution's Tenth Amendment mandated that federal government powers were limited to those specifically granted in the Constitution, with all other powers reserved to the states (or to the people).

Consequently, it is up to the legislatures to decide what sentence – probation, prison term, or even death – is appropriate for crimes that directly affect you and me in our everyday life, such as murder, rape, kidnapping, robbery, etc. Our Constitution provides double protection of those state legislative decisions from interference by the federal courts: the insulation of the Tenth Amendment and the principle that it is legislatures, not courts, to whom enactment of legislation is delegated. That means that Congress for federal criminal law, and each state legislature for state crimes, has that responsibility – not the United States Supreme Court. That assignment of power to Congress and state legislatures encompasses the power and responsibility to decide whether the death penalty is authorized and, if so, for which crimes.

For almost two centuries, the Supreme Court affirmed and reaffirmed this understanding that courts have a "limited role," and "do not act ... as legislators," because "Courts are not representative bodies'," and therefore "'not designed to be a good reflex of a democratic society'." Courts are barred from "assum[ing] primary responsibility in choosing between competing political, economic and social pressures'."[312] In considering legislation, courts are required to "presume its validity;" and, where legislative determination of "the specification of punishments is concerned," that "deference to the state legislatures ... is enhanced ... for 'these are peculiarly questions of legislative policy.'"[313] Even after, as we shall soon relate, some Supreme Court justices suddenly started to find in the "cruel and unusual punishment" clause of the Eighth Amendment the authority to interfere with the death penalty, the Supreme Court reiterated that the courts may not "become, under 'the aegis of [that clause], the ultimate arbiter of the standards of criminal responsibility ... throughout the country'."[314] Justice Douglas, although, in the end, a vote against the death penalty, wrote in 1945 that since "our national government is one of delegated powers alone,"

> "under our federal system, the administration of justice rests with the States except as Congress, acting within the scope of those delegated powers, has created offense against the United States."[315]

"... a bare majority of justices were determined drastically to reduce the number, leading to eradication, of executions by chipping away at the death penalty procedures fixed by the legislatures."

Yet, a small majority of justices later discarded this limitation and usurped the legislatures' power to decide on the death penalty.

There is only one limitation on what Congress or any state legislature may fix as punishment for a crime: It must not violate any constitutional provision. We shall see, however, that some justices – usually not more than five, creating a slim majority – have assumed the power to overrule what legislatures have ordered to substitute the greater leniency these justices believe the law should provide, in place of what the law specifies. In recent decades, those justices have rewritten the Constitution and ignored prior decisions of the Court to impose their personal views on this country's criminal justice system. What is most amazing is that the justices do so openly. Here is an example of how a majority of Supreme Court justices explain their running roughshod over the contrary view of the Court minority, the views of the people, and the views of the overwhelming number of state legislatures: "in the end our [five justices'] own judgment ... on the ... acceptability of the death penalty" controls over what we have previously "pinpointed [as] the 'clearest and most reliable objective evidence of contemporary values [which] is the legislation enacted by the country's legislatures.'"[316]

This chapter will document that a bare majority of justices were determined drastically to reduce the number, leading to eradication, of executions by chipping away at the death penalty procedures fixed by the legislatures. The Supreme Court thereby assumed from the legislatures the power to decide what penal sentences should be. Later in this chapter, I will discuss the reasons for the death penalty to allow you to decide for yourself its advisability and value.

Some Actual Cases

No American needs to be trained as a lawyer to decide whether the Supreme Court has done injustice by rewriting the Constitution to overrule death sentences imposed on criminals by jurors and judges who heard all the evidence. Let's start here with the facts in several cases in which the Supreme Court reviewed the judgment of jurors and sentencing judge in imposing a death sentence. The death sentence was upheld in some of these cases and reversed in some. Here's an opportunity for you to be the judge: Read the facts and decide in which, if any, you would have reversed the death sentence. After you have done that analysis, I'll set forth the Supreme Court decision in each. Later in this chapter I will discuss the reasons given by the Supreme Court for most of the reversals.

1. Troy Gregg and his underage companion, while hitchhiking, were given a ride by two good samaritans. When they stopped, the driver and his companion left for a call of nature. Gregg immediately told his companion, "We're going to rob them." With a gun in hand, Gregg fired at the two men as they returned, causing both to drop

into a ditch. To finish the murder, Gregg approached the two men from behind, and "at close range, then fired a shot into the head of each ..., robbed them ... and drove away with" his fellow hitchhiker in the victims' car. Initially when arrested, Gregg lied to the police and attempted to induce his companion to lie. But when his companion later truthfully disclosed what had occurred, Gregg responded "yes" to the question: "You mean you shot these men down in cold-blooded murder just to rob them?" At trial, however, Gregg testified that he had killed in self-defense. He was then confronted with a letter that he had written to his travelling companion "recounting a version of the events similar to that to which he had just testified and instructing [his companion] to memorize and burn the letter." The jury found Gregg guilty and imposed the death penalty.[317]

2. Jerry Lane Jurek expressed to two companions "a desire for sexual relations with some young girls they saw, but one of his companions said the girls were too young." Jurek was later seen talking to Wendy Adams, age 10, "at a public swimming pool where her grandmother had left her to swim." Jurek then drove Wendy "screaming in the bed of the truck ... to the river" and, "in the course of committing ... forcible rape," "choked her and threw her unconscious body in the river." The jury found him guilty and then responded affirmatively to two questions that the statute required as prerequisites to a death sentence, which the judge imposed.[318]

3. "While serving various sentences for murder, rape, kidnapping and aggravated assault," Ehrlich Anthony Coker escaped from prison. He entered the house of Mr. and Mrs. Carver, and tied Mr. Carver up in the bathroom, after taking his money and car keys. Brandishing a knife, he raped Mrs. Carver and then kidnapped her in the Carver car. Fortunately, she was saved when Mr. Carver freed

himself and called the police. The jury convicted Coker and voted unanimously to impose the death penalty.[319]

4. Robert Franklin Godfrey, "in a coldblooded executioner's style, murdered his wife" with a shotgun, following which he struck his daughter on the head, reloaded the shotgun, entered her house and shot his mother-in-law. When arrested, Mr. Godfrey admitted "I've done a hideous crime, ... I have been thinking about it for eight years," and "I'd do it again." The jury convicted him and imposed the death penalty.[320]

5. Monty Lee Eddings, with some companions, was driving his brother's car, which he had stolen. He had a shotgun and several rifles, taken from his father. When he momentarily lost control of the car, a patrolman signaled him to stop. Eddings told his companions that, "if the mother... pig tried to stop him he was going to blow him away." He did just that. "[W]hen the officer approached the car, Eddings stuck a loaded shotgun out of the window and fired, killing the officer." Eddings later told two officers that if he were loose, he would shoot them all. He received the death sentence.[321]

6. Elwood Barclay, with four other persons, "set out in a car armed with a twenty two caliber pistol and a knife with the intent to kill ... any white person that they came upon under such advantageous circumstances that they could murder him, her or them. .... [T]hey picked up a hitch hiker, eighteen years old .... [T]hey drove him to an isolated trash dump, ordered him out of the car, threw him down and Barclay repeatedly stabbed him." One of Barclay's companions "put his foot on the [hitch hiker's] head and shot him twice ... killing him instantly." A previously prepared note was stuck to the body: "Warning to the oppressive state. No longer will your atrocities and brutalizing of black people be unpunished." Subsequently,

Barclay made a tape recording, mailed it to the victim's mother and media, which included: "He was stabbed in the back, in the chest and in the stomach, ah it was beautiful. You should have seen it. Ah, I enjoyed every minute of it. I loved watching the blood gush from his eyes. ... He died in style, though, begging, and pleading for mercy." The jury unanimously convicted Barclay of murder. By a 7-5 vote, it recommended a life sentence. However, the judge, who, under Florida law, made the final decision, sentenced him to be executed.[322]

7. James Hitchcock strangled his 13-year-old step-niece after they had sexual intercourse. Hitchcock said the sex was consensual, while the prosecutor contended that Hitchcock had raped her and killed her to avoid discovery. The jury convicted Hitchcock and recommended the death sentence. The judge agreed and sentenced Hitchcock to death.[323]

8. William Wayne Thompson told his girl friend that he was going to kill his former brother-in-law, and then he did so. He shot him twice, cut open his throat, chest and abdomen, after beating him, and chained him to a concrete block and threw him in the river. In the three years before this murder, Thompson had been arrested for several other crimes, including assault and battery and burglary. The jury convicted him and imposed the death penalty.[324]

9. Johnny Paul Penry, recently released after conviction on a rape charge, "brutally raped, beat, and stabbed" a woman "with a pair of scissors." Before she died in the hospital, she identified Penry, who then confessed. The jury convicted Penry and returned affirmative answers to three questions, based on which the judge imposed the death sentence.[325]

10. In robbing two neighbors' home, Robert Tennard stabbed one victim to death while an accomplice hatcheted the

other to death. Tennard had a prior record for rape. The jury convicted Tennard and sentenced him to death.[326]

11. Christopher Simmons and his young accomplice "broke into Mrs. Crook's home in the middle of the night, forced her from her bed, bound her, and drove her to a state park. There, they walked her to a railroad trestle spanning a river, 'hog-tied' her with electrical cable, bound her face completely with duct tape, and pushed her, still alive, from the trestle. She drowned in the water below." The jury convicted Simmons and then recommended the death penalty, which the judge imposed.[327]

12. Patrick Kennedy raped his 8-year-old stepdaughter. The U.S. Supreme Court stated that the "crime was one that cannot be recounted ... sufficient to capture in full the hurt and horror inflicted on his victim or to convey the revulsion ... the jury ... sought to express by sentencing [him] to death." When the bloodied child was taken to the hospital, an expert in pediatric forensic medicine described her injuries as the most severe that he had seen from a sexual assault. After the jury found Kennedy guilty, in the sentencing hearing, a goddaughter of Kennedy's ex-wife testified that Kennedy "sexually abused her three times when she was eight years old and that the last time involved sexual intercourse." The jury voted to sentence him to death.[328]

Compare your view as to the appropriateness of the imposition of the death penalty in each of these 12 cases with the Supreme Court's decisions. The Supreme Court upheld the death sentence in only three of these cases (Nos. 1, 2, and 6). It barred the death sentence in each of the other nine cases. My guess is that most people, who are not doctrinairily opposed to the death penalty, disagree with the Supreme Court on most or all of the cases in which the Supreme Court overruled the trial judge and jury to reverse the death sentence.

With this taste of what the Supreme Court has done in second-guessing juries and trial judges, let's turn to analyzing the law on the death penalty, what the Constitution does and does not say on this subject, and whether the reasons expressed by justices in rejecting juries' decisions to impose the death penalty have support in the Constitution – or whether these justices are simply imposing their personal views, notwithstanding the pro-death penalty views of the American public, legislators (who represent the public), and juries.

The Eighth Amendment and The Death Penalty

The central dispute within the Supreme Court, which first surfaced less than 40 years ago, is whether a death sentence is unconstitutional under the Eighth Amendment if a majority of the justices personally view that death sentence as *excessive*. The Eighth Amendment reads: "Excessive bail shall not be required, nor excessive fines imposed, nor cruel and unusual punishments inflicted." The drafters of that amendment used "excessive" twice – to limit "bail" and "fines" – but carefully did not employ it to limit "punishments" to be imposed. Hence, it should be obvious that the Framers did not intend also to bar excessive punishments. If the Framers had sought to provide a constitutional bar of "excessive" penalties, all they had to do was to say "nor excessive punishments imposed." That the Framers opted to use words other than "excessive" to describe prohibited "punishments" compels the conclusion that they did not intend to prohibit sentences merely because some Supreme Court justices might personally believe they were excessive or not proportional to the crime.

So what does the Eighth Amendment's bar of "cruel and unusual" punishments mean? Let's start with the every-day meaning of the words. "Cruel" means "disposed to inflict pain or suffering."[329]   The modern methods of executing condemned persons, carefully chosen to be quick and painless, cannot reasonably be defined as "cruel" under that definition. Nor is the death penalty "unusual," which means "out of the ordinary, uncommon, extraordinary,"[330] because legislatures have prescribed the death penalty for various crimes both before and after the 1791 enactment of the Eighth Amendment.

We need not rest on the dictionary definition. The history behind the enactment of the Eighth Amendment and Supreme Court decisions during the first 200 years of that amendment demonstrate that it does not prohibit death sentences because some people – even five persons who happened to be Supreme Court justices – believe a death sentences is excessive.

The words of the Eighth Amendment tracked the words used in the English Declaration of Rights of 1689.[331] What led the English to enact a prohibition against "cruel and unusual punishments"? The English had just lived through the Bloody Assizes, during which the Stuart kings decreed vicious punishment for treason, involving "drawing and quartering, burning of women, beheading, disemboweling, etc."[332] To prevent a recurrence of such barbarous punishments, this prohibition against "cruel and unusual punishments" was enacted. Even after adoption of this language, England continued to punish over 200 crimes with the death penalty,[333] clearly establishing that they did not believe they had thereby prohibited the death penalty.

The debates in the states, leading up to the adoption of the Eighth Amendment, also demonstrate that it was intended only to prevent barbarous punishments, and not to create a bar against a death penalty justices personally viewed to be "excessive," meaning not proportional to the crime. For example, in the January 1788 Massachusetts Convention, it was argued that the Constitution, without the Eighth Amendment, did not restrain the Congress "from inventing the most cruel and unheard-of punishments, and annexing them to crimes; and there is no constitutional check on it, but that racks and gibbets may be amongst the most mild instruments of its discipline;"[334] as the death penalty was employed generally at that time, the void in the Constitution later filled by the Eighth Amendment was unrelated to the death penalty. Similarly, in the Virginia Convention, the famed Patrick Henry bemoaned the omission of a bill of rights in the Constitution, which would include a "restriction of not imposing excessive [fines], demanding excessive bail, and inflicting cruel and unusual punishments." Henry spotlighted the reason for a cruel and unusual punishment clause: "What has distinguished our ancestors? – That they would not admit of tortures, or cruel or barbarous punishment."[335] Obviously, he did not include, and was not referring to, the death penalty, which, because it was accepted by legislatures at that time, did not distinguish Americans from their ancestors.

Notice also that there was no mention of any objective to have the Bill of Rights include a "proportionality" standard to govern criminal sentences – a standard that would have barred sentences that justices thought were "excessive" as compared to the crime. That omission clearly was intentional because both drafters and proponents of the Eighth Amendment knew that certain state constitutions then contained a proportionality requirement. For example, the Pennsylvania Constitution mandated that punishments should be "more proportionate to the crimes"; South Carolina the same; in New Hampshire, "All penalties ought to be proportioned to the nature of the offense."[336] Nor could there have been any serious contention that the words "cruel" and "unusual" encompassed a proportionality rule, because they knew that some states had included both in their constitutions.[337] That the authors of the Eighth Amendment did not add a proportionality clause to the "cruel and unusual" provision warrants holding the Eighth Amendment to be limited to the "cruel and unusual" prohibition. Six states subsequently recognized that limitation in the "cruel and unusual" language by adding a proportionality requirement to the prohibition against cruel and/or unusual punishments.[338]   If the cruel and unusual prohibition had prohibited excessive sentences, there would have been no reason to add "proportionality."

Punishments prescribed by the United States Congress after it adopted the Eighth Amendment demonstrate congressional recognition that the amendment neither outlawed the death penalty nor created a proportionality rule. Congress imposed the death penalty for a variety of offenses, from treason and murder down to forgery of United States securities, and "running away with a ship or vessel or any goods or merchandise to the value of fifty dollars."[339]   Death penalty for theft of $50 cannot be a punishment that Congress could have enacted if it believed that the Eighth Amendment required punishments to be proportional to the crime.

Early American commentators made clear that the "cruel and unusual punishments" prohibition was limited to preventing "the use of the rack or the stake, or any of those horrid modes of torture, devised by human ingenuity for the gratification of fiendish passion;"[340] it prohibits "breaking on the wheel, flaying alive, rending asunder with horses, various species of horrible tortures inflicted in the inquisition, maiming, mutilating, and scourging to death."[341] They thereby confirmed that the Eighth Amendment was "adopted as an admonition against such violent proceedings as had taken place in the arbitrary reigns of some of the Stuarts."[342]

The language in the Fifth Amendment, adopted at the same time as the Eighth Amendment, also helps establish that the death penalty was not considered to be "cruel," nor outlawed. It says: "No person shall be held to answer for a *capital* crime ... unless on a presentment or indictment of a Grand Jury ...."[343] As a "capital" crime is "any criminal charge which is punishable by the death penalty,"[344] this phrase used in the Fifth Amendment expressly recognizes the continuing existence of capital punishment. Also, it prohibits being "twice put in jeopardy of life

..." – repeating the acceptance of capital punishment. One of the last provisions of the Fifth Amendment is that no person shall "be deprived of life ... without due process of law" – a third express recognition that a death sentence may be imposed if due process is afforded. This recognition of the constitutionality of the death penalty was reaffirmed in 1868 in the Fourteenth Amendment, which imposed on the states the same prohibition against depriving "any person of life ... without due process of law."

The earliest reported court decision construing "cruel and unusual punishments" confirms what I have written. In 1824, the Virginia Supreme Court explained that the provision "denouncing cruel and unusual punishments ... was never designed to control the Legislative right to determine ... the adequacy of punishment." Rather, its purpose was only to exclude "the wanton cruelty of many of the punishments practised in other countries."[345]

The United States Supreme Court, in its first opportunity to interpret the Eighth Amendment in 1878, unambiguously held that the death penalty is not prohibited by the Eighth Amendment. The Court explained that the "cruel and unusual" language was adopted to prohibit "atrocities," such as "where the prisoner was drawn or dragged to the place of execution ..., or where he was embowelled alive, beheaded, and quartered ..., public dissection ..., burning alive ...."[346] Note the acceptance of "execution," and instead focusing on prohibiting unacceptable cruelty in connection with performing an execution. Twelve years later, in 1890, the Supreme Court reaffirmed that "the punishment of death is not cruel within the meaning of that word as used in the Constitution." It explained that "cruel and unusual" is "something more than the

> *"In 1890, the Supreme Court reaffirmed unanimously that 'the punishment of death is not cruel within the meaning of that word as used in the Constitution.'"*

extinguishment of life." "Cruel and unusual" is limited to "something inhuman and barbarous," such as "burning at the stake, crucifixion, breaking on the wheel, or the like."[347]

Significantly, the Court in each of these cases was unanimous. Not one justice even hinted either that the death penalty could be considered to be unconstitutional or that they could evaluate the proportionality of the sentence to the crime to overrule the legislature's determination. And, about 70 years later, in 1958, the Supreme Court reiterated that "the death penalty ... cannot be said to violate constitutional concepts of cruelty."[348] Keep this in mind when we discuss below the Supreme Court rulings, almost two centuries after the Eighth Amendment was enacted,[349] in which some justices suddenly found in it the power to rule that a death penalty, authorized by the legislature, was prohibited. In most decisions against a death penalty, the justices were split 5-4, with five justices substituting their personal opinions for the views of thousands of legislators who had voted for the death penalty.

Also in 1958, the Supreme Court expressly declared that it had no jurisdiction to consider the issue of "excessiveness" or proportionality of the sentence to the crime – what it called "the proper apportionment of punishment." That subject, the Court explained, was one "peculiar[ly] of legislative policy," concerning which "[t]his Court has no such power."[350] This principle was reiterated by the Court the following year when it was asked to overturn a death sentence for kidnapping as "disproportionate" or "excessive." The Court, by a vote of 8-1, rejected the appeal, explaining that nothing "in the Constitution require[s] a State to fix or impose any particular penalty for the crime it may define or impose the same or 'proportionate' sentences for separate and independent crimes."[351]

As recently as 1971, the Supreme Court upheld death penalties in two separate cases, expressly rejecting the idea that it was the Court's "function" to impose on states "... what might seem to us a better system for dealing with capital cases."[352] The Court explained the constitutional limitation on its power to interfere with legislative decisions on sentencing: "the Federal Constitution, which marks the limits of our authority in these cases, does not guarantee trial procedures that are the best of all worlds, or that accord to the most enlightened ideas of [some], *or even that measure up to the individual predilections of members of this Court.*"[353]

> *" Our federal system allows each state to 'serve as a laboratory,' undisturbed by the Supreme Court."*

Non-interference with state legislative choice on sentences is consistent with Justice Louis Brandeis' famous admonition against such judicial interference: "It is one of the happy incidents of the federal system that a single courageous state may, if its citizens choose, serve as a laboratory; and try novel social and economic experiments without risk to the rest of the country. We may strike down the statute ... [b]ut in the exercise of this high power, we must ever be on our guard, lest we erect our prejudices into legal principles."[354] Our federal system allows each state to "serve as a laboratory," undisturbed by the Supreme Court.

Thus, for 180 years, the Court, without exception, limited the Eighth Amendment to prohibit barbarous sentences, and rejected that it allowed the Court to overturn legislative determinations regarding the death penalty, or the procedures mandated by legislatures for a criminal sentencing. The *stare decisis* rule, as previously discussed, requires justices to follow earlier Supreme Court decisions unless shown to be clearly wrong. Subsequent justices have not asserted that any of the death penalty decisions discussed above were clearly wrong when rendered. Hence, one would expect that the Supreme Court would have continued to rule that the death penalty is constitutional, that the procedure employed in criminal sentencing is set by the legislatures, that the Supreme Court is without power to rule on the proportionality of sentences fixed by legislatures, and that Supreme Court justices will not impose their personal sentencing views. Yet, the opposite has occurred.

The Court's Revision Of The Eighth Amendment

The shift followed a 1958 opinion in which Chief Justice Earl Warren introduced the idea that the Eighth "Amendment must draw its meaning from the evolving standards of decency that mark the progress of a maturing society," and its "scope is not static."[355] The case did not concern a death penalty. Rather, it involved a federal statute that mandated the withdrawal of American citizenship from a native-born deserting soldier (in addition to the statutory penalty for desertion). The Court held this to be "a form of punishment more primitive than torture, for it destroys for the individual the political existence that was centuries in the development."[356]

Chief Justice Warren offered no basis for his "evolving standards of decency" formula. Nor did he even suggest that his words should be used to bar as "unusual" any practice, common at the adoption of the Eighth Amendment, and for at least 150 years after, as subsequent Supreme Courts have applied it.

Warren's "evolving standards of decency" formula was accepted by most justices without regard to their position on the death penalty. Whether it was strictly consistent with the Constitution, it had a superficial attraction. If Americans, perhaps as reflected in polls and/or in the decisions of state legislatures, rejected the death penalty, it might be said that the death penalty was no longer accepted as common or usual.

Most important, the Court, later in 1989, made clear that it was rampantly held societal views to which it was referring, and not the personal views of five (or even nine) justices: "[O]ur job is to identify the 'evolving standards of decency'; to determine, not what they should be, but what they are. We have no power under the Eighth Amendment to substitute our belief in the scientific evidence for the society's apparent skepticism. .... It has never been thought that this was a shorthand reference to the preferences of a majority of this Court."[357] For this reason, the Court has frequently held that the best measure of "evolving standards of decency" is what state legislatures say. The "judgment of the representatives of the people"[358] "weighs heavily in ascertaining contemporary standards of decency."[359] It also includes what juries decide, as they "reflect the evolving standards of decency that mark the progress of a maturing society."[360]

As we shall see, this standard was misused to override the actual current standard of decency as expressed by state legislatures and the public, substituting instead what some justices personally believed *should be* the standard of decency. This invasion by certain justices of legislative prerogatives started slowly, but the slippery slope of this assumption of judicial power continued until the Court had completed its power grab.

Starting in 1972, a bare majority of Supreme Court justices – generally only five – did not exercise the constitutionally-required self-discipline that their predecessors had shown. They ignored prior Court rulings to hold unconstitutional penalties and procedures previously approved by the Court. They thereby substituted their own personal views of what is an appropriate sentence for the judgment of many legislatures, and they ruled that the long-standing death penalty for various crimes had somehow become unconstitutional. While most justices continued to pay lip service to the constitutionality of the death penalty – a few justices openly opposed *any* death sentence – the barest majority of justices repeatedly chipped away at the death penalty by changing the controlling procedural rules (thereby voiding all death penalty statutes and requiring legislatures to enact new ones), and excluding certain crimes and categories of people from a death sentence. And they did so by asserting that it was required by the "cruel and unusual punishments" language in the Eighth Amendment – although the amendment remains unchanged from the almost 200 years of opposite interpretation by the Supreme Court.

The Jury's Exercise Of Discretion In Voting A Death Sentence

Early in our country's history, legislatures enacted two different procedures to impose a death penalty. One was to specify crimes for which a death penalty was mandatory.[361] Once the jury convicted a defendant of that crime, the death sentence was fixed. The second procedure was to give to the jury the discretion to decide whether a defendant, convicted of a crime for which the death penalty had been authorized, should live or die. Providing an option to the jury was advantageous to the defendant, as it provided a means by which the defendant might avoid execution.

Where the jury was granted that discretion by statute, the judge could not overrule the jury's decision. In 1899, the Supreme Court, in fact, reversed a death sentence where the judge had incorrectly instructed the jury that it was required to impose the death sentence unless it found "palliating circumstances that tend to show that the crime is not heinous."[362] As the Court explained, in enforcing this statutory delegation "to the judgment and the conscience of the jury": "How far considerations of age, sex, ignorance, illness, or intoxication, of human passion or weakness, or sympathy or clemency, or the irrevocableness of an executed sentence of death, or an apprehension that explanatory facts may exist which have not been brought to light, or any other consideration whatever, should be allowed weight in deciding the question whether the accused should be capitally punished, is committed by [statute] to the sound discretion of the jury and of the jury alone."[363]

In the following 72 years, the Supreme Court twice reaffirmed the constitutionality of according a jury the absolute discretion to decide whether to impose a death penalty. In 1948, the Court held that "whether the accused should or should not be capitally punished [is] entirely within the discretion of the jury ... [which] could be based on any consideration which appealed to the jury."[364]   And in a 1971 ruling,[365] where the judge had instructed the jury that, in determining the punishment, "you are entirely free to act according to your own judgment, conscience and absolute discretion,"[366] the Supreme Court concluded, "we find it quite impossible to say that committing to the untrammeled discretion of the jury the power to pronounce life or death in capital cases is offensive to anything in the Constitution."[367]   It continued by explaining the practical reasons for its decision: "To identify before the fact those characteristics of criminal homicides and perpetrators which call for the death penalty, and to express these characteristics in language which can be fairly understood and applied by the sentencing authority, appears to be tasks which are beyond present human ability."[368]

Despite this clear admonition by the Supreme Court, the march of the anti-death-penalty justices began the next year. As the first step in what has become a clear march to eradicate the death penalty, the Court focused on the procedure used to apply a death penalty, not the constitutionality of a death sentence. We have already seen that in 1971 the Court expressly sustained the jury's discretion to impose a death sentence. Yet, in 1972 the Supreme Court by a 5-4 vote, in a case known as *Furman v. Georgia*, did an about-face and overturned a death sentence on the ground that giving the jury the discretion to make the decision is unconstitutional. [369] Two of the majority said that they would hold *any* death penalty to be unconstitutional, noting "that the Court ... may have in the past expressed an opinion that the death penalty is constitutional is not now binding on us"[370] – itself an arrogant assumption of power to change the meaning of the Constitution as found by their predecessors, without any change in the wording of the Eighth Amendment. These two made a majority with three justices who suddenly decided that affording juries discretion on the death penalty is unconstitutional.[371]

Before further discussion of this *Furman* decision, it will help to know that, while it remains a binding ruling, the Supreme Court thereafter, at times, expressed second thoughts. Six years later, the justices conceded that "[t]his Court had never [even] intimated prior to *Furman* that discretion in sentencing offended the Constitution."[372] As late as 11 years after the *Furman* ruling, a majority of the justices questioned the basis for it.[373] Four justices wrote, in upholding a death penalty: "We have never suggested that the United States Constitution requires that the sentencing process should be transformed into a rigid and mechanical parsing of statutory aggravating factors .... [T]he moral, factual, ... judgment of [trial] judges and juries [should] play a meaningful role in sentencing. We expect that sentencers will exercise their discretion in their own way and to the best of their ability .... [A]s long as the decision is not so wholly arbitrary as to offend the Constitution, the Eighth Amendment cannot and should not demand more."[374] Two concurring justices created a majority of six by concluding: "The sentencing process assumes that the trier of fact will exercise judgment in light of his or her background, experiences, and values."

Yet the five justices in the *Furman* decision had taken the first step on this slippery slope: They had succeeded in reinterpreting the Eighth Amendment to regulate the procedure to be used by a jury in deciding upon a death penalty; it barred juries from exercising their discretion. And despite the noted attempts to return the Court to the contrary long history of decisions, the *Furman* decision, in the end, permanently changed the death penalty jurisprudence.

The "earthquake" proportion of the *Furman* decision was accurately predicted by the four dissenting justices in that case: "the capital punishment laws of 39 States and the District of Columbia [are] struck down" and the "federal statutory structure that permits the death penalty ... are voided," including even for treason, assassination of the president, the vice president, espionage, explosive offenses where death results, and train-wrecking.[375] In rendering this decision, the majority-of-one ran roughshod over the language of the Eighth Amendment, ignored Supreme Court precedents, and disregarded public opinion and overwhelming legislative views in favor of the death penalty.

As previously discussed, the Eighth Amendment does not deal with process by which judges and juries decide on punishments, it deals only with the punishment imposed, barring only punishment that is "cruel and unusual." It is the Fifth Amendment, not the Eighth, that prohibits "depriv[ation] of life ... without due process of law." Not only did the five majority justices in *Furman* ignore that fact, they also overruled the Court's prior holding that a state "is free to regulate the procedure of its courts in accordance with its own conception of policy and fairness, unless in so doing it offends some principle of justice so rooted in the traditions and conscience of our people as to be ranked as fundamental." The Court continued, "a State's procedure does not run foul ... because another method may seem to our thinking to be fairer or wiser or to give a surer promise of protection to the prisoner at the bar."[376]

The five *Furman* justices – motivated by their social engineering views -- thus substituted their personal values for those reflected in death penalty statutes and jury deliberations. In doing

> " *The five Furman justices –*
> *motivated by their social engineering views – thus substituted their personal values for those reflected in death penalty statutes and jury deliberations. In doing so, they ran roughshod over the principle of judicial restraint...* "

so, they ran roughshod over the principle of judicial restraint, voiced even by the anti-death penalty justices, who had stated that the "clearest and most objective evidence of contemporary values is the legislation enacted by the country's legislatures."[377]

When the five justices announced their decision in *Furman*, approximately 80 percent of states approved the death penalty as mandatory or optional punishment for specified crimes.[378] There are many other indications of public support for the death penalty. In 1967, a presidential commission considered the appropriateness of the death penalty and unanimously recommended that it was not a decision to be made by the federal government, but should be left to the legislature and people of each state to decide.[379] Three states, Colorado in 1966, Massachusetts in 1968, and Illinois in 1970, held referenda, with results supporting the death penalty.[380] In 1967, a bill in the United States Senate to abolish the death penalty for all federal crimes had so little support that it never reached the Senate floor.[381] In contrast, in the decade preceding the *Furman* decision, Congress had, by overwhelming vote, added crimes for which the death penalty was authorized.[382] Jury verdicts were another indication of pro-death penalty public opinion. If public opinion had turned against the death sentence, there would likely have been a reduction in the number of death penalties imposed. In fact, the opposite occurred: Juries had voted more than 1,000 death sentences in the 1960s, and the year 1970 recorded the highest annual number since 1961.[383]

Public opinion has remained overwhelmingly in favor of the death penalty. A 2009 poll reflected that 65 percent favored the death penalty for murder. The same poll found that 49 percent believed that the death penalty is not imposed often enough and 24 percent responded it was imposed the right amount, suggesting that 73 percent approved of the death penalty.[384] Even though the percentage support for the death penalty declined slightly in a 2011 poll, it remained at 61 percent,[385] -- not even close to public rejection. Most relevant to the anti-death penalty justices' position that the death sentence is immoral – the crux of their opposition – a 2010 poll found that 65 percent of Americans believe it morally acceptable and only 26 percent that it is not.[386]

Justice Stevens, who most often voted against a death penalty, recently noted a fact reflecting public support of the death penalty. He noted that "elected judges typically used" their power to override jury sentences to "impose death rather than life," while appointed judges "favored defendants."[387] Logically, this means elected judges (subject to re-election) are more inclined to act consistent with public opinion that favors the death penalty.

The five justices in the *Furman* majority not only overrode public and legislative opinion, but established an unfortunate controlling precedent. When a legislature or the people of a state vote to permit or disallow the death penalty, a later legislature or referendum can reverse the decision. A Supreme Court decision, based on the Constitution, cannot be undone unless the decision is overruled by a later Supreme Court or the Constitution is amended. As we have earlier discussed, amendments are rare, intentionally made very difficult by our nation's Founders. Justices seldom ignore the *stare decisis* principle to overrule an earlier decision. Hence, these five *Furman* justices have effectively permanently usurped the will of the people, ending the discretionary right of juries to decide whether the death penalty should be imposed. And, because the decision held that a statute authorizing the death penalty must fix the conditions a jury must find before a death penalty might be imposed, it voided all existing death penalty statutes.

Continued public support for the death penalty was dramatically demonstrated by the prompt response of 35 states and the U.S. Congress. Less than four years after the *Furman* decision, they reinstated the death penalty (for at least certain crimes), with language that precluded jury discretion.[388] Oregon, which had not previously authorized capital punishment, enacted the death penalty.[389] And, after the California Supreme Court – parroting the United States Supreme Court's bare majority – declared that California statutes authorizing the death penalty violated the California Constitution, the people of California by referendum amended their constitution to re-authorize the death penalty.[390]

Georgia was one of the states that enacted new statutes to re-authorize the death penalty. The new Georgia statute – similar to other state laws after the *Furman* decision – retained the death penalty for murder, kidnapping, armed robbery, rape, treason and aircraft hijacking.[391] To comply with the *Furman* no-discretion ruling, it added provision that a jury "may" impose the death penalty if it found beyond a reasonable doubt one of 10 aggravating circumstances, which included, among others, that "the offense of murder, ... was committed while the offender was in the commission of another capital felony," or was committed "for the purpose of receiving money," or "was outrageously or wantonly vile, horrible or inhuman ... in that it involved ... depravity of mind ...."[392]

In the first case involving this Georgia statute to reach the Supreme Court, *Gregg v. Georgia*, a death sentence was upheld by a 7-2 vote. Justices Brennan and Marshall dissented, reiterating their belief that the Eighth Amendment prohibits any death penalty. The majority, composed of the four dissenters in *Furman*, plus the three justices who had held it unconstitutional for a jury to have discretion in deciding on a death penalty, concluded here that the new Georgia statute eliminated the jurors' discretion, and thus was constitutional.

But did *Furman* really withdraw discretion from the jury or was it simply a façade further to chip away at the death penalty? Let's analyze the before-and-after realistically. Under the pre-*Furman* Georgia statute, jurors would listen to the evidence and decide whether the defendant's conduct warranted the death penalty. While that statute did not enumerate factors for the jury to consider, it is logical that jurors would likely opt for the death penalty if the evidence demonstrated murder for money, multi-crime conduct or a depraved mind. Didn't the post-*Furman* Georgia statute require jurors to follow a virtually identical procedure? Jurors must listen to the evidence and decide whether the defendant committed murder for money, engaged in multi-crime conduct or acted in such a vile manner as to indicate a depraved mind, and, if so, whether death is the appropriate sentence. Just as under the pre-existing statute, there is no objective formula for jurors to reach their decision. Indeed, the Supreme Court, in approving this statutory "change," acknowledged that the "standards" jurors were to consider "are by necessity somewhat general."[393]

> *"What was their authority for this new 'grossly out of proportion' rule? Nothing beyond their say-so, as they cited only two non-death penalty cases, neither of which established a disproportionate rule was warranted by the Eighth Amendment."*

The question is thus posed: For what purpose did the Supreme Court's five-justice majority void all federal and state death penalty statutes, supposedly to end jury discretion, which still remains? The only realistic answer: They wanted to impose on the public those five justices' personal animosity to the death penalty, expecting that some legislatures would not re-enact it.

The seven justices who voted to uphold the new Georgia death penalty law in *Gregg* were so split on the reasoning that they wrote three separate opinions and one "statement." The opinion of three justices, considered to be the Court's opinion in the case, contained one sentence that presaged future weapons to be used against the death penalty. In words irrelevant to the case, they wrote for the first time in a death penalty decision that "the punishment may not be 'excessive.'"[394] This 3-justice opinion provided two definitions of what is "excessive": "First, the punishment must not involve the unnecessary and wanton infliction of pain" – the original meaning of the Eighth Amendment. And then it added a new rule: "Second, the punishment must not be grossly out of proportion to the severity of the crime." What was their authority for this new "grossly out of proportion" rule? Nothing beyond their say-so, as they cited only two non-death penalty cases, neither of which established a disproportionate rule was warranted by the Eighth Amendment.[395]

On the same day the Supreme Court issued this ruling, five justices made clear that they were not going to stop chipping away at capital punishment. They declared unconstitutional, on new grounds, the death penalty statutes of North Carolina and Louisiana in decisions that also affected death penalty statutes in eight other states.

To understand these decisions, we need to consider how the Court in *Furman* rationalized the conclusion there that giving the jury discretion to decide whether to impose the death penalty violated the Eighth Amendment. Justice Douglas provided the explanation: "The death penalty inflicted on one defendant is 'unusual' if it discriminates against him by reason of his race, religion, wealth, social position or class, or it is imposed under a procedure that allows for the play of such prejudices."[396] I agree that the vote of a juror shown to be biased should be voided. But proof of actual bias is vastly different from Justice Douglas' assertion that jurors' discretion creates the *possibility* of a sentence resulting from bias. Although every juror's vote, even on guilt or innocence, could conceivably be based on undisclosed bias, we do not discard every juror's vote merely on that "possibility." There is thus no support for Justice Douglas' position, based on the mere *possibility* of bias in a juror's "practically untrammeled discretion."[397]

North Carolina and Louisiana's legislatures, with other states, understood that the Supreme Court had ruled that, if a state wished to reinstate the death penalty, it must eliminate juror discretion. As already noted, the *Gregg* decision validated a death sentence imposed after the jury found specified aggravating circumstances existed. Another approach chosen by 10 states,[398] following the *Furman* decision, was to avoid jury discretion by making the death penalty mandatory upon conviction of specified crimes. For example, to replace its statute that gave the jury "unbridled discretion" to choose death or life imprisonment for first-degree murder,[399] the North Carolina legislature "enacted a new statute that was essentially unchanged from the old one except that it made the death penalty mandatory" for specified crimes, including first-degree murder.[400] States that adopted this approach certainly had good reason to believe it was constitutional. It eliminated the jury's discretion as to the death penalty. And these states were comforted that the procedure was not barred because, "[a]t the time the Eighth Amendment was adopted in 1791, the States uniformly followed the common-law practice of making death the exclusive and mandatory sentence for certain specified offenses."[401]

"It is difficult to follow the reasoning of the Supreme Court that had first declared unconstitutional death sentences imposed by a jury because jurors had discretion, and then declared unconstitutional mandatory death sentences because the jury had no discretion."

Yet, only four years after holding juror discretion unconstitutional, a five-justice majority declared mandatory sentences unconstitutional.[402] It is difficult to follow the reasoning of the Supreme Court that had first declared unconstitutional death sentences imposed by a jury because jurors had discretion, and then declared unconstitutional mandatory death sentences because the jury had no discretion.

The justices backtracked from their previous decision that there was something inherently wrong with affording discretion to a jury. They described "the movement away from mandatory sentences" (which were prevalent at the beginning of our country and for many years thereafter) and said it "marked an enlightened introduction of flexibility into the sentencing process."[403] This statement demands the question: If discretion in the jury was an "enlightened" way of deciding sentences, why did the same Court only recently reject discretion as unconstitutional? And the majority's turnabout on discretion is all the more difficult to understand because they recognized that the legislative decision, whether it be mandatory death penalties or granting discretion on that subject to juries, is entitled to heavy weight in favor of its constitutionality.[404]

Recall that the Supreme Court had rejected jury discretion because it might allow for discrimination and thus be harmful to defendants. Now, in rejecting the mandatory procedure, these justices found that jury discretion had been *good* for defendants, resulting in *no* death penalty in more than 80 percent of capital murder cases.[405] Apparently, instead of discriminating against defendants, juries armed with discretion carefully limited the death penalty to the most egregious criminal conduct. These contradictory rulings warrant the conclusion that, whether the death sentence was imposed under a mandatory procedure or by jury discretion, some justices simply sought to further their personal dislike for the death penalty.

Beside inconsistency, there are other flaws in these rulings. First, as previously mentioned, the Eighth Amendment doesn't govern sentencing *procedure*. It is directed solely to the end result: It forbids sentences that are "cruel and unusual," without regard to the procedure by which the judge or jury decides the sentence. Second, if the Eighth Amendment voids mandatory death penalties, it would logically void *any* mandatory sentence, without regard to the crime. Yet, these same justices declared they were not holding unconstitutional mandatory death sentences for crimes committed by "prisoners serving life sentences."[406] No explanation how a mandatory death sentence can be both constitutional and unconstitutional.

But that wasn't the end of the justices' gnawing away at the death penalty.

The Louisiana legislature enacted a death penalty statute which appeared to comply with both the anti-discretion and anti-mandatory rulings. For first-degree murder, the jury had to find one or more specified conditions: the murder was committed with specific intent to kill or to inflict great bodily harm, or while perpetrating aggravated kidnapping, aggravated rape or armed robbery. If the jury did not make such finding, the penalty would be life imprisonment.[407] While these conditions were not identical to those approved in *Gregg*, they met the Court's requirement that the jury's discretion be limited by requiring the finding of specified conditions before imposing the death penalty.

The Court, by a 5-4 vote, voided this Louisiana death penalty, finding that it was both too mandatory and too discretionary: It did not allow the jury the discretion to consider "the circumstances of the particular crime or ... the attributes of the individual offender"; and it did allow the jury too much discretion to "choose a verdict for a lesser offense whenever they feel the death penalty is inappropriate."[408] I don't know how to explain this decision other than by saying, "Heads, anti-death penalty proponents win; tails, death penalty proponents lose."

Two years later in 1978, the Supreme Court considered an Ohio death penalty statute that did not contain the provisions found fatal in the Louisiana statute. The Ohio statute fixed the penalty as death only if the jury made two determinations: (1) the jury must find the defendant guilty of murder with at least one of seven aggravating circumstances, such as "for the purpose of escaping ..."; and (2) after "considering 'the nature and circumstances of the offense and the history, character, and condition of the offender,' the sentencing judge determines" that none of three circumstances was established, including that the crime was committed because of "duress, coercion or strong provocation," or "the offender's psychosis or mental deficiency."[409] To make such findings, the judge had to consider all circumstances of the crime and the history and condition of the defendant, while having discretion to refrain from imposing a death sentence on the belief, for example, that the crime was out-of-character for this defendant.

This Ohio statute appears to have complied with the Court's own summary of what its various decisions meant: "all sentencing discretion [need not] be eliminated, but only that it be 'directed and limited,'" and "must permit consideration of the 'character and record of the individual offender and the circumstances of the particular offense."[410]   Yet, the Court plurality (joined by the two justices who rejected any death penalty) decided that the sentencing judge had been precluded "from considering as a mitigating factor any aspect of a defendant's character or record or any of the circumstances of the offense that the defendant proffers as a basis for a sentence less than death"[411] – even though the statute required the sentencing judge to take into account "the nature and circumstances of the offense and the history, character, and condition of the offender." Isn't this result best explained as a continuation of the crusade of certain justices against the death penalty without regard to precedent, consistency or reason?

In 1980 came the icing on the anti-death penalty cake. In Georgia, a defendant was sentenced to be executed after the jury found him guilty of murder and that "the offense of murder was outrageously or wantonly vile, horrible and inhuman."[412]

Because this Georgia statute had been approved by the Supreme Court only four years before in Gregg, the justices could not logically hold that the jury's finding, which met the statute's specifications, was insufficient to support the death sentence. Instead, these justices took a new tack in their campaign against the death penalty. They assumed a new power: to determine on a case-by-case basis whether the murder was sufficiently egregious to warrant a death penalty. They, thereby, second-guess the jury, the trial judge and the state's appellate courts, all of which had agreed on the barbarous nature of this double murder.

These anti-death penalty justices created a new rule that could not be found in the Eighth Amendment: It is not sufficient that the jury find the murder was "outrageously or wantonly vile, horrible and inhuman," as the Georgia statute, previously approved by the Supreme Court, required. The murder, according to the Supreme Court, must reflect a "consciousness more 'depraved' than that of any person guilty of murder."[413]

Understand what that means: For almost two centuries, murder was punishable by death under the Eighth Amendment. The crime of first-degree murder was (and still is) abhorrent to civilized society. In 1980, the Supreme Court majority discovered an oxymoron – a not-so-bad average first-degree murder for which capital punishment would not be allowed, because it is not sufficiently "depraved."

Look how far these anti-death penalty justices had taken their crusade. They had started their offensive by revising the Eighth Amendment to give them the power to decide whether a death penalty is "excessive," even though the amendment does not prohibit "excessive" punishment, but only "cruel and unusual punishment." They later expanded their power to authorize them to second-guess jury factual findings. In the process, the five-justice majority succeeded in placing capital punishment under a miasmic cloud of confusion and uncertainty. The anti-death penalty justices' admit the confusion they created: "The signals from this Court have not ... always been easy to decipher."[414] Now there's an understatement.

Their objective was to reduce and reduce again the number of death sentences until they approached zero. In 2005, these justices proclaimed that "the death penalty is reserved for a narrow category of crimes and offenders" – a rule nowhere to be found in the Eighth Amendment. Justice John Paul Stevens boasted about overcoming "local policy making" to the contrary, which, he reflected, has not "prevented Supreme Court decisions from eliminating categories of defendants … and offenses … from exposure to capital punishment nationwide."[415] No clearer admission of judicial usurpation of legislative responsibilities: "local policy making," which The Constitution and the Supreme Court had mandated is the responsibility of legislatures, has been overridden by five justices.

X.

SUPREME COURT OVERRULES LEGISLATURES BY ASSUMING POWER TO PROHIBIT HISTORICALLY APPROVED DEATH PENALTY FOR SPECIFIC CRIMES AND PERSONS

Having succeeded in substantially thwarting the death penalty for murder, as shown in the preceding chapter, these justices turned their attention to reducing further the possibility of imposing a death sentence, by removing selected crimes and persons from any possibility of a death penalty – even crimes and persons for which historically a death sentence had been held applicable and constitutional.

Prohibition Of Death Sentence For Felony Murder

The felony murder doctrine (with death as the penalty) originated hundreds of years ago in England, was brought to the American colonies, and was the law in the United States for over 200 years.[416] The felony murder doctrine essentially reflected the legal axiom that someone who aids another in the commission of a crime is equally guilty. Florida, as most states, codified the felony murder principle in a statute: "if the accused was present aiding and abetting the commission of one of the felonies listed in the first-degree murder statute, he is equally guilty, with the actual perpetrator of the underlying felony, of first-degree murder."[417]

This doctrine recognizes the reality that most felonies involve planning and a division of labor, and that each participant – perhaps lookout, driver, or procurer of weapons – is integral to the success of the crime and responsible for any ensuing murder. Yet suddenly, in 1982, in *Enmund v. Florida*, [418] five justices of the Supreme Court declared a death sentence for felony murder to violate the Eighth Amendment.

The facts in this case of two murders and armed robbery: A few weeks before, the victim-husband had revealed the contents of his wallet to Earl Enmund and bragged that he could easily "dig up $15,000, $16,000."[419] Enmund, previously convicted of armed robbery,[420] "initiated" and "planned" this armed robbery, "drove the getaway car," and "actively participated in an attempt to avoid detection by disposing of the murder weapons."[421]

On the morning of the crime, Enmund and his two accomplices were at a friend's home. They took the friend's car and drove to the farmhouse of the victims, a couple aged 86 and 74. Enmund stayed in the car while his accomplices, each armed with a loaded gun, approached the back door on the pretext of asking for water for their "overheated" car. When the elderly husband retrieved a water jug to help them, one accomplice held a gun to him and told the other accomplice to take the man's wallet. The victim-wife, hearing her husband's cry for help, ran out with her gun and shot one of the robbers, both of whom returned fire, killing both the husband and wife. After taking the husband's money, they ran to the car, which Enmund drove away.[422] The jury recommended Enmund receive the death penalty, and the Florida courts agreed.[423]

All nine Supreme Court justices agreed that "the evidence established beyond a reasonable doubt that [Enmund] was actually present and was actively aiding and abetting the robbery ... and that the unlawful killing occurred in the perpetration of ... the robbery," thus "support[ing] the verdicts of murder in the first degree on the basis of the felony murder portion" of Florida law.[424]

Yet, five justices held that it violated the Eighth Amendment because death for Enmund was "excessive," as Enmund did not physically pull the trigger. Why was it excessive when two innocent people had been murdered in the carrying out of the armed robbery planned and participated in by Enmund? Realistically, Enmund wrote the script, produced and directed and played a requisite role in the acts that resulted in the two cold-blooded murders. The majority's suggestion that states had trended away from the death penalty for persons who had not pulled the trigger[425] was not persuasive, for two reasons. First, the facts refuted that assertion: 23 states at that time authorized the death sentence for a "felony murderer [who] has neither killed nor intended to kill his victim"[426] – amounting to about two-thirds of states that authorized the death penalty.[427] Second, given that the Court had repeatedly recognized that each state may be a laboratory in fixing the punishment for crime, a trend away, even if true, would not affect the validity of Florida's decision to retain the death penalty for felony murder.

That so many states maintained the death penalty for felony murder did not deter these five justices on their quest to create another area in which the death penalty was not allowed. They noted that, of the 362 persons executed since 1954, 339 actually committed the homicide. But the number of non-triggermen tried for murder was not provided – prosecutors always consider the specific facts surrounding a defendant's participation and would not necessarily seek a death penalty on most peripheral felony murder defendants. In addition, they ignored that juries are extremely cautious in imposing the death penalty in most cases, likely reserving it for non-triggermen who played a central role in the robbery-murder.

In the end, the majority's rationale came down to this: "Although the judgments of legislatures, juries and prosecutors weigh heavily in the balance, it is for us ultimately to judge whether the Eighth Amendment permits the imposition of the death penalty on one ... who aids and abets a felony in the course of which a murder is committed by others."[428] This is the raw invention of judicial power: Nothing in the Eighth Amendment delegates to five justices the power to override legislative choice of felony murder punishment, thereby rejecting 200 years of American history. As the Supreme Court numerous times previously ruled, but here ignored, legislatures, not courts, have the "indisputable ... authority to define and fix the punishment for crime."[429]

> *"Nothing in the Eighth Amendment delegates to five justices the power to override legislative choice of felony murder punishment."*

Most troubling is the five justices' sympathy for the offender as contrasted with their responsibility to protect victims. They conclude that "Enmund did not ... intend to kill."[430] Of course, Enmund – no different from even most robbers physically holding a loaded gun during a robbery - hoped it would be unnecessary for the guns to be used. But Enmund planned the robbery and knew each of his two accomplices had a loaded gun. The result of Enmund's planning was the deaths of two innocent people.

The five justices asserted they were influenced by the fact that "killings only rarely occur during robberies,"[431] based on data that "[a]pproximately 2,361 persons were murdered" in "548,809 robberies [that] occurred in 1980."[432] Imagine telling the relatives of 2,361 innocent victims that they should not fret because they were part of a small number. Moreover, this is an apples-to-oranges comparison as the data does not disclose how many of these robberies involved a loaded gun, as distinguished from robberies with no weapon, or perhaps a knife or unloaded gun.

More telling, the determination should not rest on numbers comparisons, but should be based on the best criminal justice procedure to protect every innocent life. The Declaration of Independence proclaimed government's central purpose to protect all (not just most) persons' right to "life." Two-thousand, three-hundred sixty-one more innocent lives were lost at the hands of robbers than should occur in a perfect society. Granted that no one realistically expects a society in which no crime occurs, but our criminal justice system must adopt all appropriate means to reduce this number, including authorizing a death penalty to deter those who plan, aid, or commit crimes that result in murder.

Indeed, these five justices recognized that a "principal social purpose[]" of the death penalty is "deterrence of capital crime by prospective offenders."[433] They nevertheless rejected the benefit of deterrence, explaining that "[w]e are unconvinced ... that the threat that the death penalty will be imposed for murder will *measurably* deter one who does not kill ...; [i]nstead it seems likely that capital punishment can serve as a deterrent only when murder is the result of premeditation and deliberation."[434] This is a shocking statement by five justices whose primary responsibility is to protect innocent people. By the use of the word "measurably," these justices admit that the death penalty would have at least some deterrence effect. No computer program or mathematical formula can "measure" the number of murders during a robbery that would have been avoided if the deterrence of a death penalty existed. But inability to fix that number is no reason to forego a deterrence that could have saved some. Yet, these five justices rejected that means to protect whatever number of innocent lives whose murder could have been deterred.

Beyond that, the majority's own words demonstrate that the death penalty does have substantial deterrence effect in felony murder cases. The murders for which Enmund was convicted were "the result of premeditation and deliberation." The careful planning is deliberation; the decision for each of Enmund's two accomplices to accost the victims with loaded guns involved premeditation of their use if the need arose. Unloaded guns would have sufficed for scare purposes.

If the threat of a death penalty can deter premeditated and planned murders, the death penalty would similarly provide deterrence in felony murder cases. Criminals like Enmund would have to recognize that planning a robbery, in which accomplices are armed with loaded guns that may be used, would subject him to the possibility of the death penalty if a murder were committed.

> *"Nothing in the Eighth Amendment delegates to five justices the power to override legislative choice of felony murder punishment."*

One glimmer of hope is that some justices recognized they do not have *carte blanche* to void death sentences: Five years after the *Enmund* decision, the Supreme Court (with one new justice and one of the majority in *Enmund* changing sides) affirmed a death sentence for a felony murder. In that case, the defendant brothers, employing a large arsenal of weapons, helped their father and his cell mate escape from prison. When their escape car experienced two flat tires, one of the brothers stood in front of the car, while the others, armed with weapons, hid by the side of the road. A family of four good samaritans who stopped to help were quickly accosted and driven into the desert, where all four were brutally murdered by the father.[435]

The Arizona Supreme Court found that the "deaths would not have occurred but for [the brothers'] assistance."[436] And the United States Supreme Court, by a slim 5-4 vote, upheld the death penalty for the brothers, even though they neither intended to kill nor personally fired the guns that killed the victims,[437] because of their "reckless disregard for human life implicit in knowingly engaging in criminal activities known to carry a grave risk of death."[438] The Supreme Court in this case returned to the original meaning of the Eighth Amendment and respect for state decisions. But, realistically, the decision in the next felony murder case to reach the Supreme Court will depend on the next appointee to the Court: Will it increase the number of justices who abide by the limitations on judicial power, or those justices who wish to legislate their own personal views?

Prohibition Of Death Penalty For Anyone Under 18 Years Old

The Eighth Amendment contains no minimum age for punishment. Age 15 was certainly above the minimum age for capital punishment in England, which also, albeit infrequently, executed minors below that age, as young as eight.[439] A rebuttable presumption of incapacity to commit a felony applied only to under-14- year-olds.[440] Between 1642 and 1899, there were at least 22 executions in this country for crimes committed by under-16-year-olds.[441] This number was a very small percentage of all those under 16 charged with serious crimes, suggesting that the death sentence was reserved for extreme cases.

Such an extreme case, in which William Wayne Thompson, age 15 when he committed the crime, was sentenced to death, was appealed to the Supreme Court in 1988. In addition to the barbarous nature of this killing (described as case No. 8 in Chapter IX's "Actual Cases"), Thompson had a record of serious felony arrests starting when he was 12: three for assault and battery, including assault with a knife, and one attempted burglary.[442] Before he was tried as an adult, the court determined, following a hearing, that Thompson was competent, that he understood the wrongfulness of his conduct, and that "there was [sic] virtually no reasonable prospects for rehabilitation ... within the juvenile system."[443] The jury rejected the defense argument that Thompson's young age was a mitigating factor.[444]

Five justices concluded, as the dissenting justices described it, that it is "a fundamental principle of our society that no one who is one day short of his 16th birthday can have sufficient maturity and moral responsibility to be subjected to capital punishment for any crime."[445] All objective evidence refuted that conclusion. Twenty-one states submitted briefs in support of the death sentence; no state opposed it.[446]   Congress had recently lowered to 15 the age at which a juvenile may be treated as an adult, and thus subject to the death penalty, after Department of Justice officials had testified that many juveniles were "cynical, street-wise, repeat offenders, indistinguishable, except for their age, from their adult criminal counterparts." [447] "In 1979 alone, juveniles under the age of 15, *i.e.*, almost a year younger than Thompson, had committed a total of 206 homicides nationwide, more than 1,000 forcible rapes, 10,000 robberies, and 10,000 aggravated assaults."[448] A majority of states that permitted capital punishment did not differentiate based on age.[449]

What then was the basis for the Supreme Court ruling that a death sentence for someone one day under 16 was unconstitutional?   They cited higher minimum ages, made applicable to all youths for voting, jury duty, driving and marriage.[450] Such legislative or administrative fixing of a minimum age was made to avoid the necessity of determining, on an individual basis, each person's maturity for these civic rights and obligations. Such ease-of-administering decisions are irrelevant to a decision on the sentence to be imposed on a specific defendant: It is the individual traits and record of the youth who commits murder, not all youths in general, that must determine whether a juvenile should be treated as an adult in criminal court. The five justices also asserted that the death penalty cannot be a deterrent to juveniles because the "likelihood that the teenage offender has made the cost-benefit analysis that attaches any weight to the possibility of execution is so remote as to be virtually nonexistent."[451]   Virtually nonexistent?   The evidence was that Thompson performed that cost-benefit analysis: He had said that "because of his age he was beyond any severe penalty of the law, and accordingly did not believe there would be any severe repercussions from his behavior."[452]

In the end, these five justices admitted it was their *personal* opinion of the "'evolving standards of decency' that mark the progress of a maturing society"[453] that controlled. They substituted their personal views of what the law should be for what the law was.

One year later, the Court again considered death sentences for juveniles, aged 16 and 17. Kevin Stanford, with a record of numerous prior crimes, at 17 years and four months of age, raped and sodomized a woman clerk at a gas station, after which he drove her to a secluded area where he shot her point-blank in the face and back of her head.[454] Heath Wilkins, age 16½, with a history of burglary, arson, theft, attempted murder and killing of animals, stabbed and murdered a 26-year-old mother of two during his robbery of a convenience store where she worked.[455]

A new majority of five justices (composed of the four dissenters in *Thompson* plus Justice Sandra Day O'Connor, who switched sides) held that the Eighth Amendment did not bar the death penalty for these two juveniles. Rejecting the assumption of power that justices had invoked to overrule legislative determinations, this new majority explained that they would not decide the case based on their "own conceptions" or "merely the[ir] subjective views," but "on objective factors."[456]

This objective approach did not last. Sixteen years later, a slightly changed roster of justices not only overruled the *Stanford* decision, but, by a 5-4 vote, double-downed it to hold that the Eighth Amendment prohibited imposing the death penalty on anyone under the age of 18.[457]

The facts of this murder case were not sympathetic to the defendant Christopher Simmons. Only seven months short of his 18th birthday,[458] he announced that "he wanted to murder someone," and planned with two younger friends – in what even the majority opinion described as "chilling, callous terms" – breaking and entering into the home of Shirley Crook, who had been involved in a car accident with Simmons, and throwing her off a bridge. Simmons, with one of the other two, broke into Crook's home in the middle of the night, dragged her out of her bed, bound her hands and covered her eyes and mouth with duct tape, drove her in her minivan to a state park, where they covered her head with a towel, walked her to a railroad trestle over a river, then hog-tied her hands and feet together with electrical wire, wrapped her whole face with duct tape, and threw her into the river where she drowned."[459]

Under Missouri statutes, at 17-plus years, Simmons was required to be tried as an adult.[460] In regard to sentencing, the judge instructed the jury that it could consider his age as a mitigating factor, but the jury recommended the death penalty and the judge imposed it.[461]

The Supreme Court majority recognized it could not "deny or overlook the brutal crimes too many juvenile offenders have committed."[462] The dissent cited a recent murder in Alabama, involving three under-18-year-olds, together with a 19-year-old, who "picked up a female hitchhiker, threw bottles at her, and kicked and stomped her for approximately 30 minutes until she died," following which "they sexually assaulted her lifeless body and, when they were finished, threw her body off the cliff," returning later "to mutilate her corpse."[463]

The five justices acknowledged that "[i]n general we leave to legislatures the assessment of the efficacy of various criminal penalty schemes."[464] The Missouri legislature had determined that sentencing decision should be made by a jury and judge, based on the specific circumstances of the crime and characteristics of the defendant. Why did these five justices then reject the legislature's choice? They did not even claim that there was a consensus in the country against executing under-18-year-olds. In fact, at least six states had fixed 16 and two at 17 as the minimum age for the death penalty; two of these states had fixed 16 as that age after the Court's decision in *Stanford*. Thirteen other states that authorized the death penalty had no minimum age, meaning that 22 states authorized a death sentence for someone under 18.[465] In addition, the United States Senate publicly expressed its support for retaining the death penalty for juveniles when, in 1992, it ratified the International Covenant on Civil and Political Rights, subject to that exception.[466]

Nor did these five Justices assert that *every* murderer under 18 – even one day under 18 – is different from someone 18 and older. They recognized that "some under 18 have already attained a level of maturity that some adults will never reach."[467] These five justices rested on generalities unrelated to the specific defendant being sentenced: "The *general* differences between juveniles under 18 and adults"; "a lack of maturity and an undeveloped sense of responsibility are found in youth *more often* than in adults"; "juveniles have a *greater claim* than adults to be forgiven"; "for *most* teens, risky or anti-social behaviors … cease with maturity"; and "a relatively *small proportion* of adolescents … develop entrenched patterns of problem behavior that persist into adulthood."[468] By that logic, *some* youths under 18 may be proverbial "bad seeds," and should not be immunized from a death sentence.

These five justices also asserted the "low likelihood" that offenders under 18 had "engaged in 'the kind of cost-benefit analysis that attaches any weight to the possibility of execution,'" concluding the "death penalty [to be] ineffective as a means of deterrence."[469] But "*low*" likelihood is not equivalent to "no likelihood." Simmons, in fact, had engaged in that "cost-benefit analysis" and concluded that he and his friends "could 'get away with it' because they were minors"[470] – further reason to recognize that severe punishment can be a deterrent to some juveniles.

These five justices again relied on state prohibitions of those under 18 from voting, jury duty, or marrying without parental consent.[471] Do they really believe that driving carefully, drinking and marrying responsibly, and voting intelligently, are on a par with understanding that brutally murdering someone is not acceptable? As the dissenters pointed out, these comparisons "involve decisions far more sophisticated than the simple decision not to take another's life."[472]

In the end, the five justices based their decision on their "independent judgment ... on the proportionality of the death penalty for a particular class of crimes or offenders," and concluded that no murderer under 18 at the time of the murder should be subject to a death penalty.[473] Again, five justices assumed the power to substitute their personal views of what the law should be for centuries of what the law actually was, and the views of the public as expressed by their legislatures.

Prohibition Of Death Penalty For Rape

When the Eighth Amendment was enacted, most states authorized the death penalty for rape.[474] While some legislatures over time eliminated the death penalty for rape, until the 1972 *Furman* decision that invalidated all existing death penalty statutes as allowing jury discretion, rape remained a capital offense in 16 states and at the federal level.[475]

Yet, suddenly, the Supreme Court, in 1977, announced that a death sentence for rape of an adult woman is "cruel and unusual punishment."

Ehrlich Anthony Coker, the defendant whom a jury unanimously recommended be executed, was not simply an impetuous young man who had made one mistake. The facts[476] demonstrated his barbaric nature. In December 1971, Coker raped and then stabbed to death a young woman. Less than eight months later, Coker kidnapped and twice raped a 16-year-old, following which he stripped her, severely beat her with a club and dragged her into a wooded area, where he left her for dead. On being apprehended, he pled guilty to various crimes, and was sentenced by three separate courts to three consecutive life terms. About 20 months later, he escaped from prison and promptly raped another 16-year-old in the presence of her husband. Following the rape, Coker robbed the victim's husband, kidnapped the victim, and threatened that he would kill the woman if the police pulled him over.

The Georgia statute allowed the jury to recommend the death penalty only if it found specified aggravating circumstances. The jury found two: The rape had been committed by a person with a prior conviction for a capital felony, and in the course of an armed robbery. Finding no outweighing mitigating evidence, the jury, not surprisingly, recommended the death sentence. The judge concurred.

The Supreme Court reversed the death sentence, ruling it "grossly out of proportion to the severity of the crime,"[477] even while finding that, "[s]hort of homicide, [rape] is the 'ultimate violation of self,'" "highly reprehensible, both in its moral sense and in its almost total contempt for the personal integrity and autonomy of the female victim, ... a violent crime ... normally involv[ing] force, ... often accompanied by physical injury to the female ... and mental and psychological damage," and "[b]ecause it undermines the community's sense of security, there is public injury as well."[478] It seems incredible to conclude, as the justices did, that the death penalty was excessive punishment because the victim wife here "was unharmed."[479] I doubt that she would have agreed that she was unharmed by that scarring violation, not to mention his prior rapes involving the death and barbaric treatment of the rape victim.

Moreover, these justices contradicted their "excessive" finding by acknowledging that the death penalty for rape "may measurably serve the legitimate ends of punishment."[480] Although these justices proclaimed that "Eighth Amendment judgments should not be, or appear to be, merely the subjective views of individual justices,"[481] all relevant circumstances suggest that their decision was just that. The Georgia state legislature, in authorizing the death penalty for rape, had proclaimed that it was not an excessive punishment, particularly given the barbarity of the crime by a repeat offender. The 12 jurors unanimously agreed that the death penalty was not excessive on the facts, and both the trial judge and the many-judge Georgia Supreme Court[482] reached the same conclusion.

The justices recognized that "[t]he current judgment with respect to the death penalty for rape is not wholly unanimous among state legislatures …."[483] More than one-third of the states authorized the death sentence for rape before the 1972 Supreme Court decision invalidated death penalty statutes because they allowed jury discretion – not because it was applied to rape - and some reinstated it in the following few years.[484] That Georgia juries had imposed a death sentence in only about 10 percent of the rape cases during the prior three years[485] hardly demonstrated a total rejection of that penalty. Rather it reflected jurors' responsibility to reserve the death sentence for the vilest criminals and most abhorrent crimes. In the end, the justices again retreated to their "own judgment … on the acceptability of the death penalty under the Eighth Amendment."[486] Once again they preferred their personal views against the death penalty over the legislatures' right to decide the punishment for specific crimes and almost 200 years of history.

In a later rape case, *Kennedy v. Louisiana*, these justices again imposed their personal view to reject the death sentence for rape because a victim was not killed,[487] notwithstanding they called it a crime "that cannot in full be recounted in these pages sufficient to capture in full the hurt and horror inflicted on [the] victim or to convey the revulsion society" felt.[488] Patrick Kennedy had so viciously raped his 8-year-old granddaughter that her injuries were described by an examining pediatric forensic expert as "the most severe he had seen from a sexual assault": "a laceration to the left wall of the vagina had separated her cervix from the back of her vagina, causing her rectum to protrude into the vaginal structure[;] [h]er entire perineum was torn from the posterior fourchette to the anus."[489] Additional evidence that the jury heard in the sentencing proceeding included that Kennedy, after the rape, had called the police and sought to blame "two neighborhood boys."[490] He had also "sexually abused" the goddaughter of his ex-wife "three times when she was 8-years-old and ... the last time involved sexual intercourse."[491] The jury unanimously imposed the death sentence, and the Louisiana courts concurred.

Five justices of the Supreme Court substituted their "own [personal] judgment"[492] for that of the jurors and the judges of the Louisiana courts, and voided the death sentence. In doing so, they insulted those jurors and judges and undermined our society, by describing our criminal justice system as one in which, when "the law punishes by death," it "risk[s] its own sudden descent into brutality," thereby "transgressing ... decency and restraint."[493] Of course, no factual basis was provided to support this scathing assertion. [494] Indeed, these five justices acknowledged that the "death penalty for this crime has been most infrequent,"[495] thereby recognizing that America had not, despite the availability of the death sentence for rape, descended into this so-called brutality. It remained decent and restrained in limiting the death penalty to rapists who deserved it.

Again, these justices admitted that they could find no clear consensus against the death penalty for rape throughout the country.[496] Americans overwhelmingly (55 percent to 38 percent) support the death penalty for child rape.[497] As already noted, until the Supreme Court's 1972 decision in *Furman*, at least 20 jurisdictions had enacted the death penalty for rape. After the Supreme Court's wholesale invalidation of those statutes – because of the jury discretion issue, not the rape issue – as the Court conceded, six states quickly reinstated the death penalty for child rape (some states did so for all rapes), only to have the Supreme Court immediately strike those statutes down (on grounds unrelated to the crime of rape). Within a few years, six states again authorized death penalty for child rape,[498] precluding finding a consensus against the death penalty. Moreover, Congress in 2006 authorized a death penalty for rape of a minor for the military.[499] These five justices ignored the then recent congressional endorsement of the death penalty for child rape to assert incorrectly that Congress' vote (on a different bill) reflected its rejection of the death penalty for child rape.[500]

These five justices recognized – but ignored – the "moral grounds to question a rule barring capital punishment" unless a death resulted.[501] They also agreed that "the victim's fright, the sense of betrayal, and the nature of her injuries caused more prolonged physical and mental suffering than, say, a sudden killing by an unseen assassin… [In addition] rape has a permanent psychological, emotional, and sometimes permanent physical impact on the child."[502] But they rejected even the possibility of capital punishment because of their doctrinaire motivation to "insist upon confining the instances in which capital punishment may be imposed."[503]

These five justices also conceded that child rape was, in some senses, more of a threat than murder: "5,702 incidents of vaginal, anal, or oral rape of a child under the age of 12 were reported nationwide in 2005; this is almost twice the total incidents of intentional murder for victims of all ages (3,405) reported during the same period."[504] From 1976 to 1991, America experienced a 7,200 percent increase in reported cases of child sexual abuse, from 6,000 to 432,000.[505] One would logically conclude from those numbers that deterrence from a death penalty for the most vicious conduct was all the more necessary. Indeed, they expressly conceded that the death penalty for child rape could well serve a "deterrent … function."[506] But, motivated by "the necessity to constrain the use of the death penalty,"[507] these justices recognized that the universe of so many child rapists could result in more executions, and thus thwart their aim to eliminate death sentences. Nothing in the Constitution supports such a result.

Barring Death Penalty Because Justices Disagree With Jury Finding Of Mental Competency

It is universally agreed that a death sentence may not be imposed where a defendant is incompetent and thus cannot understand what is happening or assist his lawyer. Whenever a defendant raises an issue of competency to stand trial, the court will hold a factual hearing and, with the aid of psychiatric testimony, the judge and/or jury

> *"The anti-death penalty justices of the Supreme Court have furthered their anti-death penalty crusade even to insert their personal feelings to reject competency decisions made by trial judges and juries."*

will rule on his competency. Unless held competent, he will not stand trial.

The anti-death penalty justices of the Supreme Court have furthered their anti-death penalty crusade even to insert their personal feelings to reject competency decisions made by trial judges and juries.

The 1989 case of *Penry v. Lynaugh*[508] is an example. Johnny Paul Penry was indicted for the brutal rape, beating and murder by stabbing of a woman, who identified Penry as her assailant before she died. Penry had recently been released on parole after he was convicted and imprisoned on another rape charge.[509] A jury found him competent after hearing evidence establishing that he was mildly to moderately retarded.[510] At trial for the murder and rape, the jury rejected his insanity defense on psychiatric testimony that he was legally sane with a "full-blown anti-social personality."[511]

Implementing the Texas statute that had been approved 23 years earlier by the Supreme Court,[512] the judge posed three questions to the jury requiring affirmative answers for a death sentence. On these questions, the jury found that (1) the defendant acted deliberately with reasonable expectation that death would result, (2) his conduct was not in response to provocation, and (3) there was probability that he would again commit criminal acts of violence and was a continuing threat to society.[513] These three answers met the criteria mandated by the Supreme Court's own prescription in its *Furman* opinion to ensure that "the sentencing authority would focus on the particularized circumstances of the crime and the defendant."[514] The defense was given wide latitude in presenting evidence to the jury of Penry's mental retardation and abused background, and his counsel, in summation, argued to the jury that that evidence warranted an answer favorable to his client on these three questions because, he said, those questions are "inquiring into the mental state of the defendant in each and every one of them."[515] The prosecutor argued the reverse, in support of the death penalty. The jury returned answers that supported the death penalty and it was imposed.

Yet five justices reversed the death sentence. They did so despite their recognition that the defendant "will be dangerous in the future," and without disputing the prosecutor's argument that "[e]ven in a prison setting, Penry could hurt doctors, nurses, librarians, or teachers who worked in the prison."[516] Three of those five justices also agreed that executing a mentally retarded defendant is not contrary to any evolving standard of decency, as demonstrated by the paucity of state legislatures prohibiting it, thereby providing "the clearest and most reliable objective evidence of contemporary values."[517]

So why did the five justices reject the death penalty? Their reason: "a juror who believed that Penry's retardation and background diminished his moral culpability and made imposition of the death penalty unwarranted would be unable to give effect to that conclusion if the juror also believed that Penry committed the crime 'deliberately.'"[518] This makes no sense. A juror who found a lack of sufficient moral culpability could not find an ability to commit the crime deliberately. The word "deliberately" means "done with or marked by *full* consciousness of the nature and effects."[519] The jury concluded that, to whatever extent he was retarded, Penry was still fully aware of what he was doing, and of the difference between right and wrong. The jury reached that conclusion after having listened to and considered Penry's mitigation evidence, including his degree of mental retardation and his attorney's argument that Penry did not, because of his retardation, act deliberately. That the jury rejected the defense and found against him on the evidence does not make their decision unconstitutional – unless you are a justice who simply wants to use judicial power to eat away at the death penalty.

Thirteen years later, in 2002, the anti-death penalty justices expressly expanded this bar of the death penalty by ruling that the Eighth Amendment prohibits the death sentence for a defendant who is even slightly retarded, although found to be competent by psychiatrists, judges and jurors. In that case, Daryl Renard Atkins and his colleague, as part of a planned robbery, abducted a young Air Force airman and drove him to a nearby ATM, where they forced him to withdraw $200. They then drove him to a deserted area, where they ordered him out of the car and killed him by shooting him eight times.[520]

At the sentencing hearing, the jury learned of Atkins' 16 prior felony convictions. Prior victims providing "graphic depictions of [his] violent tendencies: He hit one over the head with a beer bottle; he slapped a gun across another victim's face, clubbed her in the head with it, knocked her to the ground, and then ... [shot] her in the stomach."[521] The defense focused on Atkins' mental retardation, which became "a central issue at sentencing."[522] The defense psychologist "testified that [Atkins] was mildly retarded with an IQ of 59," while the prosecutor's psychologist testified that he had "found 'absolutely no evidence other than the IQ score indicating that [he] was in the least bit mentally retarded,' and concluded that petitioner was 'of average intelligence at least.'"[523]

After hearing the evidence, two different juries[524] chose the death penalty, which the judge imposed and Virginia appellate courts affirmed. The Supreme Court majority was not persuaded. They voided the death sentence based on their apparent conclusion "that no one who is even slightly mentally retarded can have sufficient 'moral responsibility to be subjected to capital punishment for any crime.'"[525]

This decision had no basis in the wording or history of the Eighth Amendment nor in earlier Supreme Court rulings. Twenty states had left "the question of proper punishment" for persons asserting mental retardation "for the individuated consideration of sentencing judges or juries."[526] Thus, unable to find support in the actions of state legislatures – which the majority Justices recognized to be "the 'clearest and most reliable objective evidence of contemporary values'"[527] – the majority retreated to "our own judgment ..., by asking [themselves to decide] whether there is reason to disagree with the judgment reached by the citizenry and its legislators."[528] And that is what these justices did: They disagreed with the judgment of society and legislatures to hold that the jury was wrong to impose a death sentence on Atkins or any slightly retarded defendant.

To rationalize their decision, they asserted that "executing the mentally retarded will not measurably further the goal of deterrence," because "'capital punishment can serve as a deterrent only when murder is the result of premeditation and deliberation.'"[529] "Measurably" suggests that the majority admitted inability to foreclose some deterrent effect from the death sentence. On that basis, the decision whether the death sentence is appropriate should have been left to the jury and judge who heard the evidence and observed the defendant. Moreover, Atkins' conduct established "premeditation and deliberation," in that he planned the crime to include a loaded gun, and deliberated on the murder during the drive from the ATM to the deserted area where the murder occurred. The five justices' reliance on doubting the deterrence impact on another mentally retarded murderer raises a straw man; death sentences have a deterrent effect upon *any* prospective murderer, whether retarded or not, who knows that, if you commit murder, there is a good chance that you will be executed. The nuance of retardation is not what makes or breaks the deterrence effect of a death sentence; rather, the failure to execute a murderer such as Atkins sends the wrong message – that another vile murderer did not lose his life – signaling to every one that execution is not the likely punishment.

> *"Death sentences have a deterrent effect upon any prospective murderer, whether retarded or not, who knows that, if you commit murder, there is a good chance that you will be executed."*

The five justices, in rejecting the death penalty for mentally challenged persons, focused upon "retribution and deterrence of capital crimes by prospective offenders."[530] Not only were they wrong on deterrence, but they ignored a third purpose of the death penalty, previously identified by the Court:[531] "incapacitation of dangerous criminals and the consequent prevention of crimes that they may otherwise commit in the future." Being retarded does not prevent an inmate from killing guards or other inmates, or innocent persons, during an escape.

It may be said that Supreme Court justices took the most extreme step in their anti-death penalty crusade in 1986, in *Ford v. Wainwright.*[532] Alvin Bernard Ford had been convicted of murder and sentenced to death. No suggestion of incompetency was raised before or during the trial or sentencing.[533] But in the 12 years between his sentencing and the Supreme Court's review, two psychiatrists, retained by Ford's attorney, relying solely on what

Ford said to them, concluded that Ford suffered from mental disease that substantially affected Ford's ability to assist in the defense against the death penalty, and had no understanding of why he was being executed.[534] Ford's counsel invoked Florida's statutory post-sentencing procedure, pursuant to which the governor appointed a panel of three independent psychiatrists to determine whether Ford had the "mental capacity to understand the nature of the death penalty and the reasons why it was imposed upon him."[535] Their conclusion was that, while he suffered mental problems, he understood what was to happen to him. Based on that report, the governor ordered Ford's execution.[536]

The Supreme Court plurality recognized that, 36 years earlier, it had ruled that a condemned prisoner did not have a due process right to a new determination of his sanity before execution.[537] It had never held that the Eighth Amendment prevented executing a defendant who had been found competent to stand trial.[538] Yet, the Supreme Court plurality in the *Ford* case suddenly found such a constitutional right,[539] and prohibited the execution. They did so without explaining how a sentence that was not cruel and unusual when imposed became cruel and unusual years later, merely because the defendant claimed to have developed a mental illness. Nor did they explain why a murderer, held to be competent at his sentencing, and soon to be dead, if executed, must recognize the reason, as long as the execution has a deterrence impact on the public.

This decision provided defendants with a heads-I-win-tails-the-public-loses option. As several justices have noted, mental illness "symptoms ... can readily be feigned."[540] A death row defendant risks nothing by claiming mental illness – he can only benefit.

Why wasn't the governor's finding that the defendant had sufficient awareness, based on the report of three independent psychiatrists, an adequate assessment of competency? After all, "at common law it was the executive who passed upon the sanity of the condemned."[541]   Even the justices, who set aside the death penalty, claimed that each state should have the right to "develop... appropriate ways to enforce the constitutional restriction."[542]   That is exactly what Florida had done here, in mandating the procedure by which the governor heard and relied upon three independent psychiatrists in reaching his decision of competency. Yet, the Supreme Court halted the execution.

One of the concurring justices correctly assessed the Court's decision: "[r]egardless of the number of prior adjudications of the issue, until the very moment of execution, the prisoner can claim that he has become insane sometime after the previous determination to the contrary."[543]   This decision thus invited an unending – up to infinity – parade of motions to bar the execution that can repeatedly delay and effectively prevent any execution. So much for justice delayed is justice denied – a truism here in denying to society the death sentence properly imposed.

The Supreme Court in 2007 again addressed this issue of competency to be executed.[544]   In 1992, defendant Scott Louis Panetti, dressed in camouflage, drove to the home of his estranged wife's parents, broke the lock, and, in front of his wife and daughter, shot and killed his in-laws.[545]   After being found "competent to be tried and [even] to waive counsel," a jury, in 1995, rejected his defense of not guilty by reason of insanity, "found him guilty and sentenced him to death."[546]

By 2003, eight different court decisions – the trial court, twice by Texas appellate courts, a federal district court, a federal court of appeals, and three times by the Supreme Court in refusing to review – sustained the competency ruling.[547]   Suddenly, on December 10, 2003, after the judge had set his execution date for February 5, 2004, Panetti first raised the issue of his competency to be executed.[548]   He did so without providing any "medical reports or records, ... sworn testimony from any medical professional, [or] diagnosis of any medical condition."[549]   The court appointed two mental health experts, who examined Panetti and reported that

Panetti "'knows that he is to be executed, and that his execution will result in his death,' and, moreover, that he 'has the ability to understand the reason he is to be executed.'" Significantly, these experts concluded that Panetti's "uncooperative and bizarre behavior was due to calculated design."[550]

Having failed in state court, Panetti then continued in federal court his claim of incompetency to be executed. Granted a hearing, he presented testimony of four experts; the prosecution presented testimony of two experts and three correction officers. The most favorable testimony Panetti adduced from one of his experts was that "although [Panetti] claims to understand 'that the State is saying that it wishes to execute him for his murders,' he believes in earnest that the stated reason is a 'sham' and that the state in truth wants to execute him 'to stop him from preaching.'"[551] The Federal District Court and the Court of Appeals both sustained his competency, with the latter holding that the record "'necessarily demonstrat[ed] that a prisoner is aware of the reason for his execution.'"[552]

A bare majority of five Supreme Court justices, relying, as had the Court in another case, on their "*intuition* that such an execution simply offends humanity [that is] evidently shared across the nation,"[553] reversed all the lower courts. These justices, unlike the trial judge and the experts, had not personally observed the defendant or listened to expert testimony. Yet, they refused to allow the execution to proceed, pending further proceedings, because they decided that Panetti may remain unaware of why he is to suffer the punishment. Thus, despite the evidence that the murderer hears and understands that he is told he is being executed because of his murders, he can continue avoiding being executed 15 years after his double murders by voicing an easily feigned assertion that he believes the execution is for a different reason. Does that make any sense? The answer is obviously "no."

Arguments For And Against The Death Penalty

As already discussed, it is the state legislatures and Congress that have the responsibility to determine available punishments for each crime, not the Supreme Court. Just as the Constitution, properly read, does not prohibit capital punishment, it does not require it. Anti-capital punishment advocates are fully within their rights to lobby each legislature to bar it.

In 1971, Justices Brennan and Marshall, joined by Justice Douglas, while dissenting from the Court's affirmance of a death penalty, expressed their agreement that "whether the death penalty is appropriate punishment" is a "determination ... for the States."[554] Yet, one year later, Justices Brennan and Marshall wrote concurring opinions in which they declared that the Eighth Amendment barred *all* death penalties.[555] The Constitution had not changed in that one year; hence, their votes to bar all death penalties can be attributed solely to their personal views on the subject.

Justice Brennan acknowledged that, "[w]hen this country was founded ... [t]he practice of punishing criminals by death ... was widespread and by and large acceptable to society."[556] Justice Marshall recognized that the Court had repeatedly upheld the death penalty as not "cruel or unusual punishment"; yet, without basis, he proceeded to declare that those rulings were "not now binding on us."[557] He also recognized that the public, as reflected both in polls and through their legislators, favored the death penalty, but suggested, in a most elitist expression, that he knew better: "Assuming knowledge of all the facts presently available regarding capital punishment, the average citizen would, in my opinion," agree with him that the death penalty is "shocking to his conscience and sense of justice."[558] This statement demeans the knowledge and intelligence of the pro-death penalty American people and legislatures. There is no basis for his conclusion that these two justices – or even a majority of five – know more than the thousands of state legislators who have enacted statutes authorizing the death penalty.

Four years later, anti-death penalty justices had to face the reality that the legislatures had overwhelmingly re-enacted capital punishment. Justice Marshall recognized that, "I would be less than candid if I did not acknowledge that these developments have a realistic assessment of the moral acceptability of the death penalty to the American people."[559] But that did not deter him from repeating that he knew better than the American people as to the death penalty: "the American people, fully informed as to the purposes of the death penalty and its liabilities, would in my view reject it as morally unacceptable."[560]

Is there merit to this absolute anti-death penalty position? Do our citizens benefit from including the death penalty in, or excluding it from, the quiver of arrows which law enforcement has available to protect lives and safety? Let's look at the arguments on both sides.

Their arguments against the death penalty have no greater merit than their assertion that "they know better than the American people." In 2006, four dissenting justices voted to void a death penalty (which had been imposed over 24 years earlier) for a murder committed in 1981.[561] Fernando Belmontes, while burglarizing a home, armed with an iron dumbbell, killed a 19-year-old woman by striking her head with it. The four justices asserted two grounds for reversal. One was that he had already, since his arrest, "spent more than half of his life on death row."[562] The reason: He and his lawyers had taken every possible step to prevent his execution. That ground for being against the death penalty sounds as meritless as the murderer who killed his parents and then asked for mercy because he is an orphan.

The second ground was that the judge's instruction to the jury "barred the jury from considering" whether he would likely live a constructive life if imprisoned instead of executed.[563] Is speculation about how a defendant will live in prison to trump the jury's view of the gravity of the crime? Clearly, it should not. To my knowledge, no court had even previously considered instructed a jury on such a factor. These justices deserved an "A" for their imagination in inventing a new ground to allow them to avoid a death sentence.

Another ground for opposing the death penalty appears as greater sympathy for the accused than for the innocent people who are killed and raped. Yes, they are correct that no criminal justice system can operate perfectly because it cannot be run by infallible computers – if that could ever exist – but by imperfect humans, serving as judges and jurors, who may make unintended mistakes. As with any other judgment call, there has to be a comparison of the risks if you proceed with carefully reviewed death sentences, contrasted with the risks if you bar all death sentences.

> *"Contrary to claims of DNA testing having established the innocence of already executed defendants, in every instance in which DNA testing has been used to determine the guilt or innocence of executed criminals, the result has confirmed guilt."*

Anti-death penalty justices emphasize the possibility of error in executing an innocent man. There is no proof that even one innocent person has been executed in modern times. Contrary to claims of DNA testing having established the innocence of already executed defendants, in every instance in which DNA testing has been used to determine the guilt or innocence of **executed** criminals, the result has confirmed guilt.[564] For example,

Roger Coleman, sentenced to die for the "gruesome rape and murder of his sister-in-law … became the poster-child of the" anti-death penalty activists, having his picture on a Time Magazine cover, with the caption "This Man Might Be Innocent. This Man Is Due To Die." He was executed in 2002, over the objection of anti-death penalty Justice Blackmun, who sought to stay the execution because "Coleman has now produced substantial evidence that he may be innocent."[565] After his execution, his supporters claimed that "they had proved" his "innocence and had even identified 'the real killer.'" Then, in 2006, "a DNA test ordered by a later Governor of Virginia proved that Coleman was guilty" and the defense team settled a defamation suit against them by the alleged "real killer," whom they had falsely named.[566] Similarly, DNA tests, following their executions, confirmed the guilt of Rick McGinn and Derek Barbenei, refuting their supporters' assertions that they were innocent.[567]

As evidence of the execution of innocent persons, the dissent cited a 1987 study detailed in an article by Charles S. Lanier and James R. Acker.[568] Only one execution, in 1984, was recent enough to permit effective DNA testing. The guilt of that defendant, James R. Adams, executed in 1984, was confirmed. Here is some of the evidence, which Lanier and Acker did not mention: "upon arrest on the afternoon of the murder Adams was found with some $200 in his pocket – one bill of which was stained with type O blood. When Adams was asked about the blood on the money, he said it came from a cut on his finger. His blood was type AB, however, while the victim's blood was type O." The authors had also ignored the fact that the "victim's eyeglasses were found in Adams' car, along with jewelry belonging to the victim, and clothing of Adams stained with type O blood."[569] The authors were finally forced to concede that, "We agree with our critics that we have not 'proved' these executed defendants to be innocent; we never claimed that we had."[570] Yet, this undisputedly flawed article was cited by three justices as an "impressive study" that had "concluded that 23 innocent people have been executed in the United States in this century, including one as recently as 1984."[571]

Anti-death penalty advocates also used a play, entitled "*The Exonerated,*" to propagandize about supposedly innocent persons on death row. Oregon District Attorney Joshua Marquis explained: "The script never mentions that two of the play's six characters (Sonia Jacobs and Kerry Cook) were not exonerated but were let out of prison after a combined 36 years behind bars when they agreed to plea bargains. A third (Robert Hayes) was unavailable to do publicity tours because he is in prison, having pleaded guilty to another homicide almost identical to the one of which he was acquitted."[572]

Another frequently cited article, "*Exonerations In The United States 1989 Through 2003,*"[573] listed supposedly innocent persons who were convicted of capital offenses. But analysis shows that the authors misused data relating to dismissal of cases against defendants. One example was a case dismissed on grounds unrelated to guilt or innocence: The double jeopardy doctrine barred a retrial, following a conviction thrown out due to prosecutorial misconduct. Another case was dismissed when the accomplice, who had confessed and implicated the defendant in a rape and murder, committed suicide in jail, barring use of that evidence. Significantly, civil suits for monetary damages, brought by each of these two released defendants, were decided against them based on the facts that refuted their claims of innocence.[574] Thus, the article's claim that it listed "340 exonerations," a term which it defined as "an official act declaring a defendant not guilty,"[575] is false.

For argument sake, let's assume that 340 felony defendants were wrongly charged. Further, let's assume that the article "understated the number of innocents by roughly a factor of 10, that instead of 340, there were 4000 people who weren't in the crime in any way. During that same 15 years, there were more than 15 million felony convictions across the country. That would make the error rate .027 percent – or to put it another way, a success rate of 99.973 percent."[576]

I am second to no one in regretting the failure of our criminal justice system when any innocent person is convicted. Realistically, given that judges, lawyers, witnesses and jurors are all human beings, there can be no guaranty of perfection. There is no computer that could be substituted for the humans in our system, into which the evidence could be input, and from which one could expect an infallible verdict. And even if there were, it could never employ the understanding and sympathy that people can bring to bear. Realistically, we have two choices: continue with our criminal justice system, with the very small probability of error, or have no criminal justice system. No one seriously makes that latter proposal.

Anti-death-penalty advocates argue that it is intolerable that some innocent defendants are executed. There are no facts establishing that assumption is valid, given the intense judicial scrutiny of death sentences. But again, let's assume the possibility of undiscovered errors in the conviction and execution of innocent defendants, and apply the .027 percent error rate established above to the 1,238 executions in the more than 35 years from 1976-2011.[577] The mathematical conclusion is that one-third of one person who was executed was innocent .

Opponents of the death penalty assert that we should avoid even that miniscule possibility of execution of an innocent person by prohibiting the death penalty and substitute a life sentence without parole. Interesting idea, *if* it would not result in an equal or greater number of deaths to innocent people than our computed one-third of an executed person. Unfortunately, it has and would continue to result in many more deaths of innocent people.

A prisoner serving a life term without parole, where capital punishment is prohibited, has nothing to lose by escaping and killing people while he is free or killing a guard or other inmate in prison. The worst sentence he could receive is what he is already serving. These killings of people by inmates have resulted in the deaths of many more innocent people than the death penalty opponents' mathematical construct of innocent defendants. Some examples:

Three convicted murderers escaped from an Arizona prison on July 30, 2010, and murdered Linda and Gary Haas, both age 61.[578] A Georgia inmate escaped and committed rape, burglary, auto theft, and assault and battery.[579] Another Georgia inmate, effectively serving a life term, escaped, raped and threatened with death a 16-year-old.[580] After escaping from Georgia prison, another inmate beat, robbed and shot and killed his victim.[581] A jailed murderer escaped from an Arizona prison and murdered a father, mother, 2-year-old son and 15-year-old niece.[582] These innocent victims would not have been killed if their murderers had been executed rather than sentenced to jail.

Even other inmates deserve protection from lifers who have nothing to lose by killing a fellow prisoner. An example: John David Duty, serving three life sentences for rape, robbery, and shooting with intent to kill, murdered his cellmate.[583]

Then there is the deterrence effect of the death sentence. I concede that a spur-of-the-moment killing – often in a family, sexual partner, or road-rage context – would likely not be meaningfully deterred by the existence of a death penalty. But

> *"A prisoner serving a life term without parole, where capital punishment is prohibited, has nothing to lose by escaping and killing people while he is free or killing a guard or other inmate in prison. The worst sentence he could receive is what he is already serving."*

murders that occur as part of planned deliberate criminal activity may well be deterred by the knowledge that a death sentence can be imposed. Even justices who voted to overturn a death penalty conceded that a "principal social" purpose of a death penalty is "deterrence of capital crime by prospective offenders."[584] Justice John Paul Stevens, one of those justices, reiterated for the public that, "[d]eterring crime is a valid reason to punish."[585]

The institution of the death penalty for kidnapping in 1932, in response to the Lindbergh baby kidnapping, supports the deterrent effect of capital punishment for deliberate, planned, premeditated crimes. Starting in the 1920s, the number of kidnappings for ransom rose substantially. For example, in Chicago alone in 1930 and 1931, there were 200 such kidnappings.[586] Following "a new series of laws [in 1932] that allowed the death penalty for kidnapping, ... [s]lowly, the kidnapping for ransom era dissipated. Isolated cases of abductions still occurred, but the classical scenario in which children were abducted from wealthy parents and held for money, all but disappeared."[587]

Unfortunately, the deterrence impact has been undermined by enormous delay in execution of defendants sentenced to die. Between 1976 and 1981, it was not unusual for the Supreme Court to issue its death penalty decision less than three years after the crime.[588] More recent Supreme Court decisions evidence that executions have been delayed for 10 to 25 years after the commission of the crime.[589] These long delays, together with the increased number of decisions saving defendants from the death penalty, give comfort to those planning crimes that they will never face execution.

Chief Justice Warren E. Burger described the effect of delay in the justice system as causing "incalculable damage to society; that people come to believe that inefficiency and delay will drain a just judgment of its value ...."[590] Justice John Paul Stevens likewise recognized that delay vitiates much of the deterrent effect:

"A lengthy and elaborate legal process has become a central feature of American capital punishment. As a result, several executions have occurred after a delay of more than twenty years, and some prisoners currently have been awaiting their executions for more than three decades.... Such delays do not just undermine their death penalty's deterrent effect; they spoil its capacity for satisfying retribution" – another appropriate societal benefit from the death penalty.[591] Justice delayed is certainly justice denied to the public. And eliminating the death penalty certainly eliminates that deterrence effect.

XI.

FIVE JUSTICES EXTEND MISUSE OF EIGHTH AMENDMENT TO VACATE EVEN PRISON SENTENCES

As already discussed, what the Eighth Amendment precludes is any "cruel and unusual" punishments. Note that it did not proscribe a cruel *or* unusual punishment, but only punishment that is both cruel *and* unusual. A prison sentence epitomizes a sentence that is neither cruel nor unusual. It is not cruel because it does not involve infliction of torture or barbaric pain. And sentencing to prison for crimes is not unusual as it was the commonly accepted punishment for non-capital crimes in England before the American colonies existed and continually thereafter to the present day.

That a justice may personally believe a punishment imposed by a trial judge is "excessive" does not make the sentence "cruel and unusual." For example, a Supreme Court justice, reviewing a 50-year jail sentence, might prefer a shorter term.

That punishment, imprisonment, no matter the length, remains imprisonment, a means of punishment not held to be cruel or unusual. A well-publicized prison sentence of 150 years recently imposed on Bernard Madoff, who defrauded many people of billions in a Ponzi scheme, exemplifies this definition. While many disagree with that duration – more than a life sentence – it is not "cruel and unusual" because imprisonment is an accepted form of punishment. As discussed in the previous chapter, the Supreme Court had held – before it suddenly assumed a new interpretation of the Eighth Amendment – that it is up to the legislatures to decide the allowable duration of a prison sentence, unaffected by justices' view of its proportionality to the crime.[592]

> *"The Supreme Court had held – before it suddenly assumed a new interpretation of the Eighth Amendment – that it is up to the legislatures to decide the allowable duration of a prison sentence, unaffected by justices' view of its proportionality to the crime."*

Is our American Supreme Court, contrary to all legislative decisions, heading our criminal justice sentencing to the leniency that we recently saw in Norway? There, a man killed 77 innocent people, including numerous children whom he purposely targeted, and, after conviction for this mass killing, was sentenced to the maximum: only a 21-year prison term.[593]

While the Supreme Court majority has not yet gone so far, it may not be out of the question in the future. Already, having so successfully eaten away at the death sentence, various of the justices, who had joined in that crusade, started invoking the Eighth Amendment to attack legislative authority to authorize even extended prison sentences in certain circumstances.

Life Sentences For Recidivist Criminals

Recidivist statutes were enacted early in our country by all states and the federal government. They authorized greater punishment, including life imprisonment without parole, for repeat offenders.[594]

Statistics show that keeping recidivists in prison meaningfully insulates our lawful citizens from criminal harm and loss. "About 67 percent of former State prisoners and 40 percent of former federal prisoners are rearrested within three years of release."[595] Even Attorney General Eric Holder, who appears to want fewer persons in prison, conceded that a seven-fold increase in prison population "over the past 40 years ... has something to do with the crime rate dropping 40 percent since 1991," because "[m]ost crimes in America are committed by people who have committed crimes before."[596]

Those recidivist statutes received the Supreme Court's early approval as proper under the Bill of Rights. Among several Supreme Court decisions to that effect was an 1895 unanimous ruling upholding a Missouri statute which authorized life imprisonment for a recidivist, explaining that, "the state may undoubtedly provide that persons who have been before convicted of crime may suffer severer punishment, for subsequent offenses than for a first offense."[597] The same conclusion was reached by a unanimous Court in 1912, in which a defendant received a life sentence following three thefts totaling only $310.[598]

One would have thought the issue was closed. But that would be asking too much of those justices who were actively seeking to alter the criminal justice systems to reflect what those justices believed the law should be, rather than what the various state legislatures (and Congress) had decided the law was. Therefore, when the issue was considered again by the Supreme Court in 1980, the decision sustaining the Texas recidivism statute was a surprisingly close 5-4 vote.[599] While the dissent complained that the Texas recidivist statute "was the most stringent found in the 50 States," the majority quoted the respected Justice Oliver Wendell Holmes, who, in 1905, explained that "our Constitution 'is made for people of fundamentally differing views.'" Because of that, "some State will always bear the distinction of treating particular offenders more severely than any other State," which is permitted under our "traditional notions of federalism."[600]

The four dissenters used the same arguments they had used to declare various death sentences to be in violation of the "cruel and unusual punishments" clause of the Eighth Amendment. They quickly recognized, and just as quickly ignored, that the one "certain" purpose of the authors of the Eighth Amendment was "to proscribe inhumane methods of punishment"; they did not, and could not, even try to assert that a prison sentence was "inhumane." Instead, the dissenters turned away from that purpose of the Eighth Amendment to argue that certain life sentences are "excessive," because they are "grossly disproportionate."[601] Again, as with their death penalty opinions, they did not even try to explain how they found a prohibition against "excessive" punishment when the Eighth Amendment expressly prohibited "excessive fines" and "excessive bail," while not proscribing "excessive" punishment, but only punishments that are "cruel and unusual" – which a jail sentence is not. The dissent also conceded that "[e]ach State has sovereign responsibilities to promulgate and enforce its criminal law,"[602] and for that reason "this Court has not heretofore invalidated a mandatory life sentence under the Eighth Amendment."[603] Yet, these dissenters voted to overturn precedent and overrule state legislatures because, in their personal "view," the life term was unacceptable.[604]

Three years later that minority view became the majority ruling by the change of position of one justice (Blackmun), causing Chief Justice Burger to say that "[w]hat the Court means is that a sentence is unconstitutional if it is more severe than five Justices think is appropriate."[605]

The facts in this case, called *Solem v. Helm*, were even more compelling to support recidivism penalties than facts of earlier cases. The defendant had been convicted of six felonies between 1964-1975; his recidivist life sentence without parole took effect upon his seventh conviction in 1979.[606] Despite again paying lip-service to the principle that a "state is justified in punishing a recidivist more severely than it punishes a first offender,"[607] this new majority imposed their personal views that the sentence was "significantly disproportionate to his crime."[608] Chief Justice Burger, writing for the four dissenters, adopted the words of Justice Hugo Black:

> "... about judges overruling the considered actions of legislatures under the guise of constitutional interpretation: 'Such unbounded authority in any group of politically appointed or elected judges would unquestionably be sufficient to classify our Nation as a government of men, not the government of laws of which we boast. With a "shock the conscience" test of constitutionality, citizens must guess what is the law, guess what the majority of nine judges will believe fair and reasonable. Such a test wilfully throws away the certainty and security that lies in the written constitution, one that does not alter with a judge's health, belief, or his politics'."[609]

Eight years later, this decision was overruled, with the retirement of some justices and the appointment of new ones; the principals of Justice Black's excellent words became the majority view. This new case involved the constitutionality of a Michigan statute that imposed a mandatory sentence of life imprisonment without parole for possessing more than 650 grams of cocaine.[610] While it thus did not concern a recidivist sentencing statute, it necessarily raised the issue of whether the Eighth Amendment guaranteed that sentences must be proportional to the crime – the basis for the Court's voiding of the recidivist sentencing statute in *Solem*. This time the Court minced no words: "Solem was simply wrong" because "the Eighth Amendment contains no proportionality guarantee."[611] Further, the Court reiterated that, in order for a sentence to be in violation of the Eighth Amendment, it must be both cruel *and* unusual. A "disproportionate punishment," while it "can perhaps be considered 'cruel,' ... will not always be (as the text also requires) 'unusual.'"[612]

This time, the Constitution was enforced as written, not as rewritten by five justices. Of course, this decision will remain the law of the land only as long as the majority of justices abide by their oath of office that their role is not to substitute for legislatures. Unfortunately, as the decisions discussed in the rest of this chapter establish, the march by five justices to overrule legislative decisions, and usurp for those five justices the legislative role, continued unabated.

Voiding Most Life Sentences Without Parole For Juveniles

Five justices went further to restrict legislatures' right to determine how best to deal with criminals. Starting their slippery slope in a new area, they held that the Eighth Amendment forbade a life sentence without parole on any juvenile for any offense other than homicide, no matter how bad, frequent and recurring the juvenile's conduct. They later pressed ahead with that slide, away from allowing legislatures to decide that issue, by even holding unconstitutional the many state statutes mandating life imprisonment without parole for convicted youthful murderers.

This was the same Court that had previously rationalized interfering with legislative determinations authorizing a death penalty for convicted youthful murderers by explaining that "a sentence of death differs in kind from any sentence of imprisonment, *no matter how long.*"[613] The driving force then was to reduce the number of death sentences.[614] Indeed, they then expressly reassured the public that they would not interfere with prison sentences: They explained that the length of a prison term was "properly within the province of legislatures, not courts,"[615] because what is involved is "invariably" a "subjective determination, there being no clear way to make 'any *constitutional* distinction between one term of years and a shorter or longer term of years.'"[616] The Court went so far as to indicate that it would not interfere with legislative determinations prescribing life terms without parole, by expressly noting the availability of a life without parole sentence for some juvenile offenders.[617] That certainly was a ruling that the Eighth Amendment, by its terms, did not bar a life without parole sentence.

Yet, these five justices, only five years later, voided life without parole sentences for persons under 18, save only murderers (at that time).[618] In this case, Terrance Jamar Graham, then age 16, together with another youth, attempted to rob a restaurant. His accomplice hit the manager on the head with a metal bar, causing a serious head injury. Charged as an adult under Florida law, Graham pleaded guilty to armed robbery with assault and battery, a first-degree felony carrying a maximum sentence of life imprisonment without parole. The Florida trial court took into account Graham's youth and accepted Graham's statement that "this is my first and last time getting into trouble." It thus imposed a very lenient sentence of 12 months in the county jail followed by two years of probation.[619]

Less than six months after his release from that short prison term, Graham was rearrested, just 34 days short of his 18th birthday, allowing resentencing on his earlier crime due to his probation violation. He had attempted two new robberies, one home invasion, and one in which his accomplice was shot. With three handguns in his car, Graham tried to elude pursuing police, and crashed his car into a telephone pole. It turned out he had also been complicit in other robberies since his release.[620]

Faced with this record, the judge sentenced Graham to life

without parole: "Given your escalating pattern of criminal conduct, it is apparent ... that you have decided that this is the way you are going to live your life and that the only thing I can do now is to try and protect the community from your actions."[621] Does the judge's decision sound irrational? Certainly not, and three different state courts in reviewing this sentence did not think so.[622]

Yet, five Supreme Court justices substituted their personal judgment for that of the sentencing judge and the other state courts, and rejected the sentence of life without parole. Amazingly, much of what they wrote in their opinion, in fact, justified such a sentence. They recognized that one goal of sentencing may be "incapacitation" – *i.e.*, protecting society from being further harmed by the offender.[623] In fact, these five justices agreed, "incapacitation is an *important* goal," because "[r]ecidivism is a serious risk to public safety" with "67 percent of former inmates released from state prison [being] charged with at least one serious new crime within three years."[624] Further, they recognized that a life without parole sentence may well deter the commission of crime "in a few cases."[625]

These five justices also acknowledged that it "it is for legislatures," not the courts, "to determine what rehabilitative techniques are appropriate and effective," with the possibility of "[t]hose who commit truly horrifying crimes as juveniles ... turn[ing] out to be irredeemable, and thus deserving of incarceration for the duration of their lives."[626] At that time, 37 states, the District of Columbia and the federal government authorized life without parole for defendants under 18.[627] Unable to say that there was a consensus among state legislatures against life without parole, these five justices rejected the consensus that existed in favor of that sentence, and substituted their own personal opinions as to how the standards of decency *should have* evolved.

Chief Justice John Roberts concurred in the result without joining in the reasons, noting the irrationality of deciding that no one under 18 could ever be sentenced to life without parole. He offered two examples: "a 17-year-old who beat and raped an 8-year-old girl before leaving her to die under 197 pounds of rock in a recycling bin in a remote landfill" and "Florida juveniles who … gang-raped a woman and forced her to perform oral sex on her 12-year-old son."[628] Justice Clarence Thomas, in his dissent, provided a third example: shortly before the decision, an Oklahoma jury sentenced to life without parole a 16-year-old who put the head of a 17-year-old "into a headlock, and sliced her throat, raped her, stabbed her about 20 times, beat her, and pounded her face into the rocks alongside a dirt road."[629]

How is it unconstitutional to impose a life without parole sentence for such barbarous crimes, even if they did not result in death, especially if rehabilitation is unlikely? Analysis of the three "reasons" the majority justices provided in that case to ban life without parole for non-homicide under-18-year-olds demonstrates that they are mere make-weights whereby these justices interfere with states' responsibilities over crime.

The first reason: "Even if the state's judgment that Graham were incorrigible were later [borne] out, … the sentence was still [unconstitutional] because the judgment was made at the outset."[630] This is baffling, since all sentencing decisions reflect the sentencing judge's best prediction, at the time of sentencing, of how to protect society and punish the defendant.

The second reason: "sentences based on a … subjective judgment by a judge or jury that the offender is irredeemably depraved" do not "prevent the possibility that the offender will receive a life without parole sentence for which he or she lacks the moral culpability."[631] Accepting that "possibility" as a ground to withdraw sentencing discretion from a judge or jury would undermine *every* sentence because there is always the *possibility* that that defendant lacked moral culpability. But our criminal justice system accords judges and jurors the authority to apply their judgment based on the facts and evidence. This approach is fairer both to the defendant and society than the doctrinaire rule that no under-18 defendant could possibly be evaluated as likely to be a danger to society throughout his life. Apparently, these justices value returning a recidivist to society more than the innocent people who can be harmed or murdered by his recidivist propensity.

The third reason: "'The differences between juvenile and adult offenders are too marked and well-understood to *risk* allowing a youthful person to receive' a sentence of life without parole for a non-homicide crime 'despite insufficient culpability.'"632 Thus, they make clear that they would rather *risk* an innocent member of the public being harmed or murdered by a recidivist than *risk* the possibility that judge and jury and reviewing appellate judges were wrong about an offender who has already shown repeated criminal proclivities. Does that make sense? How does that risk-balancing support an Eighth Amendment bar to such a prison sentence? It clearly does not.

These five justices did not then dispute that an under-18-year-old who murders someone has

> *"All justices, including these five, have ruled that the issue of a jail sentence is for the legislature first to authorize, and then, second, for the sentencing court to apply, based on the facts unique to the defendant being sentenced. But that legal axiom was discarded in furtherance of these justices' take-over from the states of control over the states' penal systems."*

demonstrated sufficient continuing threat to society to be permanently barred from returning to society. Yet, without any basis in the Constitution, they ruled that a 17-year-old who rapes an innocent 8-year-old and leaves her for dead should never be similarly adjudicated, only because he failed in his intent to kill her. All justices, including these five, have ruled that the issue of a jail sentence is for the legislature first to authorize, and then, second, for the sentencing court to apply, based on the facts unique to the defendant being sentenced. But that legal axiom was discarded in furtherance of these justices' take-over from the states of control over the states' penal systems.

The adverse consequences of this decision holding that life without parole is cruel and unusual punishment, unfortunately, extends far beyond non-murdering juveniles, and creates a new slippery slope by which these five justices will enlarge the scope of their interference with legislative determination on penal penalties. If it is cruel and unusual punishment to provide no opportunity for release from prison to a juvenile who commits a non-homicide crime, isn't the same punishment cruel and unusual when imposed on an adult for any crime? After all, the punishment, to which the Eighth Amendment was addressed, is the same in all these situations. Indeed, the objection by an adult to a life term without parole as violating the Eighth Amendment has already been asserted. Seventy-three year-old Joseph Ligon, a Pennsylvania inmate in prison almost six decades, challenged the life without parole sentence he received for two murders when he was 15, arguing that "[t]he child who went to prison in 1953 no longer exists."[633] And, given the propensity of certain judges to assume the powers of Congress and the president, it did not take long for a judge to rule that a federal statute prescribing a minimum 5-year sentence, as applied to a 19-year-old who pled guilty to five years of distributing child pornography, was unconstitutional as cruel and unusual punishment.[634]

But that was not the end of these justices' grab for legislative power. If it is cruel and unusual punishment to sentence a juvenile to life without parole for a non-homicide crime, why isn't it similarly cruel and unusual when imposed for homicide by a juvenile? Recall that it is the sentence, not the crime, that must be evaluated to determine if it is barred as "cruel and unusual punishment."

Two years after thus striking down a life sentence without parole for a youth not convicted of homicide, five justices continued their rampage of legislative determinations on authorized sentences to answer that question. In another 5-4 decision, they held that the "cruel and unusual punishment" prohibition in the Eighth Amendment rendered unconstitutional statutes enacted by Congress and 28 state legislatures that mandated life without parole for an under-18 year old, even as applied to a conviction for murder.[635]

The facts surrounding the homicide conviction of Evan Miller, one of the two considered in that case, demonstrate that this was no simple "wild kid" who had just made one "mistake." Miller, having a history of "regularly us[ing] drugs and alcohol," had stolen the victim's wallet when the victim had passed out following jointly smoking marijuana and playing drinking games with Miller and his friend. Unfortunately, the victim awoke and grabbed Miller. When released through physical intervention of his friend, Miller repeatedly struck the victim with a bat and, "[p]lacing a sheet over [the victim's] head, told him 'I am God. I've come to take your life,' and delivered one more blow." Finally, Miller and his friend created two fires in the trailer where the victim lay; the victim "died from his injuries and smoke inhalation."[636]

Everything in the opinion of these five justices suggests that their invalidation of the life-without-parole sentence, that the statute made mandatory, is merely a continuation of their unconstitutional usurpation of legislative power, without basis in the Constitution or prior decisions of the Court.

To start with, these five justices assert their objection was to the "mandatory penalty schemes" that "prohibit" the trial court from taking account of the defendant's youth and life history to decide if treatment as an adult – including mandatory life without parole – is appropriate.[637] Even if that had presented a constitutional basis for the Court to overrule Congress and state legislatures – it is not – undisputed facts establish that it was not mandatory that the two 14-year-olds at issue be treated as adults. As the five justices wrote: Exercising his right under Arkansas law – the state of one of the two cases considered on this appeal – defendant Kuntrell Jackson (the second sentenced defendant appealing in that case) had "moved to transfer the case to juvenile court," where no mandatory life sentence existed. "[A]fter considering the alleged facts of the crime, a psychiatrist's examination, and Jackson's juvenile arrest history ..., the trial court" decided that the facts warranted treating him as an adult – an exercise of discretion affirmed by the appellate court.[638] Similarly, the law of Alabama – the state in Miller's case – provided a procedure for court determination whether the facts warranted defendant's treatment as an adult or juvenile.[639] Both trial courts decided that adult treatment was appropriate under the facts, and those decisions were reviewed and affirmed by state appellate courts.[640] That these procedures and court determinations were applied before trial, rather than after conviction, does not alter that each court examined whether the juvenile defendant should not be subject to adult treatment and a mandatory life sentence without parole. But, these five justices ignored these facts in continuing their march to assume control from legislatures of sentencing decisions.

Even without that fallacy in the opinion of these five justices, the decision flies in the face of the Constitution and the Court's prior decisions. We have already seen that a prison term, of whatever length, cannot be "cruel" punishment as understood by the authors of our Constitution and Bill of Rights. Even more incredible is how these five justices could conclude that these mandatory life without parole sentences could possibly be described as "unusual," the other required element of the "cruel and unusual punishment" prohibition. As these five justices admit, "28 states and the Federal Government make a life-without-parole term mandatory for some children convicted in adult court."[641] Yet, according to these five justices, a type of sentence imposed from the inception of our country to the present day, and still imposed by Congress and a majority of states is "unusual" – an obviously baseless finding. In an attempt to explain this incredible finding, these five justices assert that the decision by Congress and 28 state legislatures to enact a mandatory life without parole sentence for juvenile homicide defendants was "possibly (or probably) inadvertent."[642] No facts are offered from legislative history to support this Ouija-board creation of a non-existent basis for so insulting the intelligence and competence of Congress and most legislatures.

Perhaps more troubling about these five justices' decision to invalidate life without parole sentences for juvenile murderers is the unfair and devastating effect on the close relatives of the murder victims and on society in general. A recent newspaper report[643] on one such defendant, Maurice Bailey, who at age 15 viciously and with pre-planning, knifed to death his same-age lover, Kristina Grill, who was carrying his child, exemplifies consequences that those five justices did not consider.

Bailey's act snuffed out two lives immediately: his young lover Kristina and their unborn child. Add to that number Kristina's "inconsolable mother" who died within 10 months, and, shortly thereafter, Kristina's grandmother. As Kristina's sister recounted, the murder

> "wrecked my whole life. It completely changed the person I was. [Victim's families] thought this was behind them and now discover that they may have to relive the horrors again, return to the court again. Whatever sense of closure they had is gone. We were stripped of finality by five people in Washington."[644]

She said it well: Five justices who, based on the Constitution and the Court's earlier holdings, had no power to overrule legislatures that had authorized life-without-parole sentences for murder, have reopened the wounds of victims' families.

But that is not all. The murderer, Bailey himself, although proclaiming that he is different, conceded that "if the wrong juvenile lifer is let out, he [may] go[] off and kill[] again."[645] Obviously, these five justices are more interested in interfering with legislative decisions of sentences that legislators thought were needed to safeguard society from convicted murderers than safeguarding society from murderers.

Is this the end of the slippery slope toward total judicial usurpation of the legislative function of determining statutory sentences for crimes? If the past is any predictor of the future, the answer, sadly, is "no." As previously noted, in several prior decisions, the Court had explained its voiding of certain mandatory sentences for non-homicide crimes by stating "there is a distinction between intentional first-degree murder on the one hand and non-homicide crimes against individual persons, on the other."[646] Now that line they drew has been withdrawn for no reason except that these five justices found an opportunity further to expand their unconstitutional replacement of legislatures in deciding what punishment for criminal conduct should control. Thus, without the definitive distinction between homicide and other crimes, the sentence for all other crimes becomes subject to voiding by five justices because they personally believe the sentence to be excessive.

Court Extends Eighth Amendment To Order Wholesale Release of State Prisoners

This total usurpation of power by the courts was also confirmed when the Supreme Court, in 2011, again in a 5-4 ruling, held that the Eighth Amendment required California to implement a wholesale release of as many as 38,000 prisoners. The majority did not question the validity of the conviction and sentencing of these 38,000 prisoners. Nor was there even an allegation that any of these 38,000 inmates had been tortured or personally subject to any harsh treatment. Instead, it held the Eighth Amendment to require this wholesale release of convicted criminals because of prison overcrowding which *might* make it difficult for an unidentified – and unknown - prisoner to obtain medical attention *if needed*.

As already discussed, for centuries the Eighth Amendment prohibition against cruel and unusual punishment meant a sentence that was inhuman and barbarous. And, as recently as 1979, in a case in which prisoners claimed that their constitutional rights had been violated by substantial overcrowding in the prison, causing replacement of single bunk rooms with double bunks and some "sleep[ing] on cots in the common areas,"[647] the Court declined to intervene; recognizing the Constitution's limitation on its power, it held "the operation of our correctional facilities is peculiarly the province of the Legislative and Executive Branches of our Government, not the Judicial."[648] For that reason, the Court ruled that, in making decisions of how best to handle an increase in prison population, "[t]he wide range of judgment calls … are confided to officials outside of the Judicial Branch of Government."[649] The Court reaffirmed that principle in 1981, with only one justice dissenting, when it declined to take action against overcrowding in a state's prisons, again explaining that overcrowding in prisons is to be "weighed by the legislature and prison administration rather than by a court."[650]

The Supreme Court reiterated this principle as late as 1996, when it rejected a prisoner's lawsuit that alleged inadequacy of the legal research facilities in Arizona prisons that deprived prisoners of access to courts.[651] In that opinion, the Court again explained that "it is not the role of courts, but that of the political branches, to shape the institutions of government."[652] And almost clairvoyant of the case it would have to decide in 2011, the Court clearly rejected the thought that "a healthy inmate who had suffered no deprivation of needed medical treatment were able to claim violation of his constitutional right to medical care ... simply on the ground that the prison medical facilities were inadequate." The Court noted that, if it accepted that it was the function of the courts to assure adequate medical care in prisons, "the essential distinction between judge and executive would have disappeared."[653]

Despite these repeated holdings against the Court becoming involved in prison overcrowding litigation, five justices did an abrupt 180-degree turnabout in 2011. They took upon themselves to order the wholesale release of about 38,000 convicted prisoners in California – an order that those five justices admitted was "of unprecedented sweep and extent," causing even them "grave concern."[654]

These five justices obviously ignored why prisons exist: One reason is to protect law-abiding members of the community from being victims of repeat crimes by those who already had been convicted of crimes sufficiently serious to warrant a prison sentence.

There were very cogent reasons for those justices to feel "grave concern" in ordering this wholesale release of criminals. After all, one of the prime reasons for government – and the courts are part of government – is to protect, as much as possible, the personal safety and security of the average person. As those five justices further admitted, the "premature release of even one prisoner can cause injury and harm" to innocent people.[655]

History had shown that the release of the number they were ordering released would likely increase substantially the volume of crime in the affected community. The unquestionable high recidivism rate of prisoners[656] itself would require that conclusion. In addition, the Court had available what had happened when, in the early 1990s, a lower court in Pennsylvania had directed the release of thousands of inmates, also on the ground that those prisons were overcrowded. The result: During an 18-month period, thousands of these released prisoners were rearrested "for committing 9,732 new crimes," including "79 murders, 90 rapes, 113 assaults, 959 robberies, 701 burglaries, and 2,478 thefts."[657] With this factual history in mind, the California authorities warned the Court that ordering a wholesale reduction from California prisons "within a two-year period cannot be accomplished without unacceptably compromising public safety."[658] These five justices did not dispute that reality;: they agreed that "there is a risk that" the releasing of this number of prisoners "will have some adverse impact on public safety," because "some number" of prisoners released "before their sentence has been served ... can be expected to commit further crimes upon release."[659] But these five justices appeared to find some comfort in their reliance on the trial judges' opinion that the prisoner release would "not increase crime to a *significant* degree."[660] Let them tell the family of even one such murder victim or the rape victim herself that they shouldn't think it "significant." I am sure that they – and probably each reader – would agree with me that any single victim, who wouldn't have been a victim without this release of prisoners, is a travesty and therefore significant.

Not only did these justices disregard the record of substantial crime increase following the wholesale release of prisoners in Philadelphia, but they also ignored the facts showing that the "overcrowding" of California prisons had had the desirable impact of reducing the number of crimes: From 1992 to 2009 – the same period in which the prison population had so increased to culminate in the "overcrowding" - the incidence of violent crimes had decreased by 57.8 percent from 1,119.7 to 472.0 per 100,000 California residents – a reduction most welcome to law-abiding Californians.[661]

The error of these five justices was not limited to usurping the authority of the executive and legislative branches and ignoring the adverse consequences from their decision. These five justices purported to base their decision on finding that California caused "serious constitutional violations" by its "fail[ure] to meet prisoners' basic health needs."[662] The Court's factual basis for creating this constitutional violation was that "[p]risons were unable to retain sufficient numbers of competent medical staff," resulting in "timely access ... not [being] assured," and the justices' conclusion that "the California prison medical care system is broken beyond repair."[663] That finding, of a constitutional violation, was essential as, without it, the federal court would have had no jurisdiction to intervene.

> *"You can read the Constitution 100 times and you won't find any provision requiring the government to provide people – whether in or out of prison – with prompt medical care. Moreover, to sustain this constitutional right for prisoners would require acceptance of the unsupportable conclusion that prisoners have more constitutional rights than law-abiding people."*

You can read the Constitution 100 times and you won't find any provision requiring the government to provide people – whether in or out of prison – with prompt medical care. Moreover, to sustain this constitutional right for prisoners would require acceptance of the unsupportable conclusion that prisoners have more constitutional rights than law-abiding people. Many experts have used the same words, "broken beyond repair," to describe America's health system that is available to people who have committed no crimes and thus are not incarcerated.[664] Yet, no court has held that a non-prisoner person can sue the government to obtain medical care on that basis.

Many parts of our country, like prisons, have great shortages of physicians, resulting in "limited access to health care."[665] For example, "about 20% of the U.S. population - more than 50 million people - live in rural areas, but only 9% of the nation's physicians practice in rural communities."[666]   Nothing in the Constitution gives rural citizens a right to sue the government over the reality that most doctors do not opt to practice in rural areas – just as most doctors do not opt to practice in prisons.   No court would order a mass removal of people living in rural communities in order to create a better ratio of doctors to potential patients.   But that is what these five justices did here with the prison population.

To bolster their holding of a constitutional violation, these five justices pointed to a prisoner who "died of testicular cancer after a 'failure of MDs to work up for cancer of a young man with 17 months of testicular pain.'"[667]   But this anecdote does not support the justices' decision in this case.   First, that unfortunate prisoner who died is not a plaintiff in this case.   It had been, up to this decision, a rule that the court will not consider a claim unless the plaintiff has "suffered, or will imminently suffer, actual harm."[668]   None of the plaintiffs in this lawsuit even claimed that they had been so harmed, so as to have standing to sue.   These five justices, so anxious to direct California prison authorities how they should operate their prisons, ignored this rule that had been always applied without exception.

Second, and even more telling, that anecdote of the deceased prisoner, however sad and disparaging of the attending doctor's ability – and both are certainly true – does not become a constitutional violation.   If it had occurred to a person outside of prison – and that and other mistakes by doctors have unfortunately occurred – it would amount to malpractice, entitling the patient to sue for money damages, not for a violation of constitutional rights. These five justices provide no basis for having converted an ordinary medical malpractice cause of action into a constitutional violation.

Given this incredible extension of the Eighth Amendment by these five justices, we simply do not know where this Supreme Court's usurpation of the power the Constitution gave to legislatures will end.

XII.

PORNOGRAPHY -- THE SUPREME COURT REJECTS CONSTITUTIONAL MORALITY

Protecting Morality: An Objective Of The Constitution

Our country's founders, including the signers of our Declaration Of Independence and the authors and signers of our Constitution, considered the protection and enhancement of morality as one purpose of the country and government being created.

Samuel Adams, one of the first leaders of the American "revolutionaries," less than three months before the Declaration Of Independence, which he signed, wrote that morals were essential to the survival of liberty in any country.[669] In the following few years, he reiterated that "good morals" were a requisite "foundation of public liberty," and that once a people "lose their virtue they will be ready to surrender their Liberties."[670]

As early as 1774, our Continental Congress declared that there was nothing inconsistent between freedom of the press and the "advancement of ... morality."[671] (As we shall see later in this chapter, some of our more recent Supreme Court justices have taken a contrary view, asserting that the First Amendment's guaranty of freedom of speech and the press precludes government from advancing public morality by restricting such immoral activities as obscenity/pornography.) The Continental Congress itself adopted a resolution in 1778 that, because "good morals are the only solid foundations of public liberty," it "recommended to the several states, to take the most effectual measures for the encouragement" of morality.[672]

John Adams, another signer of the Declaration Of Independence, wrote, shortly before that signing, that the "only foundation of a free constitution is pure virtue."[673] In 1798, after the Constitution was ratified, Adams described it as "made only for a moral ... people."[674] Other signers of the Declaration or the Constitution also expounded on the necessity for maintaining morality if our country was to survive: Charles Carroll – "Without morals a republic cannot subsist any length of time";[675] Benjamin Franklin – "Only a virtuous people are capable of freedom";[676] Richard Henry Lee – "It is certainly true that a popular government cannot flourish without virtue in the people;[677] Benjamin Rush – "Without virtue there can be no liberty."[678]

The proverbial "Father of our Country," George Washington, himself declared that "virtue or morality is a necessary spring of popular government."[679]

The framer of the First Amendment, Fisher Ames, declared that he did not believe that the First Amendment in any way inhibited the government's ability or obligation to ensure the morality in our people: "Our liberty depends on" and "is founded on morals."[680]

> "*The Supreme Court early recognized that Congress rightfully could enact legislation to protect the 'public morals' of the Country.*"

Thomas Jefferson frequently wrote of the importance of instilling morality. He specified that an essential ingredient of a civilized country was a "political code" with "a chapter of morality."[681] To him, it was "not expected" that "nations so honorably distinguished by their advances in science and civilization," would suddenly turn their backs on morality.[682]

The Supreme Court early recognized that Congress rightfully could enact legislation to protect the "public morals" of the Country.[683] Indeed, in one of its first pronouncements on this issue, it specified that it was the legislature's *responsibility* to choose and then "exert ... what measures are appropriate or needful for the protection of the public morals."[684] The Court thereafter repeatedly reaffirmed "the authority of the state to enact laws to promote the ... morals, and general welfare of its people,"[685] and criminalize conduct that would "corrupt the morals of the people."[686] Later, the Court described the legislature's power to protect the morals of a community as including "the well-being and tranquility of a community."[687]

Justice Louis Brandeis, one of the most respected justices ever to sit on that Court, and well-known as a civil libertarian, wrote that the Constitution was intended by the Framers "to secure conditions favorable to the pursuit of happiness," that considered "man's spiritual nature, ... his feelings and ... his intellect," thereby to "protect Americans in their beliefs, their thoughts, their emotions, and their sensations," and not only their "material things."[688]

Unfortunately, as shown below, this morality-supporting direction from our forefathers has been discarded by contemporary justices who have thereby opened our society and culture to pornography and sex-everywhere bombardment. In the following chapter, I also show that the constitutional protection of morality has fallen victim to the Supreme Court's green light to immoral conduct, including by allowing the uninvited invasion of our privacy by sexual depictions, simulated child pornography, profanity on public airwaves, horrible public displays of animal torture, and violent video games for minors. Our forefathers must be turning over in their graves on the current generation's allowing these morality-degrading rulings to exist under the Constitution they bequeathed to all future generations.

The Serious Pornography and Sex Bombardment Problem

A Real-Life Example of Pornography's Destructive Impact

Granted leniency after his conviction for robbery, Thomas Schiro was serving a three-year suspended sentence residing at a halfway house, where he was supposed to receive counseling and treatment, while also working in a work-release program. His job was across the street from the residence of a young lady, Laura Luebbehusen. One day, although he was supposed to attend a counseling session, he instead went to see pornographic movies, where he exposed himself to the female clerk. He then went to Ms. Luebbehusen's residence, knocked on her door, and asked to use her phone on the pretext that his car would not start. After pretending to use her phone, he asked to use her bathroom. When he came out, he exposed himself, raped her three times, "hit her on the head with a vodka bottle until it shattered, ... picked up an iron and beat her with it," and then "strangled her to death." After she was dead, "he performed vaginal and anal intercourse on the corpse and chewed on several parts of her body."[689]

This conduct was not something new by Schiro. At trial, an expert retained by Schiro's lawyer testified that Schiro had committed between 19 and 24 rapes. One woman testified that Schiro had broken into her home, held a gun to her son's head and raped her in front of her six-year-old daughter, who suffered from cerebral palsy.[690]

Schiro's lawyer also conceded that his client "was a sexual sadist" and asserted that "extensive viewing of rape pornography ... rendered him unable to distinguish right from wrong."[691] Schiro himself gave the following written statement:

"I can remember when I get horny from looking at girly books and watching girly shows that I would want to go rape somebody. Every time I would jack off before I come I would be thinking of rape and the women I had raped and remembering how exciting it was. The pain on their faces. The thrill, the excitement."[692]

Expert witnesses testified to the causal connection between pornography and Schiro's conduct: "Schiro's viewing of pornography actually encouraged him to commit the acts of violence at issue."[693] Indeed, after a short exposure to aggressive pornography, "non-rapist populations begin to endorse myths about rape. .... They begin to say that women enjoy being raped and they begin to say that using force in sexual encounters is okay."

Professionals' Views On Pornography's Impact

Various professionals – not retained by a defendant seeking to avoid severe penalties, including death, for such horrible crimes, and therefore not subject to monetary inducements to provide favorable testimony – concur on "the links between pornography consumption and a wide number of psychological, social, and family pathologies."[694] They quote with approval one clinician who "testified, 'Those who claim pornography is harmless entertainment, benign sexual expression or a marital aid, have clearly never sat in a therapist's office with individuals, couples, or families who are reeling from the devastating effects of the material.' Research and data suggest that the habitual use of pornography—and especially of internet pornography—can have a range of damaging effects on human beings of all ages and of both sexes, affecting their happiness, their productivity, their relationships with one another, and their functioning in society."[695] A 2004 "nationally representative study of 531 internet users ... found that those who had an extramarital affair were more than three times more likely to have used internet pornography than were internet users who had not had an affair."[696]

The particular adverse impact of pornography on young people has also been amply established. Mary Eberstadt and Mary Anne Layden report various studies:[697] "children and adolescents use pornography to coerce each other into sexual behavior; ... adolescent girls who report using pornography are more likely to report being victims of passive violence, where they experience sexual harassment or forced sex at the hands of male friends or acquaintances"; a study of 30 juvenile sexual offenders established 29 of them admitted to exposure to pornography as a child, starting at an average age of 7½; "Habituation to pornographic imagery predisposes some adolescent girls to engage in sexually risky behavior," including oral and anal intercourse, raising health issues of females "more likely to be exposed to sexually transmitted diseases via anal and oral-genital contact"; research with first-year college students underlined the harm from pornography, including "increased tolerance toward sexually explicit material, thereby requiring more novel or bizarre material to achieve the same level of arousal or interest, misperceptions about exaggerated sexual activity in the general populace and the prevalence of ... group sex, bestiality, and sadomasochistic activity" – all of which results in an "increased risk of developing a negative body image ... and acceptance of promiscuity as a normal state of interaction."

I have never understood the nay-sayers who argue that watching a pornographic film or reading an obscene book has no negative effect on the individual, and, they have contended, no greater negative impact than watching a war movie. This argument, in reality, strikes at the roots of a basic belief, not long ago generally accepted, that reading good books, seeing good plays and movies, visiting good museums, and viewing good art and architecture enriches individuals, helps develop better character, and moves people up the ladder of good and successful citizenship. The reverse of that must also be true: Graphic pornography, with no socially redeeming value, has to affect the observer adversely. And the social scientists' findings, enumerated above, demonstrate the validity of this logical conclusion.

An "Expert" Who Used Pornography To Feed His Own Sexual Appetite

It is a legal truism that an "expert" can always be found for any side of a legal issue. A good lawyer, however, will carefully vet the expert before using him to be certain that nothing in the expert's background will backfire. Justice William O. Douglas, who regularly opined that the First Amendment protects even obscenity/pornography from any restrictive or punitive government action, failed to do any vetting when, in one of his opinions, he cited an expert in support of his vote against holding a book to be obscene. It concerned a book purporting to be a "sexual autobiography detailing with complete candor the author's sexual experiences from age 3 to age 36," described by the defendant's own expert as "entirely without literary merit."[698] Justice Douglas cited, as an expert supporting the social value of the book, the Rev. George Von Hilsheimer III, a Baptist minister, whom he further commended as having done "graduate work in psychology and studied analysis and training therapy," with "extensive experience as a group counselor, lecturer, and family counselor," as a "consultant to President Kennedy's Study Group on National Voluntary Services," and as "a member of the board of Directors of Mobilization for Youth."[699]

Justice Douglas quoted the Rev. von Hilsheimer that he "used the book 'insistently in my pastoral counseling and in my formal psychological counseling,'" because it provides "the history of a woman who has had sexual adventures outside the normally accepted bounds of marriage" and therefore "gives the women to whom I give the book at least a sense that their own experiences are not unusual," and "that they themselves should not [feel] guilty because" of their sexual activities.[700]   Relying on this "expert testimony," Justice Douglas opined that "I would think the Baptist minister's evaluation would be enough to satisfy the Court's test" that the book is not obscene.[701]

In fact, Rev. Hilsheimer *was* very expert, but not at being an objective, uninvolved, upstanding evaluator.   Investigation into the clergyman, now made much easier through Google, establishes a flood of evidence that he was expert in using this book – that he admits to plying women who came to him – to aid in fulfilling **HIS** sexual desires.   Women who attended his "school" have written that he "was a violent sexual predator, a serial rapist and a pedophile who raped and brutalized countless underage female students, as well as some staff women"; "he raped me in 1969," and "I know at least 7 other girls, now women, who were also raped by him"; he "stag[ed] orgies where he invited selected friends to avail themselves of sex with several of us."[702]   The camp/school that he ran was described as a "'free love' camp."[703]   And on March 20, 1998, due to his conduct, the State of Florida revoked his license to practice psychology.[704]   While I am relatively certain that Justice Douglas was unaware of the fact that his "expert." Rev. von Hilsheimer, had such a nefarious sexual predator record, it speaks volumes of the lack of support that Justice Douglas had for his pro-obscenity position that he relied on one whose life was directed so illegally toward feeding his prurient interests.

Another Erroneous Court Decision

I will shortly detail how, in a 10-year period between 1957 and 1966, the Supreme Court effectively emasculated anti-obscenity enforcement.   As our lower courts are required to accept Supreme Court decisions, including those that repudiate long-standing prior rulings, the deleterious consequences of such Supreme Court about-faces is often best observed in lower court decisions.   Here is one of them.

Only seven years before being required to review Thomas Schiro's horrible conduct, that same Federal Court of Appeals – the second highest court, just below the Supreme Court, for the geographic area it covered – considered the constitutionality of a City of Indianapolis statute to bar pornography. The Court had no doubt as to the pornography's harmful effect: "[p]ornography is a systematic practice of exploitation and subordination based on sex which differentially harms women" and "leads to ... insult and injury at home, battery and rape on the streets."[705] While the record in that case contained "materials depicting sexual torture, penetration of women by red-hot irons and the like,"[706] it did not involve the guilt of any specific offender and crime. Rather, this federal appellate court had to determine an issue having an even greater impact on the ability of a state to protect all of its citizens from the harm that flows from pornography: whether that Indianapolis anti-pornography statute was constitutional. In a dramatic example of how our courts have lost their way from the pro-morality instruction provided by our country's forefathers, this court held it unconstitutional, as violative of the First Amendment.

The Indianapolis statute, attacked in that case, was very clear and specific: Pornography was defined as "the graphic sexually explicit subordination of women, whether in pictures or in words, that includes one or more of the following:

"(1) Women are presented as sexual objects who enjoy pain or humiliation;

"(2) Women are presented as sexual objects who experience sexual pleasure in being raped;

"(3) Women are presented as sexual objects tied up or cut up or mutilated or bruised or physically hurt, or as dismembered or truncated or fragmented or severed into body parts;

"(4) Women are presented as being penetrated by objects or animals;

"(5) Women are presented in scenarios of degradation,

injury, debasement, torture, shown as filthy or inferior, bleeding, bruised, or hurt in a context that makes these conditions sexual; or

"(6) Women are presented as sexual objects for domination, conquest, violation, exploitation, possession, or use or through postures or positions of servility or submission or display."[707]

It is hard to believe that any court would hold that content that fit into any of these specific categories provided meaningful "social value as a step to truth" – part of the standard the Supreme Court fixed in order for any content to be protected by the First Amendment.[708] Why did three judges, who ruled in this case, reject that Indianapolis statute? They did recognize that "[s]exual responses often are unthinking responses." But they analogized pornographic stimuli to "religious ceremonies," or teaching by teachers, both of which likewise "condition their participants," and which are First Amendment protected. Relying on that analogy, that court held that, "[i]f the fact that speech plays a role of conditioning were enough to permit government regulation, that would be the end of freedom of speech."[709]

Can you believe that three judges would consider that pornography is no different than what a minister, priest or rabbi says in a religious ceremony or what a teacher says in a classroom? Of course, one would expect that listeners to a person of the cloth or to the teacher will have some reaction to what was said. But, unlike the pornographic stimuli, no one seriously suggests that a listener to either of them is going to be incited to commit a heinous crime or engage in morally unacceptable attacks on women. This Court's reliance on these analogies is obviously meritless. Unfortunately, it exemplifies that lower courts are required to follow the Supreme Court's trend of almost "anything goes" in dealing with this serious American problem.

Hard-core pornography is now rampant

Two-thirds of men aged 18-34 make at least a monthly visit to a pornographic web site. Between 1988 and 2005, the number of pornographic video and DVD titles that were released increased over 1,000 percent, from 1,300 to 13,585. Four billion dollars are spent annually on video pornography in this country, with close to one billion pornographic videos and DVDs being rented. That is more than spent on football, baseball and basketball.[710] This ready availability of hard-core pornography has had, understandably, a tidal wave impact on our youth. A 2004 Columbia University study found that 45 percent of teenagers "have friends who regularly view internet pornography and download it. .... 34% of adolescents reported being exposed to unwanted sexual content online. .... 70% of youth aged fifteen to seventeen reported accidently [*sic*] coming across pornography on line."[711] Our young cannot hide from pornographic communications as "pornographic references are frequently laced into popular video games, advertisements, television, and music, and also are ubiquitous in music videos."[712]

The General Sexual Bombardment

The "anything goes" court decision, which struck down Indianapolis' statute against pornography, is mirrored by what we see today in everyday life. Times and conduct have changed since I was young – the period between 1931 and 1955. During those earlier years of my life, we were not subjected to a constant bombardment of pornography, perversion or promiscuity in magazines, movies, radio, TV (when it arrived in the 1940s), or computers (a much later arrival), or sexually suggestive billboards and other advertisements.

For example, when I attended Yale Law School from 1952-1955, I never had an inkling of any public debunking of society's moral codes on sex. Women law students were housed in totally separate living quarters, apart from male students in a distant building. Yes, sometimes, a guy sneaked a female into his room contrary to the rule, but all knew it was not allowed and that it risked a meaningful sanction. Now, years after I graduated, acceptable mores are the antithesis of the moral code under which we had lived. Starting in the 1990's, the Yale Daily News had a sex columnist whose column included a description about how she had lost her virginity as well as detailing methods of self-pleasuring. Other college campuses have no problem with the same type of college spotlight on sex, sex and more sex. Tufts University had a regular "Between the Sheets" column, authored by a co-ed. Another campus featured a weekly column entitled "Wednesday Hump." Bestiality, erotic asphyxiation, and sex while dressed in animal costumes were other subjects presented by campus columnists. A Carnegie Mellon University sex columnist publicly addressed those who are troubled by this type of education that America's young are receiving: "Lighten up a little bit. .... It's just sex."[713]

The University of Tennessee Chancellor announced his "support" for a campus "Sex Week," initially attempted to be funded by taxpayers' funds, with classes and workshops on such topics as "How Many Licks Does It Take" (oral sex), "Loud and Queer," and "Transgender Sexuality."[714] And, perhaps to top all, the University of Cincinnati authorized twelve billboard-sized photographs of vaginas to be exhibited outdoors on the campus, which the college President inexplicably described as nothing more than an "intellectual exchange ... protect[ed by] the First Amendment."[715]

We are today bombarded with sex in almost every waking hour in our homes and communities. Stand in line at the check-out counter at most supermarkets and we are hit with magazines applauding and romanticizing sex. Here is an example: the cover of the April 2008 Cosmopolitan magazine – which I saw while

waiting in my doctor's office, but is also sold in supermarkets –
headlined "Be A Sex Genius!: These Brilliantly Naughty Bed
Tricks Will Double His Pleasure …. And Yours," and "Little
Mouth Moves That Make Sex Hotter." Television likewise has
many popular programs spotlighting sex. The title of the very
popular series "Sex And The City" honestly describes what it
involved while it serves as a magnet to induce watching. In the
first episode of "90210," advertised as a teen drama TV series, two
students engage in oral sex.[716] Sex has become so rampant on
television, and in contemporary music and movies, that its
frequency caused the American Academy of Pediatrics, in 2010, to
issue a public, flashing-red-light warning policy statement:

> "On television, which remains the predominant medium in
> terms of time spent for all young people, more than 75% of
> prime-time programs contain sexual content …. Talk
> about sex on TV can occur as often as 8 to 10 times per
> hour. Between 1997 and 2001 alone, the amount of sexual
> content on TV nearly doubled. …. Music … [is] a major
> source of sexual suggestiveness. …. An analysis of the 279
> most popular songs in 2005 revealed that 37% contained
> sexual references and that degrading sexual references were
> common. …. Virtually every R-rated teen movie since the
> 1980s has contained at least one nude scene and, often,
> several instances of sexual intercourse. …. Teen magazines
> are popular with preadolescent and adolescent girls, … the
> overarching focus [of which] seems to be on deciding when
> to lose one's virginity. …. Advertisements often use sex to
> sell. Women are as likely to be shown in suggestive
> clothing (30%), partially clad (13%), or nude (6%) as they
> are to be fully clothed. …. [The] United States has some
> of the most sexually suggestive media in the world.
> American media makes sex seem like a harmless sport in
> which everyone engages."[717]

Even the sex-prevalent TV shows, while not pornographic, have had substantial adverse impacts on our children. A research project among our youth reported that teenagers who watched the sexiest TV shows – *e.g.,* Sex And The City – were twice as likely to become pregnant over the following three years than those who watched few such programs.[718]

Over-the-top sex has become so prevalent that clubs exist to provide a "safe space" to act out erotic fantasies involving sadism/masochism, in which, for example, a man and woman engaged in "fire play, which involved accelerant placed on strategic points of a woman's body and set ablaze in short dramatic bursts," and, in another part of the club, "a middle-aged man was lashing a middle-aged woman's bare back with a single tail whip."[719] And, almost too hard to believe, Harvard University, which proclaims that it is dedicated "to the pursuit of excellence,"[720] recently gave accreditation to Harvard College Munch, a student group focusing on such "kinky interests."[721] (An aside: do the current administrators really believe that this is what John Harvard, a minister, intended to create when he left half of his estate to start Harvard College?[722]).

One of America's top sex symbols, Raquel Welch, well described the impact of this bombardment of sex that we all are compelled, whether we like it or not, to live through: "I think we've gotten to the point in our culture where we are all sex addicts, literally. We have equated happiness in life with as many orgasms as you can possibly pack in, regardless of where it is that you deposit your love interest."[723]

Objections To Anti-Obscenity Laws

Given this inundation of American society with obscenity and sex in general, the question to be answered is whether society should accept it and do nothing to curtail it. I have shown above the many facets of the harm it does, which conclusively responds to the contention, often voiced, that society should calmly accept it as reflecting a simple human activity. Yes, sex is a wonderful human activity when properly practiced, but not when it causes the adverse consequences already described.

Another criticism often voiced against the anti-obscenity laws is that they would return America to the cultural wasteland of the stifling Victorian-era code of conduct in which, the argument goes, all enriching culture was stifled. The facts refute that contention. During the 19th century in America, great cultural contributions were made while (as I will demonstrate immediately following) the courts strictly enforced the laws that prohibited obscenity and public crass sex. Here is a sampling of the 19th century imaginative and still-valued cultural contributions that strict enforcement of the anti-obscenity laws did nothing to curtail: American authors Washington Irving, Ralph Waldo Emerson, Henry David Thoreau, Margaret Fuller, John Muir, Frederick Douglass, Herman Melville, Samuel Clemens (better known as Mark Twain), Louisa May Alcott, and Harriet Beecher Stowe; American philosophers (in addition to those included as authors) Charles Sanders Pierce, William James, and John Dewey.

This sampling, and many more who could be named, undoubtedly led the Court, in one of its opinions, to reject, as without evidentiary support, the contention that "the stern 19th century American censorship of public distribution and display of material relating to sex, ... in any way limited or affected expression of serious literary, artistic, political, or scientific ideas. On the contrary, it is beyond any question that the era following Thomas Jefferson to Theodore Roosevelt was an 'extraordinary vigorous period,' not just in economics and politics, but in *belle lettres* and in 'the outlying field of social and political philosophies.'"[724]

In the last quarter of the 20th century, defendants in obscenity prosecutions started seriously asserting that their First Amendment rights of freedom of speech and press were being violated if they were not permitted to distribute what was held to be obscene material. As we shall see as we proceed through the years to more contemporary times, that assertion has now found favor with a substantial minority of the Court, and has undoubtedly helped to move the Court to reject many obscenity statutes and their application. But the Court, very early by a unanimous vote and continually for many decades, later with meaningful dissents, rejected the contention that anti-obscenity statutes violated the Bill of Rights: "[T]he object of [these statutes] has not been to interfere with the freedom of the press, or with any other rights of the people, but to" prevent "distribution of matter deemed injurious to the public morals."[725]

Justice Joseph Story, whose early 18th century treatise, written while he was a justice on the Supreme Court, remains the standard treatise on the subject of the meaning of the Constitution, described the contention that the First Amendment "was intended to secure to every citizen an absolute right to speak, or write, or print whatever he might please," as "a supposition too wild to be indulged by any rational man." Rather, Justice Story explained, freedom of speech and press does not immunize speech or writing that injures "any other person in his rights, person, property, or reputation" or "disturb[s] the public peace."[726] For that reason, the Supreme Court has made clear that "[l]iberty of speech and of the press is not an absolute right, and the state may punish its abuse."[727]

Consider some examples of accepted limitation on free speech and press: We have already discussed that the free speech right does not allow anyone to yell "fire" in a crowded theater. But lawful restrictions on free speech are not limited to those that protect the physical safety of others. Many speech limitations have been upheld on the ground that the speech would be an unfair imposition on society's general welfare or on other persons. You and I could not, with impunity, publish a book or make a speech that contains a false defamatory statement about another. Even in financial and business matters, some statements when made can result in criminal convictions and jail terms. Making statements about a company that you started, in order to induce another to buy stock in that company, can be enjoined and result in your going to jail, if you made any statements without first obtaining acceptance by the Securities & Exchange Commission of a full factual description of the company and limit your oral statements to what is in the writing. And you can be prosecuted for making any statement found to be materially false. Congress has been held to have the constitutional right so to limit your free speech rights because Congress is thereby protecting the general welfare of our country and people.[728]

The Supreme Court, in 1942, unanimously reiterated that the free speech right must give way when "outweighed by the social interest in order and morality" that would be torpedoed by protecting "the lewd and obscene [and] the profane." The Court explained that limitation on free speech by describing such speech as having "such slight social value as a step to truth that any benefit that may be derived from them ... [to be] clearly outweighed" by the obvious value of "order and morality."[729] In 1957, the Court, in an opinion written by the liberal Justice William J. Brennan, expressly recognized that "the Court has always assumed that obscenity is not protected by the freedoms of speech and press," because "implicit in the history of the First Amendment is the rejection of obscenity as utterly without redeeming social importance."[730] Justice Brennan was there referring to the earlier Supreme Court holding that the First Amendment only protects ideas that have "social value as a step to truth," that are not "outweighed by the social interest in order and morality."[731]

Even Justices Douglas and Hugo Black, who frequently – including in this case – dissented on the ground that the First Amendment is an absolute prohibition against government interference with any speech, including obscenity, agreed, totally inconsistently, "that there is nothing in the Constitution which forbids Congress from using its power over the mails to proscribe conduct on the grounds of good morals."[732]   Further, they proceeded to explain the logic behind that conclusion: Since "[n]o one would suggest that the First Amendment permits nudity in public places, adultery, and other phases of sexual misconduct,"[733] it would be irrational to suggest that the First Amendment allows the substitution of pictorial or textual showing of the same forbidden conduct. They never even attempted to explain how the First Amendment allowed the government to censor the content of what is mailed, but not permit government prohibition of the same objectionable content by other distribution means. There simply is no way to obtain consistency out of this totally inconsistent position.

Chief Justice Burger, in a 1973 opinion, summarized the reason for the majority rejection of a dissent based on the First Amendment: "to equate the free and robust exchange of ideas and *political* debate with commercial exploitation of obscene material demeans the grand conception of the First Amendment and its high purpose in the historic struggle for freedom."[734]

American Courts' Long-Time History Of Enforcing Anti-Obscenity Laws

Both before and immediately after the adoption of our Constitution, the American colonies and, after independence, the American states made criminal the publishing and distribution of obscenity, a synonym for pornography.[735] Originally, prohibition and criminalization of obscenity was brought to the colonies as part of English law.[736]   As early as 1712, for example, Massachusetts, by statute, made it criminal to publish "any filthy, obscene, or profane … pamphlet."[737]   On independence, all 13 states that ratified the Constitution had enacted laws criminalizing profanity and blasphemy.[738] As other states joined the Union, all enacted their own obscenity laws; and, over the years, Congress itself enacted at least 20 laws prohibiting obscenity."[739] The anti-obscenity codification was not unique to the United States; the international *Agreement For The Suppression Of The Circulation Of Obscene Publications* has been signed by over 55 countries.[740]

The law of Great Britain, from which, as already noted in this book, our courts adopted much of our controlling legal rules when we became independent, had very strict prohibitions against public dissemination of obscenity. The decision by a British High Court announced in 1868 – many years after our independence – was frequently cited by our Supreme Court in upholding anti-obscenity laws, until the Supreme Court more recently did a 180-degree turn to allow much obscenity. Hence, knowledge of that British case, *Regina v. Hicklin*,[741] provides a good start on the history of the courts' treatment of obscenity in this country.

The defendant there was convicted for distributing a pamphlet, purportedly to expose "the errors of the church of Rome, and particularly the immorality of the confessional," containing in its second half recitations of confessions that were "grossly obscene, as related to impure and filthy acts, words, and ideas." While the British court found that the defendant's "intention was honestly and *bona fide* to expose the errors and practices of the Roman Catholic Church in the matter of confession," it held the defendant was validly convicted, explaining that "the test of obscenity is … whether the tendency of the matter … is to deprave and corrupt those whose minds are open to such immoral influences." The pamphlet was held to violate that test because "it is quite certain that it would suggest to the minds of the young of either sex, or even to persons of more advanced years, thoughts of a most impure and libidinous character."[742] Note that this test of whether the matter is obscenity required a factual finding of its impact on "those whose minds are open to such immoral influences," with the "young" as one example, not on "normal" or "average" adults – to which, as we will see, the Supreme Court majority later restricted it.

In the last quarter of the 19th century, long after the 1791 enactment of the First Amendment protection of freedom of speech and the press, the Supreme Court unanimously reaffirmed its acceptance of that English ruling, declaring that it still had "no doubt" as to "the constitutionality" of a statute that made it a crime to use the mails to distribute any "obscene, lewd, or lascivious book [or] pamphlet ...."[743]

Almost 20 years later, the Court again upheld the constitutionality of statutes making it criminal to distribute "obscene, lewd, or lascivious" material.[744] It there considered the conviction of a defendant for mailing a "paper" named "'Broadway'" that contained "pictures of females" in "different attitudes of indecency," even though they were "partially covered with lamp black."[745] The Court quickly rejected any claim of ambiguity to the prohibition: "Every one ... must take notice of what, in this enlightened age, is meant by decency, purity, and chastity in social life" – what the law protects – "and what must be deemed obscene, lewd and lascivious."[746] The Supreme Court approved the trial judge's instructions to the jury to guide them through that standard:

> "the test of obscenity is whether the tendency of the matter is to deprave and corrupt the morals of those whose minds are open to such influence, and into whose hands a publication of this sort may fall. Would it suggest or convey lewd thoughts and lascivious thoughts to the young and inexperienced?"[747]

It was obvious that the Supreme Court was thereby reaffirming the acceptance for United States law of the British test, quoted above, under which a writing is criminal if its "tendency ... is to deprave and corrupt those whose minds are open to such immoral influences," such as "the minds of the young."[748]

Supreme Court's Sudden Emasculation Of Anti-Obscenity Enforcement

Thus, from our country's birth through 1956, the standard for enforcing anti-obscenity laws was clear and enforcement-favorable: It delegated to jurors (or a judge, if a jury trial was waived) to determine whether, applying contemporary standards of the community, the tendency of included obscenity was to deprave and corrupt susceptible people. Yet, in a 10-year period, between 1957 and 1966, the Supreme Court repudiated this long-time American (and British) standard to substitute an almost impossible standard for the government to meet. The impact of these game-changing new rules was substantial. They made anti-obscenity law enforcement well-nigh impossible in most factual contexts.

This effect of these Supreme Court revised rules is seen in two decisions, one in 1964 and the other in 1966. Both decisions allowed distribution of matter that would not have been allowed under the pre-existing rules.

The 1964 Supreme Court decision concerned the movie "*Les Amants*," or, in English, "The Lovers." It contained "an explicit love scene" – explicit sexual intercourse – by a married woman, "bored with her life and marriage who abandons her husband and family for a young archaeologist with whom she has suddenly fallen in love."[749] Those of us who are old enough to have seen movies – very popular and award winners – before the introduction of explicit sex into movies – and there were many applauded movies without explicit sex – can remember seeing and enjoying movies that presented a very similar plot. For example, the 1945 film, "Brief Encounter," starring Trevor Howard, Stanley Holloway and Celia Johnson, dramatized a similar triangle, but without any sexual relations or nudity. The producers, directors and actors in "Brief Encounter" were able, through the movie, to express their views on the issue of a wife's boredom in marriage and search for better love and excitement – and thus exercise their

First Amendment free speech rights – without any explicit sex.

I grant that more tickets might well have been sold for "Brief Encounter" if advertising trailers had shown a scene of a nude adulterous Celia Johnson doing "what comes naturally" in bed with her lover. But nothing in the First Amendment guarantees the speaker's right to say anything merely because it would enhance his economic profit. As already discussed, First Amendment rights are not absolute but subject to constitutional restrictions imposed by the legislature to protect welfare, safety and morals of the community. All Ohio state court judges, 13 in total in three different Ohio state courts that reviewed the film, found it obscene. Yet a smaller number in the Supreme Court, six, disagreed, overruling the judgment of the 13 judges in Ohio, and thus allowed this film to be shown.

Two years later, in 1966, the Supreme Court majority continued its turnabout from almost 200 years of enforcing anti-obscenity laws when it considered an appeal from a decision of the Massachusetts Supreme Judicial Court concerning the mid-18th century book *Memoirs Of A Woman Of Pleasure* (commonly known as *Fanny Hill*).[750] That highest Massachusetts court had affirmed the trial court's holding that the book was obscene. Yet this new majority on the Supreme Court reversed to hold it not obscene, despite conceding that the book may well "possess the requisite prurient appeal and ... be patently offensive."[751] And one of the other majority justices, Justice Douglas, wrote specifically that he agreed that the book "concededly is an erotic novel."[752]

The validity of these descriptions of this novel was made obvious in a dissenting opinion that identified the book as "nothing more than a series of minutely and vividly described sexual episodes," which were then further detailed as follows:

"The book starts with Fanny Hill, a young 15-year-old girl, arriving in London to seek household work. She goes to an employment office where through happenstance she meets the mistress of a bawdy house. This takes 10 pages. The remaining 200 pages of the book detail her initiation into various sexual experiences, from a lesbian encounter with a sister prostitute to all sorts and types of sexual debauchery in bawdy houses and as the mistress of a variety of men. This is presented to the reader through an uninterrupted succession of descriptions by Fanny, either as an observer or participant, of sexual adventures so vile that one of the male expert witnesses in the case was hesitant to repeat any one of them in the courtroom. These scenes run the gamut of possible sexual experience such as lesbianism, female masturbation, homosexuality between young boys, the destruction of a maidenhead with consequent gory descriptions, the seduction of a young virgin boy, the flagellation of male by female, and vice versa, followed by fervid sexual engagement, and other abhorrent acts, including over two dozen separate bizarre descriptions of different sexual intercourses between male and female characters. In one sequence four girls in a bawdy house are required in the presence of one another to relate the lurid details of their loss of virginity and their glorification of it. This is followed the same evening by "publick trials" in which each of the four girls engages in sexual intercourse with a different man while the others witness, with Fanny giving a detailed description of the movement and reaction of each couple.

"In each of the sexual scenes the exposed bodies of the participants are described in minute and individual detail. The pubic hair is often used for a background to the most vivid and precise descriptions of the response, condition, size, shape, and color of the sexual organs before, during and after orgasms. There are some short transitory passages between the various sexual episodes, but for the most part they only set the scene and identify the participants for the next orgy, or make smutty reference and comparison to past episodes."[753]

Before 1957, based on the rules fixed by the Supreme Court itself, under the unchanged Constitution which the Court was enforcing, the Court would have affirmed the state court decisions holding the material to be obscene and, thus, properly banned. These decisions to the contrary occurred only due to the new majority of justices who repudiated all determinative rules that the Supreme Court had so long accepted and applied. I will now show how they changed these rules.

Until 1957, as already discussed, the test of obscenity was the impact of any obscene part of the subject material on particularly susceptible people, such as the young and immature – reflecting not only our court's adoption of the English rule, but also our country's guidance from the biblical text that it is directed to "[r]escue the weak and the needy; deliver them from the hand of the wicked."[754] Suddenly, matter would be obscene only if, applying contemporary community standards, the dominant theme of the material taken as a whole appeals to the prurient interest of the "normal" or "average" person. The effect of this change was obvious: What is obscene and is more problematic for the young and immature to digest is less problematic for most "average" persons. Hence, it lowered the gate of access to the public for matter that would have been rejected as obscene when looking at the effect on the young and immature. The Court

> *"For what possible reason did the majority redefine 'community' into nationwide? It was necessary in order to support these justices' grab of power over decisions essential to enforcement of anti-obscenity laws that had previously been reserved to local juries and trial judges: the power to decide whether, as a factual matter, the material at issue was obscene."*

never even attempted to rationalize its throwing the young and immature to the wolves, and abrogating the long-accepted responsibility of the Court to "protect[] the well-being of our youth."[755]

Another departure from prior rules involved the requirement of applying "contemporary community standards." While this new majority pretended to continue that prior measure, they totally redefined the meaning of "community," away from its ordinary meaning of a more local community (certainly no larger than the state involved), to the nation as a whole. This Court majority never explained how a juror or judge from Oshkosh could possibly know nationwide standards – if such existed – given that it encompassed large areas far removed and different from the Oshkosh-residing juror or judge. Indeed, the majority Justices were candid in noting the impossibility of this new "nationwide" standard, by recognizing that "local communities throughout the land are in fact diverse," including in "their toleration of alleged obscenity."[756]

Given this admitted impossibility of having a nationwide standard, for what possible reason did the majority redefine "community" into nationwide? It was necessary in order to support these justices' grab of power over decisions essential to enforcement of anti-obscenity laws that had previously been reserved to local juries and trial judges: the power to decide whether, as a factual matter, the material at issue was obscene. The jurors and trial judges obviously would be best to perform that task if, as it had been until then, the standard to be considered was the more local "community" standard. But make the standard nationwide, local jurors and trial judges have no special knowledge of that standard, given that each community would not necessarily have the same standard as other diverse parts of the country.

This change of standard from community to nationwide substantially altered the fact-finding process on who decides whether the matter is obscene. Before this 1964 Supreme Court decision, that determination was made by the jury or, if a jury had been waived or not required, by the local judge or judges serving as the trier of fact. Such members of the local community were more likely than high-office office-holders, whom some would call elitists, in Washington, to find sexually descriptive material to be obscene. And as long as there was not a total void of reasonable factual basis for the jury's obscenity finding, appellate judges, including Supreme Court Justices, were required to accept this factual finding.

That division of responsibility, between appellate judges and the trier of fact, was not unique to the obscenity issue, but prevailed in all trials, even where constitutional rights were involved. A most obvious example of the application of this rule is where a defendant is convicted and sentenced to prison, or even death, based on a jury verdict. Of course, the Fifth Amendment guarantees that defendant must not be "deprived of life [or] liberty ... without due process of law." One might easily argue that, since due process requires a defendant not be convicted unless the facts establish his guilt beyond a reasonable doubt, an appellate judge would be authorized to overturn the conviction if he simply disagrees with the jury finding as to the facts. But appellate judges may not. Unless there were no reasonable construction of the facts that supported guilt, the appellate judge is bound by the jury's interpretation of those facts.

Therefore, until this 1964 Supreme Court opinion, appellate courts were bound by the jury finding of obscenity. Indeed, in the 1957 decision that contained the first tranche of changes in the obscenity standard, Justice Brennan expressly approved of the trial court instruction to the "ladies and gentlemen of the jury, you and you alone are the exclusive judges of what the common conscience of the community is"[757] – meaning that it is the jury that alone may decide whether the material is obscene. Yet, seven years later, he did a 180-degree reversal to hold that as few as five justices superseded jurors in their fact-finding role.

The impact of this transfer of fact-finding authority from the local jurors or trial judges to the justices in Washington is seen in the 1964 appeal from the Ohio conviction for showing the film "*Les Amants.*" The Supreme Court faced a serious head-wind against finding that it was not obscene. Both the Ohio intermediate court and its Supreme Court had accepted the trial court's factual finding that the film was obscene. Thus, in all, 13 local judges had found the film obscene, with no dissenting judge. The United States Supreme Court disagreed by a vote of 6-3, pitting only six Washington-based justices against 13 local judges (not to mention the three justices who had agreed with the local state judges). Yet, these six justices overruled the factual finding of the three local trial judges who served as the trial jury, and the concurrence of 10 other Ohio judges.

Other than ego and a power-grab, there is no basis for these six individuals, who happened to be United States Supreme Court justices, to believe that they could better apply "contemporary community standards" to this film than 16 other judges; on that issue, as on all issues of fact on which jurors make the decision, all individuals, regardless of rank, are equally capable. Therefore, the need for the power-grab: In order to give to appellate judges, including, as the final decider, Supreme Court justices, the decisional authority on whether the film was obscene, the determination no longer could be treated as the factual determination that it is, because factual determinations are to be made by juries, not by appellate judges. Ignoring the reality that whether a film is obscene requires an evaluation of the evidence, particularly the film itself, which is a responsibility of fact-finders, typically the jury, the Supreme Court suddenly converted it into a matter of law on which the opinion of Supreme Court justices is determinative.

A third major change in the anti-obscenity legal principles was made by the Court majority in this 1964 decision. Suddenly the Court majority held that the presence of explicit sex, no matter how lewd or lascivious, is not obscene, as long as it deals with that explicit sex "in a manner that advocates ideas" or has "any other form of social importance."[758] This standard totally departed from the standard in the English decision, *Regina v. Hicklin*, that had been the basis for our Supreme Court decisions until after the mid-20th century. Recall that the printed work declared criminal in *Hicklin* was a pamphlet "for the purpose of exposing what [the defendant] deemed to be the errors of the Church of Rome, and particularly the immorality of the confessional."[759] That was certainly an advocacy of an idea on a matter of social importance. Yet, that pamphlet was held criminal because the sexual descriptions "would most likely suggest ... thoughts of a most impure and libidinous character," and thus have "the tendency to corrupt the minds and morals into whose hands it might come."[760]

Without viewing the text of the confessions found to make the pamphlet obscene in that early English case, it is easy now to question the fairness of that decision and criminal prosecution. But it is clear that for over 150 years the rule enunciated in that case was the accepted law of this land, as it had been almost 100 years before when our Framers wrote and enacted both the Constitution and the First Amendment. And there was good reason for it, and good reason against the Supreme Court majority's 20th century rejection of that rule. Take this example: A hard-core pornographic film, by itself, would be banned, and a defendant who had distributed it validly convicted. But camouflage it with the title "Understanding Why Pornography Is Harmful," add a preface explaining the adverse consequences of pornography, perhaps with apt references to the events in the film, conclude with a short summation that also refers to the film, and suddenly a hard-core pornographic film is converted into a lawful advocacy of ideas on a matter of social importance, and thus protected by the First Amendment. That is the reality of this new test imposed by the Supreme Court majority. And then that hard-core pornography, with all its adverse impact on the young and impressionable, could easily be sold for profit-making.

This major revision of the rules the Supreme Court had been applying since its first court session turned out not to be enough to open fully the flood gates to obscenity. In order to reach the 1966 majority decision allowing distribution of *Woman Of Pleasure*, the majority had to fiddle again with the test they had just prescribed in 1964. To understand this, what I would call, incredible decision, both on the facts and in its disregard of over a century and a half of law in this country, we should analyze a little more carefully the standard applied in the preceding 1964 decision: "'whether to the average person, applying contemporary community standards, the dominant theme of the material taken as a whole appeals to prurient interest.'"[761] The definition of "prurient" is "arousing, or appealing to, sexual desire."[762] It is therefore a synonym of "erotic," which too is defined as "tending to arouse sexual ... desire."[763] Hence, since one of the majority justices conceded that the book was erotic and the Court's opinion itself recognized that it may have prurient appeal and be patently offensive – descriptions obvious from the contents of the book – by every prior decision, the Massachusetts courts' ban of the book should have been affirmed. But the Supreme Court instead reversed the Massachusetts courts.

For that result, this Court majority again revised the test to hold that a "book cannot be proscribed unless it is found to be *utterly* without redeeming social value."[764] Hence, in just a period of 10 years, a Supreme Court majority had thrice totally altered and emasculated the impact part of the test for determining obscenity: At all times before 1957, the accepted test required only that the material "suggest or convey lewd thoughts and lascivious thoughts to the young or inexperienced."[765] Under that test, the presence of any material amount of lewd and lascivious descriptions or pictures supported a finding of obscenity. Then, in 1957, the majority of the justices asserted that the test had been altered so that no longer would a matter be obscene on the basis of any material amount being lewd and lascivious; instead, the matter would not be obscene unless the "dominant theme of the material taken as a whole appeals to prurient interest."[766] But the majority was not satisfied that the law's ability to restrict obscenity had been sufficiently emasculated. Thus, in 1966, it rescinded the "dominant theme" quantification and held that a book may not be considered as obscene, no matter how much of it is obscene and appeals to the prurient interest, unless "it is found to be *utterly* without redeeming social value."[767] That imposed a virtually impossible burden to meet; what this meant is that pure pornography could be published and sold, as long as it is sandwiched between words purporting to provide a lesson with social value.

The anti-obscenity laws have thus become a paper tiger. And this total alteration was accomplished by this small number of people, who happen to compose a majority of justices of the Supreme Court. There had been no amendment of the Constitution to alter the legal structure these justices were sworn to apply. There was not even any indication of popular change of view on anti-obscenity laws; in fact, every state and Congress had continued support of these laws. But these justices made these changes to result in the emasculation of the anti-obscenity laws that Americans are now required to endure.

So what is the message that our Supreme Court is sending to Americans on their moral standards? Is it that lewd, raunchy, profane and ribald "entertainment" is acceptable? It certainly appears to be the teaching of these decisions. Is the Supreme Court's teaching inconsistent with those of other organs of government? Look at this example: In January 2011, well-commended U.S. Navy Captain Owen Honors, commanding officer of a nuclear aircraft carrier, was relieved of his duties (a Navy euphemism for being fired) because he showed his crew videos described as lewd, raunchy, profane and ribald.[768] If the Supreme Court allows such entertainment for any person, even for children, to view, why was this Navy captain fired for providing this type of entertainment for sailors while on the sea for substantial periods, away from family and loved ones. Does this suggest that our military is more in tune than the Supreme Court with the high moral standard that our forefathers expected of this country?

I hasten to note that the Court itself has recognized that it has gone too far in castrating anti-obscenity laws. With the departure of certain justices and the addition of new ones, the Court, for a short time, partially reversed course with decisions strengthening the government's ability to prevent distribution of obscene matter. In 1973, in an opinion by the newly appointed Chief Justice Warren Burger,[769] the Court by a 5-4 vote upheld a conviction for soliciting purchasers of books by the use of brochures that primarily "consist of pictures and drawings very explicitly depicting men and women in groups of two or more engaging in a variety of sexual activities, with genitals often primarily displayed," and that provided a sample of the contents of books bearing titles such as "Intercourse," "Man-Woman," and "Sex Orgies Illustrated."[770]

To affirm this conviction, the Court rescinded some, but not all, of the changes it had recently made to the obscenity test. It rejected the "*utterly* without social value" test as "a burden virtually impossible to" meet.[771] Also, it expressly stated that states had the right to bar matter as obscene if it "carries with it a significant danger of offending the sensibilities of unwilling recipients or of exposure to juveniles."[772] But, in the end, rather inconsistently, it kept the recent decade's changes that determined obscenity by the effect on "the average person," of whether "the work, taken as a whole, ... lacks serious literary, artistic, political, or scientific value."[773] The Court, however, never reconciled the states' right to bar a book with portions that carry "a significant danger of offending sensibilities of" some people – a states' right affirmed in the opinion – with the requirement that the book must be "taken as a whole." That latter requirement strongly suggested that most books that include vivid sex as part of an otherwise non-sexual plot still may not be barred.

This majority opinion also made clear that the "community" standard that the jury or judge must apply in deciding whether the matter is obscene is the local community, not a nationwide standard, recognizing there is no single nationwide standard. Rather, the Court defined "community" in this standard as the state in which the material is distributed.[774]

You may readily ask: Are we and our children protected against a tidal wave of obscenity? The answer is that we have much less protection than the authors of our Constitution believed to be needed, proper and constitutional. Even more troubling is that a change of but one or two votes on the Court could re-open the obscenity flood gates, either by accepting the dissenters' view that the First Amendment bars any restriction of obscenity or by further emasculation of the obscenity test to make it impossible to apply.

XIII.

HOW RECENT SUPREME COURT DECISIONS HAVE FURTHER DEGRADED MORALITY IN AMERICA

Easing of pornographic creation and distribution, sadly, is not the only means the Supreme Court has authorized to reduce American moral standards. Here are several other subjects that have recently been allowed to adversely affect our country's moral climate:

Allowing Obscenity To Violate Our Privacy

In many of the earlier obscenity cases, both justices upholding obscenity laws and those who dissented repeatedly made clear that erotic material may not be shown or distributed in such manner that any person is deprived of his choice not to see it. For example, Justices William J. Brennan Jr., Potter Stewart and Thurgood Marshall, although dissenting from a decision sustaining Georgia's right to ban two obscene films, agreed that a "'communication of [erotic material], imposed upon a person contrary to his wishes, has all the characteristics of a physical assault'" and "constitutes an invasion of his privacy."[775] Even where the Court had reversed obscenity convictions, it noted that the decision would be different if the obscenity had been "an assault upon individual privacy by publication in a manner so obtrusive as to make it impossible for an unwilling individual to avoid exposure to it."[776]

What display of nudity would be more realistically "impossible for an unwilling individual to avoid exposure to" than a film shown at a drive-in movie that can readily be seen by drivers, and passengers including children, on the adjacent road or while stopped for a red light? Apparently recognizing that reality, the City of Jacksonville enacted an ordinance that prohibited showing nudity by a drive-in theater when the screen is visible from a public street. A theater manager was charged with violating the law in showing a movie in which "female buttocks and bare breasts were shown" on the large screen that was "visible from two adjacent public streets and a nearby church parking lot."[777] Despite all these earlier Court declarations to the contrary, a majority of the justices held that the city had no right to prevent such public showing of nudity.

Indeed, only about 25 years before, the Court had expressly affirmed the right to protect passers-by from being forced to hear anything – not limited to obscenity or nudity – they did not come to hear. In so ruling, the Court noted the vast difference between the "passer-by who may be offered a pamphlet in the street but cannot be made to take it," and when he is "on the street, ... practically helpless to escape this interference with his privacy."[778] Forty-three years before, a unanimous Court, in an opinion written by Justice Brandeis, also enforced the public right to regulate billboard displays that would not be constitutional if applied to other forms of advertising. As Justice Brandeis put it, "[t]he radio can be turned off, but not so the billboard or street car placard, ... to be seen without the exercise of choice or volition."[779] Note that Justice Brandeis did not credit that, as a physical fact, no one was forcing any person to put and keep one's eyes on the billboard or streetcar placard. The reason is obvious: It is natural that a person will view whatever is placed within his vision and not realize its distaste until after having seen and realized what it is. Ignoring this earlier decision, and its obvious logic, the majority in this Jacksonville ordinance case applied a physical impossibility – that it did not invade anyone's privacy because "an offended viewer" could "avert his eyes from such without seeing it"[780] Disregarding that it was impossible for a "viewer" to become "offended" "without seeing it;" to become offended by what is on the screen, one would have to have seen enough of what was forced on him (and any child with him) to know that it offended.

The illogic of the majority's decision that the Jacksonville ordinance was unconstitutional is readily understood. It boggles the mind that these justices could write with a straight face that someone could avert his eyes from the display of nudity without seeing it, and therefore having cause to avert his eyes. Moreover, no explanation is even attempted as to how the parent walking or driving past with his child – whom even these justices conceded that the state has "police power to protect"[781] – is supposed to be able to avert that child's eyes when nudity is displayed on that large screen.

Next, the majority held the ordinance objectionable because the statute "does not protect citizens from all movies that might offend," but "rather singles out films containing nudity, presumably because the lawmakers considered them especially offensive to passersby." Based on that, the Court majority concluded that the First Amendment does not allow the government "selectively to shield the public from some kind of speech on the ground that they are more offensive than others."[782]

> *"The Court majority concluded that the First Amendment does not allow the government 'selectively to shield the public from some kind of speech on the ground that they are more offensive than others.'"*

Are these justices thereby

suggesting that the First Amendment would be better served by shutting the theater entirely, to avoid traffic and privacy-invasion issues, rather than precluding only films with nudity? That throw-out-the-baby-with-the-dirty-bathwater conclusion is unacceptable nonsense.

Then, these justices held the statute unconstitutional because it also barred nudity which would apply to "scenes from a culture in which nudity is indigenous."[783] But the government's right to police what is imposed on non-consenting viewers by exhibiting it on a public movie screen is no different from that right to regulate similar exhibition live on a public street. No one would question the constitutionality of a New York prohibition against nudity in Times Square, even when exhibited by a culture in which nudity is indigenous. As Chief Justice Burger reasoned in his dissenting opinion, "[a] nudist colony ... cannot lawfully set up shop in Central Park or Lafayette Park, places established for the public generally."[784]

These majority justices also questioned the efficacy on traffic issues of barring nudity, explaining that "[t]here is no reason to think that a wide variety of other scenes in the customary screen diet, ranging from soap opera to violence, would be less distracting to the passing motorist." However, they admitted, even if scenes of two fully clothed men or women talking might also distract, the court has "frequently upheld underinclusive classifications on the sound theory that a legislature may deal with one part of a problem without addressing all of it."[785]

Beyond that, one has to question either the honesty or libido of these (all male) justices. They cannot be serious that seeing an attractive nude body would not be more distracting than viewing a conversation in a soap opera that could not be heard, or even witnessing some on-screen violence. Finally, they ignored the court's prior decision upholding restrictions on public speaking with sound amplifiers on the streets of Trenton, New Jersey, as a then reasonable exercise of police power, allowing the legislature the right to determine it could be "dangerous to traffic" on the business streets and disturb "in the residential thoroughfares the quiet and tranquility."[786] If denial of the use of a means needed to communicate political or religious views is constitutional, a bar to communicating nudity without intending to communicate a message must also be constitutional.

Child Pornography

Even after some justices voiced permissiveness for adult pornography and obscenity, the justices remained unanimous for some years in affirming the state's right to regulate and criminalize child pornography. For example, Justices Brennan and Marshall, both of whom frequently voted to insulate obscenity from government prohibitions, agreed that the "State has a special interest in protecting the well-being of our youth," that "afford[s] the State the leeway to regulate pornographic material, the promotion of which is harmful to children," that they would not authorize as to non-child pornography.[787] In one Court opinion, justices wrote that "the interests underlying child pornography prohibitions far exceed the interests justifying" adult pornography laws.[788]

Yet, even with child pornography, some of the justices soon interjected the First Amendment free speech provision to bar successful prosecution. In 2002, a six-justice majority held unconstitutional a federal statute that banned "virtual child pornography" – defined to cover all means used to create sexually explicit images that appear to depict minors in lewd and obscene activities, but not necessarily involving the casting of a minor. In fact, they include innocent images of real children that had been altered to make them appear to be engaged in sexual activity, adults who looked like minors, and computer-created images that looked real-life.[789] While the young-looking-adult casting and the computer-generated look-real child pornography films did not portray actual children, the objective in making them was to sell them as child pornography and, when well-made, would cause all viewers to see them as indistinguishable from child pornography. And where pictures of actual youth were altered to have them appear to be engaged in sexual activity, they were in fact children.

Recognizing that such virtual child pornography is indistinguishable by the naked eye from child pornography actually involving minors, Congress enacted the statute because of undisputed findings that such pornography could only result in encouraging a greater volume of child pornography. There was no doubt of the factual support for these findings. An earlier Attorney General's Commission on Pornography had found that "child pornography is often used as part of a method of seducing child victims" – a "child who is reluctant to engage in sexual activity with an adult or to pose for sexually explicit photos can sometimes be convinced by viewing other children 'having fun' participating in the activity."[790] Hence, Congress rightfully concluded that pedophiles could "use these materials to encourage children to participate in sexual activity."[791] If adults cannot distinguish between real children and virtual children engaged in pornography, then clearly a child being seduced to engage in child pornography cannot. And thus, such virtual child pornography is as deleterious to children as real child pornography and should be halted for the same reasons.

Congress specified a second reason why it criminalized virtual child pornography: as the technology to make virtual child pornography has been improved, "it becomes more difficult to prove that a particular picture was produced using children,"[792] thus making prosecution of pornographers, actually using children, more difficult.

In voiding this statute, this majority of the Court disregarded more than a century of its own decisions and thereby further lubricated the entry of more pornography, here, even child porn, into circulation. What is most disturbing is that, as already noted, up to this case even those justices who regularly dissented on prohibiting adult obscenity had recognized the right of legislatures to impede the child pornography industry.

Also, as already noted, Congress, in enacting this statute, made clear that it was doing so to protect children. The Court majority disagreed with Congress' reasoning, and on that basis voided the statute. By what authority did the Court substitute its views for those of Congress as to whether this statute would help protect children and reduce child pornography? There is no such authority, and the Court cites none. Indeed, it violated its own legal axiom, repeatedly pronounced and reaffirmed since the outset of this Court. For example, in 1876, the Court explained that, as to "the propriety of legislative interference ..., the legislature is the exclusive judge."[793] Again, in 1905, the Court reiterated that principle:

> "It is no part of the function of a court ... to determine which one of two modes was likely to be the most effective for the protection of the public .... That was for the legislative department to determine in the light of all the information it had or could obtain."[794]

The Court went even further to make clear that "the judgment of the legislature must prevail, though it be controverted and opposed by arguments of strength."[795]

Based on its required respect for the legislature's judgment on how best to protect the public welfare, the Court has upheld legislation that was analogous to the virtual child pornography statute. In an 1887 case, the Supreme Court reviewed a Kansas legislature's decision that, to prevent the manufacture and sale of intoxicating beverages, it had to prevent the manufacture of intoxicating beverages by any individual for his own consumption, even if not for sale. The Court upheld that legislative judgment in words directly applicable to the virtual child pornography production (bracketed words added for clarity):

"If such manufacture does prejudicially affect the rights and interests of the community [to eradicate child pornography], it follows ... that society has the power to protect itself, by legislation, against the injurious consequences of ... [the virtual child pornography] business. .... Under our system that power is lodged with the legislative branch of the government. It belongs to that department to exert what are known as the police powers of the state, and to determine, primarily, what measures are appropriate or needful for the protection of the public morals, the public health, or the public safety."[796]

Beyond the Court's power-grab assumption of the legislative power, the reasons it gave for rejecting Congress' judgment in enacting it are obviously fallacious. First, this Court majority reasoned that it is not so terrible that the virtual pictures show "what appear to be 17-year-olds engaging in sexually explicit activity" as it is "undeniable that some youths engage in sexual activity before the legal age, either on their own inclination or because they are victims of sexual abuse."[797] Having already accepted in this majority opinion "the State's particular and ... compelling interest in prosecuting those who promote the sexual exploitation of children,"[798] it is not rational so casually to accept sexual activity of minors, particularly if they are victims of sexual abuse. Moreover, the legislature's proper attempt to lift the standards practiced by some young people cannot be denied merely because others are practicing a lower unacceptable standard.

Continuing along the Court's rejection of the standard the legislature has set in favor of the lowest-common-denominator contrary practices by some, these justices point to the portrayal of sexual activities by minors in contemporary movies:

"Last year's Academy Awards featured the movie, Traffic, which was nominated for Best Picture. .... The film portrayed a teenager, identified as a 16-year-old, who became addicted to drugs, ..., which in the end leads her to a filthy room to trade sex for drugs. The year before, American Beauty won the Academy Award for Best picture. .... In the course of the movie, a teenage girl engages in sexual relations with her teenage boyfriend, and another yields herself to the gratification of a middle-aged man."[799]

It is incredible that Supreme Court justices would look to Hollywood, over Congress, to determine what is in the public's best interest. We all know that Hollywood has filled movies with gun killings, knifings, bombings, and much more violence. Because such movies are popular does not mean that Congress, and the courts, must allow people in real life to engage in such conduct. Nor do movie portrayals of sexual escapades of the young deny Congress its right, and its responsibility, to seek a better life for our young.

The Court also rejected Congress' finding that the prohibition of virtual child pornography was necessary to prevent pedophiles from inducing children to engage in sexual activity. Despite the legal rule that it is Congress, not the courts, that determine the value of legislation, these justices substituted their different judgment from that voted by Congress. These justices found the "causal link" between the virtual child pornography and "actual instances of child abuse" to be "contingent and indirect" because the "harm does not necessarily follow from the" exhibited virtual child pornography, "but depends upon some unquantified potential for subsequent criminal acts."[800]

> *"It has always been held that Congress has the right to proscribe the cause of a harm that it concludes is more important to prevent than other possible causes."*

Dissecting this long rationalization for rejecting Congress' judgment shows how incredible it is. These justices, by asserting that harm does "not necessarily follow," thereby admit that harm can follow from the use of virtual child pornography. Certainly, that harm may occur, even if not on every occasion, is sufficient basis for Congress to act to prevent those occasions of harm. Moreover, the rather ambiguous words that harm is dependent "upon some unquantified potential for subsequent criminal acts," actually means only the truism that the harm of inducing a child to engage in sexual activity does not automatically occur by showing the virtual child pornography. Congress never suggested otherwise. Rather, Congress concluded that showing a minor virtual child pornography images would soften the child up to accept the criminal act of then inducing the child to engage in a sexual act.

These justices' final basis for rejecting Congress' judgment that the statute was "necessary because pedophiles may use virtual child pornography to seduce children," is even more ludicrous. The Court opinion points to "many things innocent in themselves, such as cartoons, video games, and candy, that might be used for immoral purposes, yet we would not expect them to be prohibited because they can be misused."[801] Even if there were anything seriously valid in this statement, it would have no effect, as it has always been held that Congress has the right to proscribe the cause of a harm that it concludes is more important to prevent than other possible causes. Moreover, unlike candy and the other examples of "innocent" causation, child pornography, even virtual, is not innocent, but a portrayal of what these very justices wrote in their opinion is a "vice" that "the State was justified in attempting to stamp out."[802]

The obvious lack of validity to any of the Court's rationale for holding this statute unconstitutional leads to the only reasonable conclusion: that this was a continuation of certain justices' slippery slope to allow "anything goes," rather than protecting societal morality.

Profanity On Public Airwaves

In a unanimous 1969 decision, the Supreme Court expressly recognized the right of the government to regulate broadcasters' use of the public airwaves to protect "the right of the public to receive … esthetic, moral, and other ideas and experiences."[803] For this purpose, the Federal Communications Commission ("FCC") was created as "more than a traffic policeman concerned with the technical aspects of broadcasting," but to interest "itself in general program format and the kind of programs broadcast by licensees," and thereby assure that a broadcaster's programming serves "the public interest."[804]

In an earlier 1943 decision, the Court had similarly declared that broadcasters are "licensed to serve the public interest," and responsible to ensure operation "in the public interest … in accordance with the express requirements of the" statute and regulations adopted by the FCC "to carry out the provisions of" the statute. [805]

To ensure that the broadcasts that the public receives are appropriately esthetic and moral, the statute that Congress enacted prohibited any licensed broadcaster on radio and television from allowing utterance of "any obscene, indecent, or profane language."[806] The FCC, assigned responsibility for enforcing this statute, defined "indecent speech" as "language that describes, in terms patently offensive as measured by contemporary community standards for the broadcast medium, sexual or excretory activities or organs at times of the day when there is a reasonable risk that children may be in the audience."[807] In layman's terms, prohibited were four-letter words, such as the F-word and the S-word that most families would not allow be uttered at the family dinner table when children were present.

The Supreme Court later explained the purpose of the law and Congress' power to enact it:

"Patently offensive, indecent material presented over the airwaves confronts the citizen, not only in public, but also in the privacy of the home, where the individual's right to be left alone plainly outweighs the First Amendment rights of an intruder. ... Because the broadcast audience is constantly tuning in and out, prior warnings cannot completely protect the listener or viewer from unexpected program content. To say that one may avoid further offense by turning off the radio when he hears indecent language is like saying that the remedy for an assault is to run away after the first blow. One may hang up on an indecent phone call, but that option does not give the caller the constitutional immunity or avoid a harm that has already taken place."[808]

The Court continued its explanation of the rightful purpose of the statute by pointing out that radio is particularly available to children of even very young age. Referring to the government's responsibility to protect the "well-being of its youth," and "parents' claim to authority" over their children, it held that this statute and FCC regulation were justified to meet those objectives.[809]

The issue again came to the Supreme Court after a New York radio station, owned by Pacifica Foundation, on a 1973 Tuesday afternoon broadcast a 12-minute recorded monologue by a satiric humorist, George Carlin, entitled "Seven Words You Can Never Say on Television." The monologue began with Carlin's thoughts about "the words you couldn't say on the public, ah, airwaves," which he then "proceeded to list ... and repeat over and over again." A man, who heard this broadcast while driving with his young son, complained to the FCC, which, after review of the facts, held that the broadcast violated the statute.[810] This decision was consistent with a long line of Supreme Court cases, mentioned above, upholding the government's power - indeed, responsibility - to protect "the right of the public to receive ... esthetic [and] moral material."

While that line of cases has not been overruled by the Court, what is startling, and frankly scary, is that the Court upheld the FCC decision by only a 5-4 vote. Thus, a change of only one vote on the Supreme Court would open the floodgates to broadcast obscenities. In 2009, the Court again voiced support for the right of the FCC to sanction broadcasters that allowed obscenity to be broadcast during hours, when children will likely be listening, but again by a very close 5-4 division of the Court.[811] The FCC had found the broadcaster of the 2003 Billboard Music Awards had not prevented Nicole Richie from broadcasting the S-word and the F-word. This broadcaster had effectively been forewarned of this problem, as it had produced the 2000 event at which the singer Cher had also used the F-word.[812] Following both of these incidents, numerous parents, whose children had been exposed to the language, complained to the FCC.[813] The FCC found these violations particularly troubling because "they were aired during prime-time awards shows 'designed to draw a large nationwide audience that could be expected to include many children interested in seeing their favorite music stars'" – a prediction proven true by the about "2.5 million minors who watched each of the broadcasts."[814]

The fact that children would be watching spotlighted the FCC's responsibility to take action and thereby signal to broadcasters the requirement that they must prevent any repetition. "Congress has made the determination that indecent material is harmful to children." A bare majority of the Court agreed on the grounds, hard to dispute, that "children mimic the behavior they observe—or at least the behavior that is presented to them as normal and appropriate." Therefore, the "government's interest in the 'well-being of its youth' ... justified [this] regulation."[815] Although the Supreme Court explicitly declined to decide its constitutionality in order to allow the lower court first to consider that issue,[816] the language employed by the majority all but said that it was constitutional: "[barring] references to excretory and sexual material 'surely lie at the periphery of First Amendment concern.'"[817]

As noted, the Supreme Court was only one vote away from holding that the FCC could not enforce its rule that implemented Congress' direction that it prevent radio and television from being inundated with four-letter profanities. The reasoning expressed by those in the opposing camp is telling in its reliance on a lowest-common-denominator standard. One of the four dissenters pooh-poohed the presence of obscenities on the public airwaves by calling them "the stuff of everyday conversations."[818] The lower appellate court, whose decision overturning the FCC's action was reversed by the Supreme Court, commented that it was "skeptical that the Commission can provide a reasoned explanation ... that would pass constitutional muster" because "children today 'likely hear this language far more often from other sources than they did in the 1970's when the Commission first began sanctioning indecent speech.'"[819] Both convey nothing more than a defeatist view that Congress and the FCC cannot succeed in their aim of providing "conscientious parents a relatively safe haven for their children" to listen to acceptable programming.[820] Being so negative here makes as little sense as considering an increase in juvenile crime as a reason for not taking extra steps to reduce the crime rate.

Another dissenter used slightly different reasoning, while also relying on the supposed current norms. According to Justice Stevens, the prevalent use of the S-word, in such places as a golf course when the golfer shanks a short approach, means that it was not being used to describe excrement, the required category under the FCC regulation in order for it to be prohibited.[821] This argument demonstrates how removed from reality those who favor opening the flood gates to obscenity must go. What else but "excrement" did Justice Stevens conceive the S-word meant? If he did not know, a quick visit to the dictionary would have shown that "excrement" is the first definition provided.[822] Justice Stevens was certainly correct, but his reasoning spurious, that this hypothetical golfer was using the S-word to express an emotion. Some people who are not prone to use obscenities might in that golfing circumstance utter "darn it" or "oh, my God"; the obscenity-prone golfer, however, would use the S-word because it describes his golf shot as foul waste – the meaning of "excrement."

But all of these dissenting rationalizations ignore the crux of the issue: Do parents have the right to teach their children that use of these four-letter words in civilized social conversation, including at the family dinner table or in church, synagogue or mosque, is unacceptable? If the answer is yes – and I believe all would agree that is the parents' right – then the government, through Congress and the FCC, is within its right to support that parental right by denying a stamp of approval to the use of such words in family entertainment. The Constitution denies the Supreme Court any right to interfere with that Congressional and administrative exercise of judgment. That four Supreme Court Justices voted to assume that power once again highlights for America the danger facing this country from Supreme Court Justices who seek to impose their personal views of what the law should be for what the Constitution and Congress have mandated what the law is.

Commercialization of Animal Torture and Cruelty

People seek to make money on the distribution of depictions of animal torture and cruelty. An example of these, what are called, "crush videos":

> "A kitten, secured to the ground, watches and shrieks in pain as a woman thrusts her high-heeled shoe into its body, slams her heel into the kitten's eye socket and mouth loudly fracturing its skull, and stomps repeatedly on the animal's head. The kitten hemorrhages blood, screams blindly in

pain, and is ultimately left dead in a moist pile of blood-soaked hair and bone."[823]

Another example of this type of for-profit films, entitled "Catch Dogs And Country Living," depicts "the use of pit bulls to hunt wild boar, as well as a 'gruesome' scene of a pit bull attacking a domestic farm pig."[824]

One doesn't have to be an animal lover – I confess that I am – to regard such films as disgusting, vile and sadistic. And certainly, it is very difficult to assert that these films "are [an] essential part of any exposition of ideas, and are of such [meaningful] social value as a step to truth that any benefit that may be derived from them is [not] clearly outweighed by the social interest in order and morality" – the test that the Supreme Court, 70 years ago, unanimously held must be established for a film or any other communication to be protected by the First Amendment.[825]

Congress enacted a statute that criminalized the "creation, sale, or possession" of depictions "in which a living animal is intentionally maimed, mutilated, tortured, wounded, or killed," if it is illegal under federal or state law where "the creation, sale, or possession takes place," and the depiction is devoid of any "serious religious, political, scientific, educational, journalistic, historical, or artistic value."[826] In support of this statute, Congress found that these depictions "appeal to persons with a very specific sexual fetish who find them sexually arousing or otherwise exciting,"[827] and, having considered the First Amendment issue, found that "'depictions of animals being intentionally tortured or killed are of such minimal redeeming value as to render them unworthy of First Amendment protection.'"[828]

This congressional statute, aimed to stop animal cruelty in this country by criminalizing the means of making a profit on its depiction, was far from the first statutory proscription of animal cruelty. The prohibition of animal cruelty itself in American law dates from the early settlement of the colonies. For example, in

1641, the Massachusetts Bay Colony outlawed "any Tirranny or Crueltie towards any bruite Creature which are usually kept for man's use."[829] All 50 states and the District of Columbia have laws that prohibit the acts typically shown in these crush videos.[830]

The Supreme Court considered the constitutionality of this statute in an appeal involving a jury conviction of a man who ran a business, entitled "Dogs of Velvet and Steel," with an associated web site through which he sold these films.[831] The Court, by a vote of 8-1, held the statute unconstitutional, thereby freeing the defendant whom the jury convicted and the trial judge had sentenced to be imprisoned for 37 months, followed by three years of supervised release.[832]

I am certain that you are asking on what basis those eight justices decided to assist the animal cruelty industry. I choose those words very carefully since no justice disputed the obvious, that the industry of making and selling the films recording the animal cruelty is the major profit-making vehicle for any animal cruelty; without this mass distribution method, animal cruelty would be limited to the few, and much less remunerative, small local rings that local police are more likely to discover and prosecute. The gruesome torture and killings of animals for the crush films need no audience, can be done in private and thus not readily known to local police, because the means of making money on them – the inducement to engage in such tortures – is the wholesale sale of the films recording the horror.

First, the majority justices admitted, but turned on its head, the fact that the Court has always recognized exceptions to the First Amendment free speech protection, including for obscenity, defamation, fraud and incitement. According to the majority's reasoning, because depictions of animal cruelty had not previously been included, it should not be included now.[833] These justices ambiguously write that "[f]rom 1791 to the present" categories of exceptions have been permitted, but "never 'includ[ing] a freedom to disregard these traditional limitations."[834] Except for arbitrarily so stating, these justices offer no reason for this decision. Moreover, their own opinion demonstrates the falsity of their assertion, that "from 1791" the Court had not added to the categories exempt from the First Amendment. They specifically include in the "traditional limitations" on First Amendment protection, categories with dates that had been added long after 1791, as, for example "fraud ... (1976), and incitement ... (1969)."

Further, crush movies and their means of wholesale distribution through a website could not have been envisaged when the First Amendment was adopted in 1791. That does not mean that crush movies, having, as all the justices concede, no redeeming social value, must now be granted First Amendment protection. Rather, it requires that the justices determine the application of the First Amendment as its authors would have applied it to this new category of crush movies. Just as the Court determined that the First Amendment did not insulate child pornography films – an industry not existing in 1791 – it was not precluded by the First Amendment from holding that animal torture crush films were not insulated.

The second ground used by the majority justices is that the statute is unconstitutionally overbroad in that it could be construed to criminalize hunting that is legal in most, if not all, states.[835] But the statute the justices declared unconstitutional on this ground expressly excludes any conduct that is lawful "where the creation, sale, or possession takes place." It also exempts from the statute's prohibition any depiction with "serious religious, political, scientific, educational, journalistic, historical, or artistic value." The majority's speculation that some prosecution might occur that would be unfair – which if it did occur would be stopped in its tracks by the judge, jury and appellate courts – hardly warrants throwing out this excellent-purpose, morality-enhancing statute in its entirety.

Violent Video Games For Minors

What do you think of marketing to minors the means to kill "[v]ictims by the dozens ... with every imaginable implement, including machine guns, clubs, hammers, axes, swords, and chainsaws," with victims being "dismembered, decapitated, disemboweled, set on fire, and chopped into little pieces," resulting in the victims' "cry[ing] out in agony and beg[ging] for mercy?" Then the minors are able to see that the victims' "[b]lood gushes, splatters, and [collects in] pools," with "[s]evered body parts and gobs of human remains [being] graphically shown." Or how about a product that induces a minor to "take on the identity and reenact the killings carried out by the perpetrators of the murders at Columbine High School and Virginia Tech?" Or what about others that allow a minor "to rape a mother and her daughters, ... rape Native American women, ... engage in 'ethnic cleansing' ... choose to gun down African-Americans, Latinos, or Jews, ... [or to] fire a rifle shot into the head of President Kennedy as his motorcade passes by the Texas School Book Depository?"

All of these[836] – and many more – video games are marketed to youth that induce minors to assume the role of purveyor of bloody violence, sexual assaults, mass racial attacks and many other horrible criminal acts that are prohibited by law, as well as unacceptable to any civilized moral society.

The California legislature saw in these violent games what two Supreme Court justices described "as a potentially serious social problem: the effect of exceptionally violent video games on impressionable minors, who often spend countless hours immersed in the alternative worlds that these games create."[837] To solve that problem, California enacted a statute that makes it a crime to sell or rent "a violent video game to a minor," excepting if "sold or rented to a minor by the minor's parent, grandparent, aunt, uncle, or legal guardian."[838] Further, to prevent convicting someone who reasonably believed that the purchaser was not a minor, the statute provided for a defense of reasonable reliance on evidence such as a driver's license.[839] The term "violent video game" was carefully defined as one in which (i) "the range of options available to a player includes killing, maiming, dismembering, or sexually assaulting an image of a human being," and (ii) "the game enables the player to virtually inflict serious injury upon images of human beings or characters with substantially human characteristics in a manner which is especially heinous, cruel, or depraved in that it involves torture or serious physical abuse to the victim."[840] Further defining the term, the California legislature included a paraphrase of the definition previously approved by the Supreme Court for obscenity:[841] to be a "violent video game," it must meet each of three criteria:

> "(i) A reasonable person, considering the game as a whole, would find [it] appeals to a deviant or morbid interest of minors;
>
> "(ii) It is patently offensive to prevailing standards in the community as to what is suitable for minors;
>
> "(iii) It causes the game, as a whole, to lack serious literary, artistic, political, or scientific value for minors."[842]

The California legislature had good reason for seeking to prevent youth, without parental involvement, having access to such violent games. Video games are "excellent teaching tools," regularly used for positive training purposes, because they "can help develop habits, accustom the player to performance of the task and reward the player for performing that task well."[843] That practice and habit-forming in driving a car for a new driver, or flying a plane for a pilot-cadet in the Air Force, for example, contributes to a worthwhile aim.

But training a child in proficiency in killing, maiming, torturing, and sexual assault is not a worthwhile societal aim. Playing violent video games is training to engage in prohibited and criminal acts in real life. Respected research substantiates the California Legislature's judgment that a statute barring minors' easy access to them would assist in maintaining the health and safety of its citizens. Research found "that increased exposure to video games causes an increase in aggression. …. Experimental studies in laboratories have found that subjects randomly assigned to play a violent video game subsequently displayed more characteristics of aggression than those who played nonviolent games. …. Surveys of 8th and 9th grade students have found a correlation between playing violent games and aggression. …. Cutting-edge neuroscience has shown that 'virtual violence in video game playing results in those neural patterns that are considered characteristic for aggressive cognition and behavior.' …. '[M]eta-analyses,' i.e., studies of all the studies, have concluded that exposure to violent video games 'was positively associated with aggressive behavior, aggressive cognition, and aggressive affect,' and that 'playing violent video games is a causal risk factor for long-term harmful outcomes.'"[844]

> "(The) majority held that video games are subject to First Amendment free speech protection as they 'communicate ideas.' But so does punching another person in the face communicate the idea of dislike. Yet, no one would suggest that the First Amendment immunized punching someone you don't like."

All relevant professional societies endorsed these conclusions: the American Academy of Pediatrics, American Academy of Child & Adolescent Psychiatry, American Psychological Association, American Medical Association, American Academy Of Family

Physicians and American Psychiatric Association. In 2000, they issued a joint statement reporting that "over 1000 studies point overwhelmingly to a causal connection between media violence and aggressive behavior in some children," with "the impact of violent interactive entertainment (video games ...) on young people ... significantly more severe than that wrought by television, movies, or music."[845] The American Academy of Pediatrics issued a supplementary statement in 2009 that more recent studies "have revealed that in as little as 3 months, high exposure to violent video games increased physical aggression."[846]

One would have thought that when the constitutionality of this California statute reached the Supreme Court, it would be a no-brainer that it would be upheld. After all, it was addressed to the protection of minors, previously recognized by the Court as a group appropriate for special protection: "a State's interest in 'safeguarding the physical and psychological well-being of a minor' is 'compelling.'"[847] Also, the statute paraphrased language that the Court had previously ruled made an anti-obscenity statute constitutional, and no one disputed that the California legislature had good reason to seek to limit minors from easy access to violent video games.

Shockingly, however, the Court, by a 7-2 vote, held the statute unconstitutional, and thus allowed minors free access to these violent video games.

First, this majority held that video games are subject to First Amendment free speech protection as they "communicate ideas." But so does punching another person in the face communicate the idea of dislike. Yet, no one would suggest that the First Amendment immunized punching someone you don't like. The video game communicates the idea of punching, killing, torturing, rape, etc., all of which, like an actual "simple" punch, is criminal conduct not protected by the First Amendment. The Court opinion rationalizes its ruling by indicating that books that describe violence are protected by the First Amendment.[848] But there is a vast difference in degree between reading about violence and partaking in it as the actor in a simulation of despicably violent conduct. Certainly, that vast difference allows the legislature to exercise its judgment that violent video games are a problem that must be addressed.

The majority also invoked the reasoning it had used to strike down the federal anti-animal-cruelty law: that the subject had not previously been held by the Court to be exempt from free speech protection.[849] That is as much a lame excuse here as it was in connection with the animal cruelty statute. Of course, the authors of our Constitution and the Bill Of Rights never conceived of then non-invented video computer games. But that is not the issue. Rather, the issue is whether our forefathers would have considered that training our children in committing violent criminal acts was protected by the First Amendment. Just as the Court decided that causing our children to learn about obscenity is not protected by the First Amendment, training them in criminal acts of violence requires the same ruling.

Finally, the Court majority asserts that, because any restriction of video games is within First Amendment protection, it would be unconstitutional "unless it is justified by a compelling government interest."[850] And it concludes that no such compelling interest was shown. That conclusion cannot be attributed to the lack of evidence of the compelling government interest. The unanimous expert view of the meaningful adverse impact of violent video games by itself, together with the undisputed government responsibility to protect the country's young and support parental control, are more than sufficient evidence. Moreover, the Court's denial of any showing of government interest is belied by its own language on this subject: the Court majority wrote that "[w]e have no business passing judgment on the view of the California Legislature that violent video games ... corrupt the young or harm their moral development."[851] That, by itself, applied to the violent video games involved, refutes the basis on which the majority

264

struck down this California statute.

Once again, a Court majority has ignored the Constitution and the right of legislatures to determine what is needed to protect its citizens and societal morality.

A very recent massacre strongly suggests the unfortunate consequences that might reasonably be said to flow from this decision. On December 14, 2012, 20-year-old Adam Lanza entered the local Sandy Hook Elementary School in Newtown, Connecticut, and proceeded to shoot and kill 20 of the youngest children in the school, as well as six school staff members.

Was this horrible massacre related to the prevalent violent video games that the Supreme Court majority, overruling legislatures, allowed to be readily available to our youth? Was Adam Lanza acting out in real life what he repeatedly practiced on the computer screen, thereby perfecting his prowess in murdering innocent young victims who happened to appear before him? Since both Adam and his mother are now dead, we may never know with certainty, but known relevant circumstances point to a very likely connection.

Adam was a loner who "sat in his room playing video games for hours and hours."[852] While the names of each game that he played may remain unprovable, it is known that one game that was available was entitled "Kindergarten Killer," bearing the advertised description:

> "Get inside the kindergarten and shoot down those pesky little kids with your shotgun avoid getting killed by them."[853]

Should we discard this game as irrelevant because Adam did not kill any kindergarten children, but only first-graders? Is it a coincidence to be ignored that Adam, before going on his murderous rampage, "donned black camouflage" and "a military-style vest"[854] – not dissimilar to the appearance of many shooters in computer games? Should we continue to give no weight to the unanimous medical professional conclusion of a causal connection between violent video games and the behavior of children who thereafter engage in aggressive conduct? Of course, not every child who is addicted to video games will transfer the screen-play to real life act-out, just as not every person who is addicted to pornography will proceed to commit a rape. Yet, for most of America's history, we prohibited pornography in recognition of the impact it has on susceptible people – the young and others who, for whatever reason, would likely be affected by it – even though not all or even most of the young or adults would be caused thereby to engage in improper conduct.

The question that must be asked is whether these violent computer games have such redeeming social value – indeed, any social value – that they must be allowed as a vehicle for the exercise of free speech rights. How does the Supreme Court majority find that ideas that have "social value as a step to truth,"[855] the communication of which is the purpose behind First Amendment free speech rights, are being communicated by a child playing a violent video game? I find it difficult to discover any such ideas flowing from the playing of violent video games. Moreover, not only legislators, but the American people overwhelmingly (86 percent) believe that parents should have decisional authority over whether their children can buy or rent violent video games.[856] By declaring unconstitutional the California statute granting that right to parents, these seven Supreme Court justices thus overrode not only legislators but also the view of the American people, and did so without any basis in the Constitution that required or even supported their ruling.

XIV.

FIVE JUSTICES USURP CONGRESS' POWER TO APPROPRIATE TAXPAYER FUNDS TO PAY FOR LAWSUITS TO ATTACK LAWS PASSED BY CONGRESS

Here is some icing on the cake of the history of five justices assuming the power to say what the law should be, rather than what the law, as enacted by Congress, is. Our five justices, because they disagreed with Congress, usurped the role of Congress to themselves appropriate taxpayers' funds for a purpose that Congress had expressly prohibited. And what was that prohibited purpose? To finance legal attacks on statutes enacted by Congress, and thus provide more cases in which five Supreme Court justices could overrule the Legislative branch.

In 1974, Congress enacted the Legal Services Corporation Act to provide financial support so indigent individuals could obtain legal assistance for which they were otherwise unable to pay.[857] To pass the statute, and yearly thereafter to appropriate the funds to finance it, Congress voted for "a compromise set of restrictions" prohibiting the use of taxpayers' funds for various specified purposes.[858] Congress explained that it included these restrictions because it wanted the program "kept free from the influence of or use by it of political pressures."[859]

Congress expressly prohibited "recipients from making available LSC funds, program personnel, or equipment to any political party, to any political campaign, or for use in 'advocating or opposing any ballot measures' ...., in most criminal proceedings and in litigation involving nontherapeutic abortions, secondary school desegregation, military desertion, ... violation of the Selective Service statute" or "bringing class action law suits" (without express approval from LSC). One (of many) additional statutory prohibitions against use of taxpayers' money, specifically at issue in this Supreme Court decision, was the prohibition of "funding of any organization

> 'that initiates legal representation or participates in any other way, in litigation, lobbying, or rulemaking, involving an effort to reform a Federal or State welfare system, except that [a recipient may represent] an individual eligible client who is seeking relief from a welfare agency if such relief does not involve an effort to amend or otherwise challenge existing law in effect on the date of the initiation of the representation.'"[860]

The intent of Congress in creating and financing the LSC, but at the same time specifying what the LSC may not do, was clear. Some in Congress wanted to provide legal assistance to those without funds to press their personal claims that they were being deprived of welfare benefits that the welfare laws provided. Some congresspersons, however, would not vote to create and finance the LSC if it could be used to bite the hand that fed the LSC – meaning use congressionally-appropriated funds to attempt to overturn statutes enacted by Congress. That led to what the Supreme Court called a "compromise": a statute that created the LSC, but with specifications of what the LSC could NOT do, including granting any LSC funds to an entity that sought to overturn or modify any welfare laws.

Hence, without this compromise, no LSC would have been created and no funds would have been appropriated for lawyers to represent indigents who believed that they, personally, were being unlawfully deprived of welfare benefits that Congress or state legislatures had granted. If this compromise had not been reached and no LSC created, indigents seeking legal assistance to obtain their personal welfare benefits would have had no place to complain – other than the ballot box – as nothing in the Constitution or laws required Congress to establish and finance free legal assistance for indigents in non-criminal actions.

Both as simple logic and based on many prior Supreme Court decisions, the result should have been simple and clear, when, in 2001, the Court considered an attack on the congressional prohibition against the use of any LSC's funds as grants to any entity that worked to invalidate or alter a welfare law. It would have been expected that the Court would have ruled that Congress, not the Court, decides the purpose for which taxpayers' funds are appropriated, and the restrictions, if any, on the use of the funds, and the Court has no power to overrule Congress. And finally, such a compromise reached in Congress, to prevent a logjam impeding passage of legislation, is certainly to be applauded, not rejected.

Many Supreme Court precedents had endorsed that logic and conclusions. Here are some examples:

- In 1977, the Court upheld a welfare regulation that authorized Medicaid recipients to receive payments for childbirth, but denied payments for non-therapeutic abortions, explaining that the government may "make a value judgment favoring childbirth over abortion, and ... implement that judgment by the allocation of public funds."[861] The Court also pointed out that the state's decision to fund childbirths, but not abortions, leaves the indigent woman in the same position in which she would have been if the state had never decided to fund *any* childbirths.[862]

- In 1983, the Court unanimously upheld Congress' right to prohibit tax-exempt entities from using tax-deductible contributions to perform lobbying to influence legislation.[863] The Court explained that Congress had the right "simply" to choose "not to pay for" lobbying,[864] analogizing it to Congress' right to "grant funds to an organization dedicated to combating teen drug abuse, but condition the grant by providing that none of the money received from Congress could be used to lobby state legislatures."[865]

- In 1988, the Court upheld a statute that denied participation in the federal food stamp program to any household in which a member is on strike, explaining that the Court's "review of distinctions that Congress draws in order to make allocations from a finite pool of resources must be deferential, for the discretion about how best to spend money to improve the general welfare is lodged in Congress rather than the courts."[866]

- In 1998, the Court upheld a statute that required the National Endowment Of The Arts, in making grants of federal funds, to give weight to "general standards of decency and respect for the diverse beliefs and values of the American public,"[867] reaffirming a prior ruling that "Congress may 'selectively fund a program to encourage certain activities it believes to be in the public interest, without at the same time funding an alternative program which seeks to deal with the problem in another way.'"[868]

These are four – of many - examples of Supreme Court rulings, during the 22-year period from 1977 through 1998, in which the Court repeatedly reaffirmed two basic principles: (1) Congress may appropriate funds for activities it chooses and refuse funding for alternative activities that others might prefer; and (2) any individual who seeks funding for such alternative activities is not injured by Congress' selection, as that individual is denied nothing more than if Congress had refused to fund any alternative.

These two basic principles, as applied to the Legal Services Corporation Act, should have resulted in rejecting this court attack on Congress' decision not to fund any entity working, through litigation or lobbying, to alter any welfare system. As declared in these Supreme Court decisions, Congress had the right to specify for what purposes taxpayers' funds may be used and not used. And anyone who wished to work to alter a welfare system remained free to do so, but only with his/her funds, as would have been the reality if Congress had never approved the Act.

> *"Instead of recognizing that Congress would not have agreed to appropriate these funds without the assurance that they would not be used for the prohibited purposes, the Court simply directed that the funds could be used for both the purposes authorized by Congress AND the purposes that Congress had prohibited."*

Yet, despite all of these prior Supreme Court rulings, in 2001, five Justices struck down Congress' decision not to fund any entity that engaged in lobbying and litigation to alter existing welfare statutes. And then instead of recognizing that Congress would not have agreed to appropriate these funds without the assurance that they would not be used for the prohibited purposes, the Court simply directed that the funds could be used for both the purposes authorized by Congress AND the purposes that Congress had prohibited. In so ruling, these five justices ignored another long-standing Supreme Court axiom: that the Court may not "rewrite a statute and give it an effect altogether different from that [Congress] sought by the measure as a whole," but must presume a congressional "intent that, unless the act operates as an entity, it shall be wholly ineffective."[869]

The LSC statute enacted by Congress, by its words, made clear that Congress was not appropriating any funds to finance recipients to attack Congress' (and state legislatures') welfare legislation. These five justices themselves described the statute as a "compromise," a word that means "a settlement of differences in which each side makes concessions."[870] In simple terms, these five justices recognized that, unless these prohibitions against activities to alter welfare statutes had been included, Congress would have refused to enact the statute and appropriate funds to give life to the Legal Services Corporation.

It is no answer to say that the recipient would use other funds, not funds appropriated by Congress, to finance its lobbying or legal attacks on existing welfare laws. Money is fungible. An entity that has an operating budget of $2 million, of which $1.8 million comes from Congress' LSC appropriation and $200,000 from non-Congress sources, that seeks to spend $200,000 on attacking welfare laws, can continue to do so merely by asserting that it is using the non-Congress source money for that purpose, even though, without the $1.8 million of funding from Congress, the entity would not exist. Recognizing this reality, Congress did not want to give life to an entity that would seek to destroy Congressional decisions.

Hence, these five justices went whole hog in violating the constitutional delegation to Congress, not to the Court, of the power to decide the purpose for which taxpayers' funds are to be appropriated. These five justices ignored Congress' express provision that prohibited the use of funds for the purpose that these five justices wanted to finance. And although these five justices recognized that Congress would have appropriated no funds if the prohibitions had not been included, they directed that the statute should be implemented and financed in a manner that allowed the prohibited activities.

Why did these five justices so bastardize what Congress had expressly enacted and so clearly intended? One can only conclude that, overall, it was to grasp more power than the Constitution delegated to judges, thereby altering the express division of powers that our forefathers designed. It is thus contrary to our Founders' plan for America.

But this case presents an even greater and growing legal cancer that five justices appear to be feeding: the misuse of supposed *pro bono* litigation by the legal profession. Chief Judge Dennis G. Jacobs of the United States Court of Appeals For The Second Circuit well-described this problem in a 2008 speech[871] as one allowing lawyers "to promote their own agendas, social and political—and (on a wider plane [to which I am now referring]) to promote the power and the role of the legal profession itself."

> *"What part of the legal profession has the power to direct enlargement of the legal profession's power? The answer is judges, who are themselves lawyers, and have, as shown in this book, assumed powers that the Constitution did not give them."*

What part of the legal profession has the power to direct enlargement of the legal profession's power? The answer is judges, who are themselves lawyers, and have, as shown in this book, assumed powers that the Constitution did not give them. Thus, when lawyers – the litigating part of the legal profession – bring societal-impact cases before judges – the ruling part of the legal profession – the loop is closed on the legal profession's stranglehold on power to control decisions that were intended to be made by Congress and state legislatures.

No other profession has this control over our country. Yes, almost every profession, in our democracy, properly seeks to push for what they believe would be best for themselves (while, of course, using good PR tactics, phrasing it as what is best for our country). But no profession other than lawyers brings its quest-for-change to fellow members of the profession with the power to decide: judges who are members of the legal profession. As Chief Judge Jacobs well explained: "Cases in which the lawyers can and do make an impact are (by the same token) cases in which the judges can make an impact; and impacts are exercises of influence and power." Hence, lawyers, pushing their own political agendas through supposedly *pro bono* cases, bring them to fellow members of the legal profession who love these cases, in which, generally, the judges can overrule the other branches of government: legislatures (whether federal or state) and executives (whether president or state governors).

Let me be clear that I support true *pro bono* work by lawyers who provide legal assistance to indigents, otherwise financially unable to retain a lawyer, to help such persons obtain their individual legal rights. Lawyers should contribute their time and expertise to help, for example, a poor person obtain welfare payments to which the controlling statute or regulation entitles him or her. That meets the *pro bono* definition of being in the public interest, because all individuals, without regard to wealth or poverty, should be able to obtain benefits to which our elected representatives have determined they are entitled, only to be effectively overruled by some bureaucrat.

But why should it be considered to be in the public interest for some lawyer, who disagrees with legislation adopted by our elected representatives, to commence a lawsuit to overrule their decision? Nothing advances the public interest more than our democratic elections that allow our public to choose its representatives, empowered to enact legislation. It is these elected representatives, who must answer to their respective voting populations through elections every two, four, or six years, and are thereby most likely to choose what is in the public interest or they would not be re-elected. Certainly, elected representatives are more likely to represent what the public wants than a lawyer who delegates to himself the power to rescind what elected representatives have enacted. It is for this reason that the Court properly declared in 1977 that, "when an issue involves policy choices as sensitive as those implicated by public funding ..., the appropriate forum for their resolution in a democracy is the legislature,"[872] and continued by reaffirming the early 20th century Court ruling, written by Justice Oliver Wendell Holmes, that "'legislatures are ultimate guardians of the liberties and welfare of the people in quite as great a degree as the courts.'"[873]

Significantly, most of these lawyers are themselves well-off and not part of the class of people the legislation was enacted to protect, such as welfare recipients. That a non-lawyer disagrees with a statute doesn't entitle him/her to claim the mantle of *pro bono*; but a lawyer who applies in court to further a personal political or social agenda, by seeking to invalidate that statute, is given that medal of honor. The same lawyer, seeking to overrule what elected representatives have enacted, would not likely dare to ask for affirmation by running for office and subjecting his view of what is in the public interest to the ultimate decision-maker: an election in which the public decides.

Chief Judge Jacobs, in his 2008 speech, provided two excellent examples of cases, commenced by lawyers proclaiming they were doing it in the public interest, that were clearly against the public interest. One involved the Sicily Island Area Levee project, a federal project, originally planned by the Army Corps of Engineers in 1975, to alleviate flooding in Catahoula Parish, Louisiana. Fast forward 30 years to 2005, and the levee project remained undone. The consequence of that 30 years of inaction was that Sicily Island was hard hit by the infamous 2005 hurricane, Katrina. We can all be certain that, if elected representatives had been responsible for this 30-year failure to fix the known problem, they would have been defeated for reelection, because it was their fault that inaction was allowed. But it was not legislators' fault; they had directed that the work be done, and it would have been except for self-proclaimed *pro bono* lawyers, with six environmental organizations as their named plaintiffs, who sought and won an order preventing levee construction until additional environmental impact studies were completed. Was that result, allowing the disastrous damage from Katrina, in the public interest? I suggest there would be near unanimity that it was not.

The second example related by Chief Judge Jacobs involved a case publicized by the late New York City Mayor Ed Koch. The city had sought the eviction of a woman living in a city-owned rental apartment with several dozen birds. The reason for the eviction: that many birds were not allowed and, most important, health experts had determined the large, private flock was creating a health menace due to bird-caused disease. Self-selected, supposed *pro bono* lawyers succeeded in delaying the eviction. That it thus allowed a health risk to all the other human tenants in the apartment project – and therefore must be considered contrary to the general public interest – was not important to these self-proclaimed *pro bono* lawyers.

With these lessons in mind, let's return to considering the Supreme Court decision forcing, contrary to Congress' decision, the government to finance entities that seek to overturn or alter welfare statutes enacted by elected representatives in Congress or state legislatures. The impact of this orphan ruling by these five justices is dramatically seen by contrasting two recent rulings on the issue by two different courts of appeal.

On August 21, 2012, the Court of Appeals for the Fifth Circuit, following the clear direction provided by the Supreme Court in the decisions enumerated above, upheld most of a Texas statute and implementing regulations that prohibited any taxpayers' funds from "'entities that perform or promote elective abortions or are affiliates of entities that perform elective abortions.'"[874] Recognizing that the "policy expressed" by the

Texas legislature was "for public funds to subsidize non-abortion family planning ... to the exclusion of abortion," it held that "Texas's authority to promote that policy would be meaningless if it were forced to enlist organizations as health care providers and message-bearers that were also abortion advocates."

Yet, on October 23, 2012, the Court of Appeals for the Seventh Circuit reached a diametrically opposite result.[875] At issue was an Indiana statute – very similar to the Texas statute upheld by the Fifth Circuit – that prohibited "abortion providers from receiving any state contracts and grants, including those involving state-administered federal funds."[876] This Indiana State statute mirrored the Hyde Amendment, enacted by Congress, that "prohibits the use of federal funds to pay for nontherapeutic abortions" (with certain exceptions).[877] Moreover, as this court admitted, "Medicaid regulations permit the states to establish 'reasonable standards relating to the qualifications of providers,'"[878] and the Senate report expressly declared that the statute "'is not intended to preclude a State from establishing, under State law, *any other bases for excluding individuals or entities* from its Medicaid program.'"[879]

So how does this court invalidate this Indiana statute? Essentially by the assumption by these judges of the power to determine what is "reasonable," a determination that is usually within the legislature's power. These judges admitted that the state legislature has the power to decide who, within the state, is qualified to perform health services: "[n]o one disputes that the states retain considerable authority to establish licensing standards and other related practice qualifications for" recipients of taxpayers' money.[880] And these judges recognized that the Supreme Court had made clear that there was "'no limitation on the authority of a State to make a value judgment favoring childbirth over abortion, and to implement that judgment by the allocation of public funds.'"[881] But, it overruled the legislature to hold that it is not "reasonable" to deny qualifications because of providing abortion services. How it is not "reasonable" for a state, using federally-supplied funds, to copy the federal statute's lead in denying federal funds to any abortion provider defies belief. The only explanation is that these judges did not agree with the view of both Congress and the Indiana legislature that it was reasonable to deter abortions by declining to finance any entity that provided abortions. On that basis, they assumed the power of legislatures to make that decision.

These judges, below the Supreme Court, thereby also ignored the rulings of the Supreme Court – rulings they are duty-bound to follow. They believed that their personal views as to what the law should be trumped the legislatures' decisions on what the law is. And they can find support in decisions of five justices of the Supreme Court who, all too often, substitute their personal views of what the law should be for what prior decisions of the court have held that the law is.

POSTSCRIPT:
ABOUT, AND FROM, THE AUTHOR

I offer the following facts about me, in case any reader experiences that curiosity.

* * * * * * * *

I started this book by explaining that my love for this country was the reason that I decided to write it. You may ask, why is it that I so love this country? The answer is that no other country, in existence today or even anytime in history, would have given me the same freedom and opportunity that I have had here – an opportunity that has allowed me to reach heights of learning, professional success, and financial comfort. Yes, I have worked hard and, fortunately, the genes that I received gave me the inner wherewithal to perform well. But the results would likely not have been the same without the basic structure in America that provides a ladder for all to reach towards the top.

To understand why I am so thankful, you have to know a little more about my life.

My Young Life

I was born in 1931 – in the midst of a terrible depression – to a Jewish family of four, that my arrival increased to five: father, mother, and two much older brothers. (I was told that I had to thank my grandmother that I was conceived and born: She kept cajoling my mother that if she had another child, it would be a girl. Despite her poor prediction, and though I hardly knew her due to her death while I was very young, I am forever thankful to her.)

It would be unreal to ignore the misfortune that my father

suffered in early life that had to have had a substantial impact on him, and, through him, on me. When he was about four years of age, his mother died and his father abandoned him and his two siblings. The result: His sister was permanently separated off and given for adoption to a non-Jewish family, while my father and his younger brother were placed in an orphanage, where he was later taught a trade but never allowed to receive any higher education – a real waste because he always exhibited great intelligence.

Economically, in my pre-adult years, we were somewhere between the poverty level and lower-middle class in the economic strata. The first residence that I recall was in the Bronx: a four-flight walkup apartment, with only one bedroom, requiring the three brothers to sleep in the bedroom while our parents slept in the living room.

My parents could not have given me (and my brothers) more love and dedication, but economically, my father, with the exception of one three-year stint, never had a secure job that brought home much money. Indicative of our economic situation are a few tidbits from that early life.

I recall, on several occasions, the bell to our apartment would ring and my mother would put her finger across her lips and quietly tell me to "shush." She did not open the door or even ask whom it was. The reason, as I would be told after the bell-ringer had departed, was that it was the man from the gas company to turn off the service in our apartment as we were in arrears in paying the bill; not letting him enter kept the gas flowing.

Then there were the times – happily infrequently, but certainly more than once or twice – when my mother would put out food for the three boys, but none for herself and my father, because there simply was not enough for all. They would go hungry so that their three children would have something, as sparing as it was.

To add some income, my mother, year after year, after taking care of her children, would work into the wee hours of night, making buttons by pasting an artificial jewel top into a base – a tedious and sight-burdening repetitive task that earned my mother miniscule piece-work compensation.

I was very fortunate to go to excellent public schools. The classes were not small in number of students, but the teacher insisted upon – and received – disciplined attention from all at all times. There were, even as early as first grade, meaningful amounts of homework and creative projects that were assigned and performed.

From about age 11, I worked to earn money. I started doing baby-sitting at night, usually on weekends, earning 25 cents an hour. Then, beginning about age 13 and continuing through high school, I worked as a messenger and delivery boy for a dressmaker, earning, as I recall, 35 cents an hour. During the summers that I was attending City College of New York ("CCNY") – then a free public college – I worked full time at whatever position I could obtain, such as an assistant bookkeeper. To earn my first year's tuition at Yale Law School, I found a job driving a retail ice cream truck in Greensboro, North Carolina, where I worked 14-hour days, seven days a week, for the entire summer, and came back with about $1,400, which covered my first semester tuition and expenses (after which, based on my performance, I obtained substantial scholarships and loans for the rest of the three years of study).

I mention all of this, not to feel sorry for myself, but to demonstrate that I was not born with a silver spoon in my mouth and worked hard to reach where I am today. That hard work, together with being in a country that provided the opportunity to move up the ladder, is what permitted me, and many others of all religions and races, to succeed.

My Mother-In-Law

I have to interject my mother-in-law, who exemplified the spirit that has made America the magnet to the oppressed from abroad. She was born and then lived in that portion of Eastern Europe that, depending on the victor of the last war in that area, was either Russian or Polish. One by one, her twelve brothers had departed, emigrating to either Canada or the United States, finally leaving only her (the youngest sibling) with her mother, with the understanding that she was next to join her brothers. Unfortunately, the First World War started, the door out of Russia was effectively closed, and she was left alone with her mother. When Russia stopped fighting, there was total lack of food. She and her mother would dig up a potato, boil it in water, resulting in "soup" and potato as the meal for the two of them, day after day. After a short time, her mother died of malnutrition, and my future mother-in-law, now alone at her young age, walked across most of Europe to reach Belgium. There, through the help of HIAS (a Jewish charity), she traveled to Canada to reunite with some of her brothers.

Years later, after my wife's birth, my mother-in-law developed multiple sclerosis, which, for many years, prevented her from walking, and then left her totally bed-ridden. She never uttered a word of self-pity for her condition. When asked, she repeatedly only said, "I thank God that I was fortunate in being able to have my children and grandchildren grow up in America." I must say that I strongly concurred because, without that, I would never have had the good fortune of meeting my wife.

College and Law School

I attended CCNY for four years from 1948 to 1952. That required a daily commute by subway from the Bronx to 138th Street and Convent Avenue in Manhattan.

While there, I was very active in student politics, finally being elected president of the student body.

Politics within the student body was, in microcosm, a serious battleground, with two major belligerents: the very leftist with some communists and pro-communists versus the liberal anti-communists. I was a leader of the latter group. Also, there was a small group of Republicans or conservatives, who generally allied themselves with those who, while liberal, were anti-communists.

Although campus politics was just that, it provided practical education in debating, convincing, and the importance of issues that affected our country, the world, and our future.

From CCNY, I was very fortunate to be able to attend Yale Law School, where I was chosen to be managing editor of the Yale Law Journal, and from which I graduated *cum laude*.

Professional Career

After law school, I had almost 10 years of government service: one and a half years as law clerk to two federal judges in New York, three years in the United States Air Force as a first lieutenant in the Judge Advocate General's Corps, and then five years as Chief of Special Prosecutions in the Office of the United States Attorney in New York. Each of those positions was immensely interesting, challenging and educational, and, most important, allowed me to serve our country. Indeed, if I had been born with that proverbial silver spoon, I believe I would have stayed as a federal prosecutor.

But I had obligations to my wife and children. The best decision of my life was marrying Sheila, without whose partnership and help I could not possibly have accomplished what I did. And with her, we jointly produced three wonderful children and, through them, six superlative grandchildren. Two of our children were born while I was a prosecutor. Recognizing that the minimal compensation in that position would not allow me to give our offspring the life and education that I wanted for them, I joined a law firm in New York, where I practiced for over 40 years, and for many years served as chairman of its over-60-lawyer Litigation Department.

I was happily continuing my law practice there, when, in 2006, I received a telephone call from the Bush White House, asking me if I would consider serving as Inspector General of the Corporation For National And Community Service ("CNCS") – the government agency better known as the "domestic peace corps" – which happened to be a government activity that I had long applauded. I talked this offer over with my wife. She gave me her "kitchen pass" to accept, although, as we both understood, it would involve a substantial reduction in compensation and my weekly commuting from New York to spend five days in Washington. We both agreed that it presented a wonderful opportunity to give back something to a country that had done so much for us. To put a limit on Sheila's hardship of being alone for five days each week, we agreed that I would do it for two years only.

My Tenure As Inspector General

On my acceptance of the offer, President Bush formally sent my nomination to the Senate, and, after some time lapse, I was confirmed and sworn in by Supreme Court Justice Samuel Alito, whom I have long admired.

I started as Inspector General in early January 2007. I inherited an excellent staff of dedicated, professional and non-political civil servants who each had had many years of government service. They included a staff of investigators and a staff of auditors, as well as an administrative staff. They succeeded in uncovering a large number of fraudulent and other misuses of taxpayers' funds, which resulted in meaningful amounts returned to the Treasury, successful prosecutions of wrongdoers, and termination of miscreants' opportunity to continue to receive taxpayers' funds.

In early 2009, pursuant to the agreement with my wife, I called a meeting of my entire staff, and informed them that, although I loved the work that I was doing and working with them, I was going to submit my resignation, explaining the agreement that I had with my wife, who was not happy with my being away from her for four nights each week.

The next morning when I arrived at the office, I found a delegation of three leading members of my staff waiting to see me. They informed me that they had been delegated by the entire staff to ask me to reverse my decision. They stated that all the staff was in agreement that they had never before had as good, dedicated, supportive, and involved Inspector General as they had with me. They acknowledged that they understood and respected my family reasons for deciding to resign, but came to suggest a solution that would give me much greater time with my wife in New York, while remaining as Inspector General. They showed me various recent governmental directives that approved substantial amounts of tele-working to reconcile family needs with government responsibilities. They therefore proposed, on behalf of the full staff, that I spend only one night, and thus two days, in Washington, and tele-work from New York the other three days of the work-week, unless an office emergency required otherwise. I responded that I would consider it, and, if there were no objection from either my wife or the CNCS leadership, I would be willing to try it for a six-month test period to allow me, my staff, and the CNCS leadership each to determine if it really was workable. I specified that I would be willing to continue it after a test period only if I could continue properly to perform my duties as IG. On communicating the proposed procedure to my wife and to the CNCS leadership, all approved giving it a try.

From January into June, the only comments that I received were that it was working very well. With modern communication methods – telephone, computer, fax – I had no problem in conferring with and directing my staff during my days in New York. The result during that test period was that my office performed its responsibilities in a manner that continued to receive accolades, including from CNCS leadership.

But then I learned first hand why President Harry Truman had made the statement that, "If you want a friend in Washington, get a dog!"

In 2008, my staff had commenced an investigation into, and an audit of, a grantee in Sacramento, California, based on certain information provided to my office by CNCS staff. As with any other leads, my staff sought to determine whether any wrongdoing had occurred by examining the grantee's books and interviewing witnesses. My staff soon provided me with a detailed report substantiating wrongdoing and the total misuse, for the personal benefit of the grantee's principal, of the large grant made by CNCS to this grantee. The report, with detailed facts and documentation, substantiated the staff recommendation of both criminal and civil proceedings against the grantee and its principal. I concurred and we proceeded in that direction.

Not that it would have changed my support for my staff's work, but I did not then know that the principal wrongdoer, Kevin Johnson, later elected as Democratic Mayor of Sacramento, was a close friend and political ally of then candidate, soon to be president, Barack Obama. After commencing a civil action against him, tremendous pressure was suddenly imposed on me to settle the matter by leaving Johnson off the hook, with only his entity, which was totally insolvent, to be held accountable. I refused to sell out my staff and the excellent work they had done. My staff, whom I kept informed, not only concurred but appreciated my support despite the pressure. The result: The White House called me on my cell phone while I was in a car, late on a Wednesday when my schedule had me travelling, and told me that I had the choice of resigning or being fired.

Significantly, when I asked the reason for being fired, nothing that I had done was stated. Rather, I was told that "the president believed that it is time that you move on." When I asked for time to make my decision, and suggested until the following Tuesday, I was told that I had one hour and no more. The White

House pressed me by calling me back in 45 minutes for my answer. I then responded that I would not resign, and was informed that I was fired.

It is hard to imagine a "peoples'" government firing someone for doing his job, and supporting his non-political staff in doing so. But that is what happened. Yet it got worse.

When members of the Senate and the House vocally objected to my firing for apparently no good reason, the White House issued an "explanation" that employed words suggesting that I was suffering from Alzheimer's! That caused over 150 leading lawyers in New York to write an open letter to the president certifying that, based on their personal knowledge of me, any such assertion was totally false, as well as various other words complimentary to me.

Post-Inspector General

Having been fired, I returned home to New York full time, making my wife very happy. Rather than reactivate a full-time practice of law, I preferred to direct my time and attention to writing this book, serving on two not-for-profit boards, accepting from the Court of Appeals for the Second Circuit the honor and responsibility of serving as a member of that Court's lawyer disciplinary committee – and spending time with my family and doing traveling.

* * * * * * * *

Given this treatment that I had from our country's government, you may ask how I could possibly continue to love this country. The answer is clear. No country, no people, no government, and certainly no person is perfect. But I know that this country – unlike any other in the world – gave me the opportunity that I have used to speak my mind freely, to practice my religion without restriction, and to use my God-given faculties to rise from a poor kid to one who, through a legal practice, is financially comfortable. I owe my country a debt of gratitude, which, in a small way, I feel that I can repay by this book, to extol and seek to strengthen what this country was intended, and, with sufficient public support, can continue to be.

My Addiction To Politics

I confess to being a political junkie from early age, having been born into a family which, as I approached my 10th birthday, was steeped in politics – not as an occupation, but solely as a civic duty. My father puts the lie to the class stereotype that Republicans are limited to the top 2 percent in wealth in this country. Although he never had much more than a penny to his name, he was a loyal Republican whose hero was President Herbert Hoover. My brothers, on the other hand, were FDR Democrats. Each of them, my father and my two brothers, remained unchanged until they died. As you must notice, we were a very democratic (with a small "d") family.

I, on the other hand, early on, changed my political loyalties. In 1940, at the age of nine, I campaigned for Wendell Willkie for President, opposing FDR's third-term candidacy. But, in 1944, when FDR was seeking a fourth term against Thomas Dewey, I campaigned for FDR. Why the conversion? In 1940, I was troubled by FDR's promise not to send Americans to war in Europe, when it was apparent that Hitler would not cease his conquering of other peoples without American military opposition. In contrast, I was impressed by Willkie's refusal to make that, what he believed to be an empty, promise, in order to be elected. 1944 presented different circumstances in that we were at war and I did not appreciate the thought of "changing horses" in mid-war.

From 1948 until the 1972 election, I campaigned for the

Democratic candidates for president. Indeed, I was asked to be a Democratic candidate for the state legislature, but rejected the offer in order to continue building my legal practice. Then, in 1972, the far left took control of the Democratic Party and nominated George McGovern, who espoused an isolationist appeasement of Communist Russia. At this takeover, I – and many others – converted to become a Republican.

Some may scratch their heads to figure out how and why I did such a 180-degree conversion. I attribute it to two causes: First, I have always believed in America's remaining strong in preventing dictators and tyrants from oppressing free people, so that we would not repeat the mistake of the 1930s, when America and Western democracies allowed Hitler to violate all treaties, remilitarize, eat up independent countries, and then commence the Second World War. If led by the United States, a coalition of democracies would have, early on, easily defeated Hitler with few casualties. Instead of doing so, we followed a mainly isolationist path and prolonged our military weakness – in the head-in-the-sand view that we would not spill any American blood on foreign soil. The result, as we all know, was a war in which more than 60 million people – too many of whom were Americans – were killed, mostly on foreign soil.

The second cause for my "right turn" was simply described by Winston Churchill, who famously said that, "if you are not a liberal when you're young, you have no heart; if you are not a conservative when you're older, you have no brain."

Actually, both causes were interconnected.

CHAPTER NOTES

Chapter I.

[1] Copy on file at Federal Bar Council, 123 Main Street, White Plains NY 10601-3104.

Chapter II.

[2] http://www.reuters.com/article/2012/04/02/us-obama-healthcare-idUSBRE8310WP20120402 (visited June 7, 2012).
[3] http://www.cbsnews.com/8301-3460_162-57464549/roberts-switched-views-to-uphold-health-care-law/ (visited on October 13, 2012).
[4] http://avalon.law.yale.edu/19th_century/lincoln1.asp (visited June 7, 2012).
[5] Remarks by President Bush at the Federalist Society's 2007 annual conference, November 15, 2007, found at http://georgewbush-whitehouse.archives.gov/news/releases/2007/11/20071115-14.html (visited on June 5, 2012).

Chapter III.

[6] Locke, *Essay Concerning Human Understanding,* c. XXI, No. 52 (1690).
[7] *Schenk v. United States,* 249 U.S. 47, 52 (1919).
[8] *Breard v. Alexandria,* 341 U.S. 622, 642 (1951).

Chapter IV.

[9] http://xroads.virginia.edu/~hyper/jefferson/ch18.html (visited June 14, 2012).
[10] http://www.beliefnet.com/resourcelib/docs/21/Benjamin_Franklins_Request_for_Prayers_at_the_Constitutional__1.html (visited on June 18, 2012).
[11] http://www.senate.gov/artandhistory/history/resources/pdf/Chaplain.pdf (visited June 18, 2012).
[12] http://docs.fdrlibrary.marist.edu/odddayp.html (visited June 14, 2012).
[13] Coinage Act of 1864 (April 22, 1864).
[14] 36 U.S.C. § 302.

[15] http://en.wikipedia.org/wiki/In_God_we_trust (visited 2/1/13).

[16] *Santa Fe Independent School District v. Doe,* 530 U.S. 290 (2000).
[17] *Id.*

Chapter V.

[18] http://nation.foxnews.com/eric-holder/2012/04/05/read-attorney-general-holders-letter-5th-circuit-court-appeals-here (visited June 12, 2012)
[19] Sen. Doc. 111-39, 111th Cong., 2d Sess. (2010) p. 201, a document prepared by the Congressional Research Service.
[20] http://www.domawatch.org/about/federaldoma.html (visited June 5, 2012)
[21] Article VI.
[22] Article III.
[23] Federalist Papers No. 78 (Hamilton)(Wills. ed.) p. 394.
[24] Federalist Papers No. 39 (Madison)(Wills ed.) p. 194 (emphasis added).
[25] http://constitutionality.us/TheConstitution.html (visited June 14, 2012).
[26] Federalist Papers No. 39 (Madison) (Wills ed.) p.194.
[27] Federalist Papers No. 45 (Madison)(Wills. ed.) p. 236.
[28] *Screws v. United States,* 325 U.S. 91, 109 (1945).
[29] *Marbury v. Madison,* 5 U.S. 137 (1803).
[30] http://www.heritage.org/research/reports/2011/10/nicaraguas-presidential-elections-how-daniel-ortega-could-shame-democracy (visited June 8, 2012).
[31] I Blackstone, *Commentaries On The Laws Of England* p. 59.
[32] Holmes, *Collected Papers* 204 (1920)(hereinafter "Holmes")(emphasis added).
[33] Holmes at 239.
[34] *Eisner v. Macomber,* 252 U.S. 189, 219-20 (1920)(emphasis added)(Holmes, J., dissenting, and quoting from opinions of the highest courts in Indiana and Florida).
[35] *Gompers v. United States,* 233 U.S. 604, 610 (1914).
[36] *Louisville and Nashville Railroad Co. v. Barber Asphalt Paving Co.,* 197 U.S. 430, 434 (1905).
[37] *Tyson v. Brother & Blanton,* 273 U.S. 418, 446 (1927)(Holmes, J., dissenting).
[38] *The Mind and Faith of Justice Holmes, His Speeches, Essays, Letters, and Judicial Opinions* 432 (Editor: Lerner 1943).
[39] Holmes at 307.
[40] *Kuhn v. Fairmont Coal Co.,* 215 U.S. 349, 372 (1910)(Holmes, J., dissenting).
[41] *United States v. Wade,* 388 U.S. 218, 249-50 (1967)(Black, J., dissenting).
[42] Senator Edward M. Kennedy's attack on Robert H. Bork, nominated by President Reagan, epitomized the political nature of the confirmation process: he called him a nominee who has opposed "civil rights, the rights of women, the right to privacy and other individual rights and liberties." N.Y. Times, *Excerpts From Debates In Senate Over Bork Nomination To The High Court,* Oct. 22, 1987.

That hearing was so debasing that it resulted in a new word in our English language: "to bork" means "to attack a candidate systematically, especially in the media." http://dictionary.reference.com/browse/bork (visited Dec. 10, 2012).

[43] Federalist Papers No. 78 (Hamilton) (Wills ed.) p. 394.

[44] Keith E. Whittington, *Political Foundations Of Judicial Supremacy: The Presidency, the Supreme Court, and Constitutional Leadership in U.S. History*, p. 220 (Princeton Univ. Press 2007).

[45] White's dissent from *Roe v. Wade* is included in *Doe v. Bolton*, 410 U.S. 113, 221 (1973)

[46] 384 U.S. 436, 526 (1966) (White, J., dissenting).

[47] http://www.nytimes.com/learning/general/onthisday/bday/0227.html (visited Dec. 10, 2012)

[48] *Abrams v. United States*, 250 U.S. 616, 629 (1919)(Holmes, J., dissenting).

[49] *Railroad Retirement Board v. Alton R. Co.*, 295 U.S. 330, 346 (1935).

[50] *Dred Scott v. Sandford*, 60 U.S. 393, 405, 407 (1857).

[51] *Id.* at 537.

[52] *Plessy v. Ferguson*, 163 U.S. 537, 544 (1896).

[53] *Brown v. Board of Education*, 347 U.S. 483 (1954).

[54] Federalist Papers No. 78 (Hamilton)(Wills ed.) p. 397.

[55] http://www.princeton.edu/~tjpapers/kyres/kydraft.html

[56] *E.g.*, Jack M. Balkin, *Living Originalism* (Harvard University Press 2011)(hereinafter "Balkin").

[57] Constitution Art. II; see Balkin p. 44.

[58] Constitution Eighth Amendment; see Balkin p. 42.

[59] Balkin, p. 43.

[60] *Id.*

[61] http://blog.constitutioncenter.org/2012/05/how-things-changed-since-1787/ (visited December 13, 2012)(34 ½ years); and http://articles.mcall.com/1987-06-28/features/2569915_1_horse-farming-rural_america (visited December 13, 2012)(38 years).

[62] http://en,wikipedia.org/wiki/List_of_Presidents_of_the_UnitedStates_by_age (visited December 13, 2012).

[63] *Id.*

[64] http://www.cdc.gov/nchs/fastats/lifeexpec.htm (visited December 13, 2012).

[65] http://en.wikipedia.org/wiki/List_of_Presidents_of_the_United_States_by_age (visited December 13, 2012).

[66] http://www.netplaces.com/america-history/the-world-war-i-era/womens-suffrage-and-the-advancement-of-womens-causes.htm (visited Dec. 20, 2012).

[67] http://www.nwhm.org/education-resources/history/woman-suffrage-

timeline (visited Dec. 20, 2012).

[68] *Spencer v. Board of Registration,* (D.C. Supreme Court 1871), referenced at http://memory.loc.gov/cgibin/query/r?ammem/naw:@field(DOCID+@lit(rbna wsan3154div12)) (visited Dec. 20, 2012)..

[69] *In re Slaughter-House Cases,* 83 U.S. 36, 68 (1972).

[70] *Id.* at 71.

[71] *Mapp v. Ohio,* 367 U.S. 643, 676-77 (1961)(Harlan, J., dissenting)

[72] *Citizens United v. Federal Election Commission,* 558 U.S. 50, 180 S.Ct. 876, 911-12 (2010). Exemplifying that precedent is not lightly to be overruled, the "sure error" found in that case was the almost axiom that "[t]here is simply no support that the First Amendment, as originally understood, would permit the suppression of political speech." *Id.* at 906.

[73] 163 U.S. 537 (1896).

[74] U.S. Constitution Amendment XIV, section 1.

[75] *Brown v. Board Of Education,* 347 U.S. 483 (1954).

[76] Federalist No. 78 (Hamilton)(Wills ed.) p. 399.

[77] Federalist Papers No 78 (Hamilton)(Wills ed.) p. 396.

[78] *Roper v. Simmons,* 543 U.S. 551 (2005).

[79] *Id.* at 578 (emphasis added).

[80] P. 35 (W.W. Norton, 2005).

[81] "Constitutional Interpretation by Justice William J. Brennan, Jr." dated October 12, 1985. Found on teachingamericanhistory.org, visited on August 27, 2010.

[82] *Roper v. Stevens,* 543 U.S. 551, 587 (2005)(Stevens, J. concurring).

[83] *Sturges v. Crowninshield,* 4 Wheat 122, 202 (1819), quoted with approval in *Jacobson v. Com. Of Massachusetts,* 197 U.S. 11, 22 (1905)

[84] *Katz v. United States,* 389 U.S. 347, 364-65 (1967)(Black, J., dissenting)

[85] *Roper v. Simmons,* 443 U.S. 551, 616 (2005)(Scalia, j., dissenting).

[86] http://www.thestate.com/2013/03/06/2663343/justice-kennedy-notes-power-shift.html (visited March 8, 2013).

[87] Federalist Papers No. 49 (Madison)(Wills. Ed) p. 257.

[88] *Day-Brite Lighting, Inc.,* 342 U.S. 421, 425 (1952).

[89] *Ferguson v. Scrupa,* 372 U.S. 726, 730 (1963).

Chapter VI.

[90] *Lanzetta v. New Jersey,* 306 U.S. 451, 455-56 (1939), quoting from *State v. Gaynor,* 119 N.J.L. 582, 197 A. 360.

[91] *Orozco v. Texas,* 394 U.S. 324 (1969).

92
http://news.google.com/newspapers?id=mDIjAAAAIBAJ&pg=4156%2C44672 68 visited on December 4, 2011.

93 *Id.*

94 I became aware of this case when it was reported in a legal periodical that I saw in my law office, years ago. Unfortunately, I did not retain the report.

95 384 U.S. 436 (1966).

96 U.S. Constitution, Fifth Amendment (emphasis added).

97 384 U.S. at 490.

98 *New York v. Quarles*, 467 U.S. 649, 654 (1984), repeating what it stated in *Michigan v. Tucker*, 417 U.S. 433, 444 (1974)(emphasis added).

99 United States Constitution, Art. I, § 8.

100 *Id.*, Art. III, § 2.

101 *Oregon v. Elstad*, 470 U.S. 298, 370-71 (1985)(Stevens, J., dissenting).

102 *Hopt v. People*, 110 U.S. 574, 583 (1884).

103 Justice Harlan's reputation as a strong supporter of constitutional rights was forever made by his dissent in *Plessy v. Ferguson*, 163 U.S. 537 (1896), from that decision's upholding segregation of African-Americans on the separate-but-equal theory.

104 *Sparf v. United States*, 156 U.S. 51 (1895).

105 *Id.* at 55.

106 *Id.*

107 *Wilson v. United States*, 162 U.S. 613, 616 (1896).

108 *Id.* at 625.

109 See, *e.g.*, *Pierce v. United States*, 160 U.S. 355 (1896); *Bram v. United States*, 168 U.S. 532, 548-49 (1897); *Powers v. United States*, 223 U.S. 303, 313 (1912); *Ziang Sung Wan v. United States*, 266 U.S. 1, 14-15 (1924); *McNabb v. United States*, 318 U.S. 332, 345-46 (1943); *Haynes v. Washington*, 373 U.S. 503, 513 (1963).

110 *Lisenba v. California*, 314 U.S. 219, 234-35 (1941).

111 357 U.S. 433 (1958).

112 *Id.* at 436-37.

113 *Id.* at 434.

114 *Id.* at 435, 438.

115 *Oregon v. Elstad*, 470 U.S. 298, 310, 312 (1985)

116 So, What Happened To Miranda? found at http://news.google.com/newspapers?id=mDIjAAAAIBAJ&pg=4156%2C44672 68

117 *Hopt v. People*, 110 U.S. 574, 584-85 (1884).

118 384 U.S. at 442, quoting the same statement made in *Brown v. Walker*, 161 U.S. 591, 596-97 (1896).

[119] 384 U.S. at 477.

[120] *United States v. Janis,* 428 U.S. 433, 448-49 (1976), repeated in *Colorado v. Connelly,* 479 U.S. 157, 166 (1986).

[121] *Watts v. Indiana,* 338 U.S. 49, 59 (1949)(concurring and dissenting).

[122] 384 U.S. at 482.

[123] 384 U.S. at 481.

[124] *Crooker v. California,* 357 U.S. 433, 440-441 (1958).

[125] 384 U.S. at 438-39.

[126] *United States v. Dickerson,* 166 F.3d 667, 687 (4th Cir. 1999) [citing, *e.g.,* Cassell & Fowles, "Handcuffing The Cops? *A Thirty-Year Perspective on Miranda's Harmful Effects on Law Enforcement,"* 50 Stan. L. Rev 1055 (1995)], *reversed on other grounds, Dickerson v. United States,* 530 U.S. 428 (2000).

[127] *New York v. Quarles,* 467 U.S. 649, 656-57 (1984).

[128] *Id.* at 657.

[129] *Hopt v. People,* 110 U.S. 574, 584 (1884).

[130] 384 U.S. at 471.

[131] *Id.,* quoting from *People v. Dorado,* 62 Cal.2d 338, 351, 398 P.2d 361, 369-70 (1965).

[132] *Lisenba v. California,* 314 U.S. 219, 234-35 (1941).

[133] *McNabb v. United States,* 318 U.S. 332, 346-47 (1943).

[134] *Haynes v. Washington,* 373 U.S. 503, 504 (1963).

[135] *Id.* at 513.

[136] *Id.* at 516-17.

[137] *Michigan v. Tucker,* 417 U.S. 433, 444 (1974); *New York v. Quarles,* 467 U.S. 649, 654 (1984); *Oregon v. Elstad,* 470 U.S. 298, 305 (1985).

[138] *Palermo v. United States,* 360 U.S. 343, 353n. 11 (1959); *Funk v. United States,* 290 U.S. 371, 382 (1933).

[139] *Dickerson v. United States,* 530 U.S. 428, 437 (2000).

[140] *Id. at* 432 (2000).

[141] *Berghuis v. Thompkins,* 130 S. Ct. 2250 (2010).

[142] *Id.* at 2256.

[143] *Id.* at 2256-57.

[144] *Id.* at 2257.

[145] *Id.* at2256.

[146] *Id.* at 2272 (Sotomayor, J., dissenting).

[147] *Id.* at 2276.

[148] *Id.*

Chapter VII.

[149] *Mincey v. Arizona,* 437 U.S. 385 (1978).

[150] *Stone v. Powell,* 428 U.S. 465, 469-70, 482 (1976).

[151] *Id.* at 471-74, 482.

[152] *People v. Mitchell,* 39 N.Y.2d 173 (1976).

[153] *Id.* at 178.

[154] NH Constitution of 1784, pt. I, Art. XIX.

[155] *Mayo v. Wilson,* 1 N.H. 53, 60 (1817).

[156] *United States v. La Jeune Eugenie,* 26 F. Cas. 832, 843-44 (C.C.D. Mass. 1822)

[157] *Adams v. New York,* 192 U.S. 585, 594-95 (1904), in part quoting from I Greenleaf, *A Treatise On The Law Of Evidence* 254a.

[158] *People v. Defore,* 242 N.Y. 13, 23-24 (1926).

[159] *Id.* at 21.

[160] *Weeks v. United States,* 232 U.S. 383 (1914).

[161] *Wolf v. Colorado,* 338 U.S. 25 (1949).

[162] *Weeks v. United States,* 232 U.S. 383, 391 (1941).

[163] *Olmstead v. United States,* 277 U.S. 438, 467 (1928).

[164] *Weeks v. United States,* 232 U.S. 383, 393 (1914).

[165] *Adams v. New York,* 192 U.S. 585, 598 (1904).

[166] *Wolf v. Colorado,* 338 U.S. 25, 31 (1949).

[167] 18 U.S.C. § 242.

[168] *Screws v. United States,* 325 U.S. 91 (1945).

[169] *Id.* at 98.

[170] *Irvine v. California,* 347 U.S. 128, 136 (1954).

[171] *Stone v. Powell,* 428 U.S. 465, 489-90 (1976), quoting, in the latter portion, from Justice Black's dissent in *Kaufman v. United States,* 394 U.S. 217 (1969).

[172] *Elkins v. United States,* 364 U.S. 206, 217 (1960).

[173] *Mapp v. Ohio,* 367 U.S. 643 (1961).

[174] *Irvine v. California,* 347 U.S. 128, 135 (1954).

[175] *Id.* at 135-36.

[176] *Elkins v. United States,* 364 U.S. 206, 219 (1960).

[177] *United States v. Leon,* 468 U.S. 897, 943 (1984)(Brennan and Marshall dissenting)

[178] *Olmstead v. United States,* 277 U.S. 438, 484 (1929)(Brandeis, J. dissenting).

[179] *Wolf v. Colorado,* 338 U.S. 25, 30 (1949).

[180] N.Y. Times, July 19, 2008, p. 1, *"U.S. Stands Alone In Rejecting All Evidence When Police Err."*

[181] *Stone v. Powell,* 428 U.S. 465, 485, 488 (1976).

[182] *United States v. Janis,* 428 U.S. 433 (1976).

[183] *United States v. Ceccolini,* 435 U.S. 268 (1978).

[184] *Pennsylvania Board Of Probation And Parole v. Scott,* 524 U.S. 357, 364 (1998).

[185] *Immigration Naturalization Service v. Lopez Mendosa,* 468 U.S. 1032 (1984).

[186] *Id.* at 1041.

[187] *Id.* at 1050.

[188] http://realcostofprisons.org/blog/archives/2009/08/prisons_not_the.html (visited 2/8/2011).

[189] *United States v. Leon,* 468 U.S. 897, 906 (1984).

[190] *McGuire v. United States,* 273 U.S. 95, 99 (1927).

Chapter VIII.

[191] 410 U.S. 113 (1973).

[192] *Id. at 116.*

[193] http://www.dailymail.co.uk/news/article-2297168/University-pulls-Sex-week-funding-outrage-state-paying-events (visited March 21, 2013).

[194] *Sturges v. Crowninshield,* 4 Wheat. 122, 202 (1819).

[195] *Passenger Corp. v Passengers Assn.,* 414 U.S. 453 (1974). As the Supreme Court there stated, "[t]his principle of statutory construction reflects an ancient maxim – expressio unius est exclusio alterius."

[196] *Roe v. Wade,* 410 U.S. 113, 153 (1973)(citations omitted).

[197] Free On-Line Dictionary

[198] The Texas statute at issue in *Roe v. Wade* made abortion a crime, as did similar statutes in 35 other States at the time the 14th Amendment was adopted. 410 U.S. at 175.

[199] 410 U.S. at 152-53.

[200] *Union Pacific Railway Co. v. Botsford,* 141 U.S. 250, 252 (1891).

[201] *Ibid.*

[202] *Stanley v. Georgia,* 394 U.S. 557 (1969).

[203] *Eisenstadt v. Baird,* 405 U.S. 438 (1972). Although, in passing, the Court's opinion gratuitously mentions right to privacy, the opinion of the four Justices rested on the Equal Protection Clause of the 14th Amendment, irrelevant to the *Roe* decision, with one of those four Justices separately explaining that the case simply rested on the 1st Amendment right to give a lecture. *Id.* at 455 (Douglas, J., concurring).

[204] *Griswold v. Connecticut,* 381 U.S. 479, 483-86 (1965).

[205] *Boyd v. United States,* 116 U.S, 616 (1886); *Katz v. United States,* 389 U.S. 347 (1967); *Terry v. Ohio,* 392 U.S. 1 (1968).

[206] *Meyer v. Nebraska,* 262 U.S. 390 (1923), with quotation at 403.

[207] 262 U.S. at 401.

[208] *Katz v, United States,* 389 U.S. 347 (1967).

[209] *Id.* at 350 & n.5.

[210] *Id.*

[211] *Id.* at 350-51.

[212] *Griswold v. Connecticut,* 381 U.S. 479. 508-09 (1965)(Black, J., dissenting; emphasis added).

[213] *Slaughterhouse Cases, 83 U.S. 36,* 71 (1872).

[214] *Loving v. Virginia,* 388 U.S. 1, 10 (1967).

[215] *McDonald v. City of Chicago,* 130 S. Ct. 3020, 3033n.9 (2010).

[216] Cong. Globe, 39th Cong., 1st Sess. 2765 (1866).

[217] *Id.* at 1088.

[218] *Slaughterhouse Cases,* 83 U.S. at 77.

[219] *Id.* at 82.

[220] *Id.* at 77, quoting with approval from an opinion of Supreme Court Justice Bushrod Washington (nephew of George Washington), on Circuit, in *Corfield v. Coryell,* 4 Washington's Circuit Court 371 (1823).

[221] 83 U.S. at 78.

[222] *Id.* at 78.

[223] *Day-Brite Lighting, Inc. v. Missouri,* 342 U.S. 421 (1952).

[224] 83 U.S. at 81.

[225] *Id.* at 78.

[226] *Katz v. United States,* 389 U.S. 347n.5 (1967)

[227] *Jacobson v. Comm. Of Massachusetts,* 197 U.S. 11, 31 (1905).

[228] *Twining v. New Jersey,* 211 U.S. 78, 102 (1908).

[229] *Meyer v. State of Nebraska,* 262 U.S. 390, 403 (1923).

[230] *Snyder v. Massachusetts,* 291 U.S. 97, 105 (1934).

[231] *Griswold v. Connecticut,* 381 U.S. 479 (1965), first quote *id.* at 493, quoting from *Snyder v. Massachusetts,* 291 U.S. 97, 105 (1934)(some internal quote marks omitted); second quote *id.* at 493, quoting from *Poe v. Ullman,* 367 U.S. 497, 517 (1961)(dissenting opinion by Douglas, J.)(some internal quote marks omitted).

[232] *Loving v. Virginia,* 388 U.S. 1, 12 (1967).

[233] *Duncan v. Louisiana,* 391 U.S. 14 r, 149 n.14 (1968)

[234] http://www.gallup.com/poll/154838/Pro-Choice-Americans -Record-Low.aspx (visited 9/23/12); see also Wall Street Journal, "Gallup's Pro-Life America," by William McGurn, June 1, 2010, p. A17.

[235] http://www.kofc.org/en/news/polls/index.html (visited 2/1/13).

[236] http://www.pollingreport.com/crime.htm (visited 9/17/10).

[237] *Snyder v. Massachusetts,* 291 U.S. at 105.

[238] See Note 7 *supra.*

[239] 410 U.S. at 116.

[240] *Roe v. Wade,* 410 U.S. at 116, 119.

[241] *Id.* at 176 (Rehnquist, CJ, dissenting)

[242] *Id.* at 139.

[243] *Penry v. Lynaugh,* 492 U.S. 302, 331 (1989).

[244] http://www.religioustolerance.org/abo_when7.htm (visited on May 7, 2010).

[245] *Roe v. Wade,* 410 U.S. at 132.

[246] *Id.* at 134.

[247] *Id.* at 132.

[248] *Id.* at 132-36.

[249] *Id.* at 136. England's abortion law, enacted in 1967, allowed an abortion under very restricted circumstances, *e.g.*, risk to the life of the mother, and only on the concurrence of "two other licensed physicians." *Id.* at 137-38.

[250] *Id.* at 141-42 (emphasis added).

[251] *Id.* at 142 (emphasis added).

[252] *Id.*

[253] *Id.* at 143.

[254] *Id.* at 176 (Rehnquist, CJ., disssenting).

[255] *Wolf v. Colorado,* 338 U.S. 25, 31 (1949).

[256] *Griswold v. Connecticut,* 381 U.S. 479, 482 (1965).

[257] *Jacobson v. Comm. Of Massachusetts,* 197 U.S. 11, 26 (1905).

[258] 410 U.S. at 116.

[259] *Ibid.*

[260] *Roe v. Wade,* 410 U.S. 113, 153-54 (1973).

[261] *Ibid.*

[262] *Griswold v. Connecticut,* 381 U.S. 479, 482 (1965).

[263] 410 U.S. at 156-67.

[264] *Id.* at 159.

[265] http://swordandspirit.com/library/writings_prolife/embryo_fetus.html (visited on July 22, 2010); Larsen. *Human Embryology,* pp. 158, 316-21, 368, 393, 419-21 (2001).

[266] 410 U.S. at 159.

[267] *Id.* at 141.

[268] *Id.* at 142.

[269] 1874 Mass. Acts, ch. 706, § 12S.

[270] http://groups.csail.mit.edu/mac/users/rauch/nvp/consistent/jackson.html (visited 6/21/12).

[271] 310 U.S. at 151.

[272] *Id.* at 150.

[273] *Id.* at 159.

[274] *Id.* at 149.

[275] *Id.* at 151.

[276] *Id.* at 151.

[277] *Frank v. Maryland,* 359 U.S. 360, 370 (1959), quoting Justice Oliver

Wendell Holmes opinion in *Jackman v. Rosenbaum Co.*, 260 U.S. 22, 31 (1922).

278 *Frank v. Maryland, supra,* 359 U.S. at 371.

279 *Id.* at 373.

280 *Id.* at 371.

281 *Ibid.*

282 http://civilliberty.about.com/od/abortion/tp/Pro-Life-vs-Pro-Choice.htm

283 *Jacobson v. Comm. Of Massachusetts,* 197 U.S. 11, 26 (1905).

284 *Id.* at 26-27, quoting from *Hannibal & St. J.R. Co. v. Husen,* 95 U.S. 465, 471 (1877)(first internal quote), and from *Crowley v. Christensen,* 137 U.S. 86, 89 (1890)(second internal quote).

285 *Jacobson v. Comm. Of Massachusetts,* 197 U.S. 11, 31 (1905).

286 *Id.* at 35.

287 197 U.S. 11 (1905).

288 *Id.* at 36.

289 *E.g.,* Cong. Rec. House p. 4737 (April 17, 2002).

290 *Moore v. East Cleveland,* 431 U.S. 494, 503-05 (1977).

291 *Planned Parenthood of Central Missouri v. Danforth,* 482 U.S. 52, 72 (1976).

292 *Roper v. Simmons,* 543 U.S. 551, 569 (2005), quoting from its prior decision in *Johnson v. Texas,* 509 U.S. 350, 367 (1993).

293 *Id.* at 569.

294 *E.g.,* the minor, no matter how young, is found to be "sufficiently mature to decide." *Lambert v. Wicklund,* 520 U.S. 292, 294 (1997)

295 *E.g.,* WorldNewDaily, December 3, 2004, http://www.wnd.com/?pageId+27841, visited July 20, 2010.

296 I learned of these two examples through an e-mail from a high reputation clinical neuropsychologist, of over 30 years experience, with a specialty practice that includes treating children and providing guidance to parents, and serves on medical staffs of seven hospitals, often consulted by schools.

297 *Planned Parenthood of S.E. Pa. v Casey,* 505 U.S. 833, 897-98 (1992).

298 *Planned Parenthood of Central Missouri v Danforth,* 482 U.S. 52, 72 (1976).

299 *Skinner v. State of Oklahoma,* 316 U.S. 535, 541 (1942).

300 *Ibid.*

301 All of the facts concerning the above-described Marotta matter can be found in the following newspaper articles: http://www.dailymail.co.uk/news/article-2255241/Sperm-donor-ordered-pay-child-support-lesbian-couple-despite-giving-rights-child.html http://www.nydailynews.com/news/national/sperm-donor-lesbian-pair-pay-child-support-kansas-court-article-1.1230524?localLinksEnabled=false and http://www.foxnews.com/us/2012/12/31/kansas-sperm-donor-to-same-sex-couple-readies-for-child-support-fight/?cmpid=NL_FNTopHeadlines

302   *Roe v. Wade,* 410 U.S. 113, 153 (1973).
303   *Lochner v. New York,* 198 U.S. 45 (1905).
304   *Id.* at 61.
305   *Id.* at 65.
306   *Roe v. Wade,* 410 U.S. at 139 & n. 37.
307   Constitution Article I, § 8.

Chapter IX.

[308] Federalist Papers No. 3 (Wills ed.)(Jay) p. 10.

[309] U.S. Constitution Art. I, § 8.

[310] *Id.*

[311] *Weems v. United States,* 217 U.S. 349, 379 (1910).

[312] *Gregg v. Georgia,* 428 U.S. 153, 175 (1976), quoting with approval Justice Frankfurter's concurring opinion in *Dennis v. United States,* 341 U.S. 494, 525 (1951).

[313] *Gregg v. Georgia, supra,* at 176, in part quoting with approval from *Gore v. United States,* 357 U.S. 386, 393 (1958).

[314] *Gregg v. Georgia, supra,* at 176, in part quoting with approval from the plurality opinion in *Powell v. Texas,* 392 U.S. 514, 533 (1968).

[315] *Screws v. United States,* 325 U.S. 91, 109 (1945).

[316] *Atkins v. Virginia,* 536 U.S. 304, 312 (2002), quoting from *Penry v. Lynaugh,* 492 U.S. 302, 331 (1989).

[317] *Gregg v. Georgia,* 428 U.S. 153, 212-14 (1976)(discussed further pp. [34-37]).

[318] *Jurek v. Texas,* 428 U.S. 262, 265-67 (1976).

[319] *Coker v. Georgia,* 433 U.S. 584, 587-89 (1977)(discussed further pp. [64-67]).

[320] *Godfrey v. Georgia,* 446 U.S. 420, 449, 426-27 (1980)(discussed further pp. [45-46]).

[321] *Eddings v. Oklahoma,* 455 U.S. 104, 106 & notes 3 & 7 (1982).

[322] *Barclay v. Florida,* 463 U.S. 939, 942-44 (1983)(discussed further pp. [29-30]).

[323] *Hitchcock v. Dugger,* 481 U.S. 393, 394-95 (1987).

[324] *Thompson v. Oklahoma,* 487 U.S. 815, 860, 862 (1988)(discussed further pp. [56-58]).

[325] *Penry v. Lynaugh,* 492 U.S. 302, 307, 310 (1989)(discussed further pp. [73-75]).

[326] *Tennard v. Dretke,* 542 U.S. 274, 276-77 (2004).

[327] *Roper v. Simmons,* 543 U.S. 551, 556-58 (2005)(discussed further pp. [59-63]).

[328] *Kennedy v. Louisiana,* 554 U.S. 407, 413-17 (2008)(discussed further pp. [67-72]).

[329] Free On Line Dictionary

[330] *Id.*

[331] http://avalon.law.yale.edu/17th_century/england.asp (visited 2/15/11): "That excessive bail ought not to be required, nor excessive fines imposed, nor cruel and unusual punishments inflicted."

[332] *Harmelin v. Michigan,* 501 U.S. 957, 968 (1991).

[333] *Id.* at 975.

[334] 2 J. Elliot, Debates On The Federal Constitution 111 (2d ed. 1854), quoted in *Harmelin v. Michigan,* 501 U.S. 957, 979 (1991).

[335] 3 J. Elliot, Debates On The Federal Constitution 447 (2d ed. 1854), quoted in *Harmelin v. Michigan,* 501 U.S. 957, 980 (1991).

[336] Pa. Const. 38 (1776); S.C. Const. Art. XL (1778); N.H. Bill Of Rights, Art. XVIII (1784), all quoted in *Harmelin v. Michigan,* 501 U.S. 957, 977 (1991).

[337] *E.g.,* New Hampshire Constitution both prohibited "cruel or unusual punishments" and required "all penalties ought to be proportioned to the nature of the offence." N.H. Bill Of Rights, Arts. XVIII and XXIII (1784), quoted in *Harmelin v. Michigan,* 501 U.S. 957, 977 (1991).

[338] Maine Const. Art I, 9 (1819); Rhode Island Const. Art I, 15-16 (1816); Georgia Const. Art I, 16, 21 (1868); Ohio Const. Art VIII, 13, 14 (1802); Indiana Const. Art. I, 15-16 1816); West Virginia Const. Art. II, 2 (1861-63).

[339] 1 Stat. 114, quoted in *Harmelin, supra,* 501 U.S. at 981 (1991).

[340] J. Byrd, A Brief Exposition of the Constitution of the United States 164 (2d. ed. 1840), quoted in *Harmelin, supra,* 501 U.S. at 981.

[341] B. Oliver, The Rights Of An American Citizen 186 (1832), quoted in *Harmelin, supra,* 501 U.S. at 981.

[342] J. Story, Commentaries On The Constitution Of The United States 1896 (1833), quoted in *Harmelin, supra,* 501 U.S. at 982.

[343] Emphasis added.

[344] The Free Dictionary. As explained in it, such crimes are called "capital" because "the defendant could lose his/her head (Latin for caput)."

[345] *Aldridge v. Commonwealth,* 4 Va. 447, 449-50 (1824).

[346] *Wilkerson v. Utah,* 99 U.S. 130, 135 (1878).

[347] *In re Kemmler,* 136 U.S. 436, 446-47 (1890).

[348] *Trop v. Dulles,* 356 U.S. 86, 99 (1958).

[349] Some anti-death penalty commentators and some justices point to *Weems v. United States,* 217 U.S. 349 (1910), as precedent for the Court to consider the proportionality of the sentence to the crime. In fact, that decision held unconstitutional a sentence imposed by a court in the Philippines (then a U.S. territory), which required "painful labor" during 15 years of imprisonment, including at *all times* "carry[ing] ... a chain at his ankle, hanging from his wrist." *Id.* at 383. While the Court also commented that "it is a precept of justice that

punishment for crime should be graduated and proportioned to the offense" (*id.* at 367), the Court did not abrogate to itself, rather than the legislature, that responsibility. The Court, in 1980, recognized that the *Weems* case was limited to the "extraordinary nature of the 'accessories' included within the punishment of cadena temporal," the name given by the Philippine legal system to the "painful labor" imprisonment described above. *Rummel v. Estelle,* 445 U.S. 263, 274 (1980).

[350] *Gore v. United Sates,* 357 U.S. 386, 393 (1958).

[351] *Williams v. Oklahoma,* 353 U.S. 576, 586 (1959).

[352] *McGautha v. California,* 402 U.S. 183, 195-96 (1971).

[353] *Id.* at 221 (emphasis added).

[354] *New State Ice Co. v. Liebmann,* 285 U.S. 262, 311 (1932)(dissenting opinion).

[355] *Trop v. Dulles,* 356 U.S. 86, 100-01 (1958).

[356] *Id.* at 101.

[357] *Stanford v. Kentucky,* 492 U.S. 361, 379 (1989).

[358] *Gregg v. Georgia,* 428 U.S. 153, 175 (1976).

[359] *Woodson v. North Carolina,* 428 U.S. 280, 294-95 (1976).

[360] *McGautha v. California,* 402 U.S. 183, 201-02 (1971).

[361] *E.g.,* Act of April 30, 1790, which mandated death penalty for murder, treason, and specific other crimes (see p. [___] *supra*). In 1897, Congress amended that law to provide that, in all convictions of murder and rape, the jury would have discretion to choose death or life. Act of January 15, 1897.

[362] *Winston v. United States,* 172 U.S. 303, 305 (1899).

[363] *Id.* at 313.

[364] *Andres v. United States,* 333 U.S. 740, 743 (1948).

[365] *McGautha v. California,* 402 U.S. 183 (1971).

[366] *Id.* at 189-90.

[367] *Id.* at 207.

[368] *McGautha v. California,* 402 U.S. 183, 319-20 (1971).

[369] *Furman v. Georgia,* 408 U.S. 238 (1972)

[370] *Id.* at 329 (Marshall, J., concurring).

[371] *Id.* at 256 (Douglas, J., concurring); *id.* at 310 (Stewart, J., concurring); *id.* at 314 (White, J., concurring).

[372] *Lockett v. Ohio,* 438 U.S. 586, 598 (1978).

[373] *Barclay v. Florida,* 463 U.S. 939, 970 (1983).

[374] *Id.* at 950-51.

[375] *Furman v. Georgia,* 408 U.S. 238, 411-12 (1972)(Blackmun, J., dissenting).

[376] *Snyder v. Comm. of Massachusetts,* 291 U.S. 97, 105 (1934).

[377] *Penry v. Lynaugh,* 492 U.S. 302, 331 (1989).

[378] *Furman v. Georgia,* 408 U.S. 238, 385 (1972)(Burger, J., dissenting)

[379] *Id.* at 462-63 (Powell, J., dissenting).

[380] *Id.* at 438-39.

[381] *Id.* at 437.

[382] *Id.* at 412-13 (Blackmun, J., dissenting).

[383] *Id.* at 441.

[384] http://www.pollingreport.com/crime.htm (visited 9/17/10)

[385] http://www.deathpenaltyinfo.org/public-opinion-gallup-poll-reports-lowest-support-death-penalty-nearly-40-years (visited 6/24/12).

[386] http://www.gallup.com/com/poll/1606/Death-Penalty.aspx (visited 9/17/10).

[387] Stevens, *On The Death Sentence*, New York Review Of Books (Dec. 23, 2010)(hereinafter "Stevens *Book Review*).

[388] *Gregg v. Georgia*, 428 U.S. 153, 179-80 (1976).

[389] Stevens *Book Review*.

[390] *Gregg v. Georgia*, 428 U.S. at 181.

[391] *Id.* at 162-63.

[392] *Id.* at 165 & n.9.

[393] *Id.* at 193-94.

[394] *Id.* at 173.

[395] The first citation, *Trop v. Dulles*, 356 U.S. 86 (1958), voided a statute which automatically deprived a soldier of his American citizenship if convicted of desertion, explaining that "citizenship is not subject to the general powers of the National Government and therefore cannot be divested in the exercise of those powers." *Id.* at 92. The other citation, *Weems v. United States*, involved a sentence by a Philippine court that inflicted undue pain. See note 42 *supra*.

[396] *Furman v. Georgia*, *supra*, 408 U.S. at 242.

[397] *Id.* at 248.

[398] *Woodson v. North Carolina*, 428 U.S. 280, 312 (1976)(Rehnquist, dissenting)

[399] *Woodson v. North Carolina*, 428 U.S. 280, 285 (1976).

[400] *Id.* at 286.

[401] *Id.* at 289.

[402] *Woodson v. North Carolina*, 428 U.S. 280 (1976). The 5-justice majority included Brennan and Marshall, who had dissented in *Gregg* because they rejected any death penalty, and the three authors of the anti-discretion opinion in *Furman* who now rejected mandatory decisions.

[403] *Id.* at 298.

[404] *Id.* at 294-95.

[405] *Id.* at 295n. 31; see also 296.

[406] *Id.* at 292 n. 25.

[407] *Roberts v. Louisiana*, 428 U.S. 325, 337-39 (1976)(dissent)

[408] *Id.* at 331-35 (majority opinion).

[409] *Lockett v. Ohio,* 438 U.S. 586, 589, 593-94 (1978).

[410] *Id.* at 601.

[411] *Id.* at 605.

[412] *Godfrey v. Georgia,* 446 U.S. 420, 426 (1980).

[413] *Id.* at 433.

[414] *Lockett v. Ohio,* 438 U.S. 586, 602 (1978)

[415] Stevens, *Book Review.*

Chapter X.

[416] *Enmund v. Florida,* 458 U.S. 782, 816-17 (1982)(dissenting opinion).

[417] *Id.* at 808 (quoting the statute).

[418] 458 U.S. 782 (1982).

[419] *Id.* at 803 n. 5 (dissenting opinion)

[420] *Id.* at 805 (dissenting opinion).

[421] *Id.* at 806 and 824 n. 40.

[422] *Id. at* 802 (majority opinion).

[423] *Id.* at 785-87.

[424] *Id.* at 785-86.

[425] *Id.* at 791.

[426] *Id.* at 822 (dissenting opinion).

[427] *Id.* at 823 (dissenting opinion).

[428] *Id.* at 797.

[429] *Ex Parte United States,* 242 U.S. 27, 42 (1916), reaffirmed in *Chapman v. United States,* 500 U.S. 453 (1991).

[430] *Enmund v. Florida,* 458 U.S. 782, 799 (1982).

[431] *Id.* at 800.

[432] *Id.* at 800 n. 24.

[433] *Id.* at 799.

[434] *Id.* (emphasis added).

[435] *Tison v. Arizona,* 481 U.S. 137, 139-41 (1987)

[436] *Id.* at 143.

[437] *Id.* at 138.

[438] *Id.* at 157-58.

[439] Blackstone's *Commentaries on The Law,* Book IV pp. 759-60 (Gavit Ed. 1941).

[440] *Thompson v. Oklahoma,* 487 U.S. 815, 864 (1988)(dissenting opinion)

[441] *Id.,* citing Streib, Death Penalty For Children, 36 Okla. L. Rev. 613, 619 (1983).

[442] *Thompson v. Oklahoma,* 487 U.S. 815, 862 (1988) (dissenting opinion).

[443] *Id.* at 819.

[444] *Id.*

[445] *Id.* at 463-64.

[446] *Id.* at 818 n.*.

[447] *Id.* at 865-66 (Scalia, J., dissenting).

[448] *Id.*

[449] *Id. at* 868 (Scalia, J., dissenting).

[450] *Id.* at 825 & n. 23 & Appendices A, B, C, & D (pp. 839-45).

[451] *Id.* at 837.

[452] *Id.* at 862.

[453] *Id.* at 821 (plurality opinion) quoting *Trop v. Dulles*, 356 U.S. 86, 101 (1958).

[454] *Stanford v. Kentucky*, 492 U.S. 361, 365 (1989).

[455] *Id.* at 367.

[456] *Id.* at 369.

[457] *Roper v. Simmons*, 543 U.S. 551 (2005); for the overruling of *Stanford, see* 574.

[458] *Id.* at 619 (dissenting opinion).

[459] *Id.* at 556-57 (majority opinion); see also facts at 600-01 (dissenting opinion).

[460] *Id.* at 557.

[461] *Id.* at 558.

[462] *Id.* at 572.

[463] *Id.* at 619.

[464] *Id.* at 571.

[465] *Id.* at 564 & Appendix A.

[466] *Id.* at 567.

[467] *Id.* at 574.

[468] *Id.* at 569-70 (emphasis added).

[469] *Id.* at 561-62.

[470] *Id.* at 556.

[471] *Id.* at 569.

[472] *Id.* at 619.

[473] *Id.* at 574-75; see also 563.

[474] http://law.jrank.org/pages/12110/Moral-Religious-Influences-Deciding-on-capital-crimes.html (visited on 2/15/11).

[475] *Coker v. Georgia*, 433 U.S. 584, 593 (1977).

[476] *Id.* at 605, 607n. 4, & 608n. 2.

[477] *Id.* at 592.

[478] *Id.* at 597-98.

[479] *Id.* at 587.

[480] *Id.* at 593n.4.

[481] *Id.*

[482] *Id.* at 599 n.15.

[483] *Id.* at 596

[484] *Id.*

[485] *Id.*

[486] *Id.* at 597.

[487] *Kennedy v. Louisiana,* 128 S.Ct. 2641, 2650-51 (2008).

[488] *Id.* at 2646.

[489] *Id.* at 2646.

[490] *Id.*

[491] *Id.* at 2648.

[492] *Id.* at 2658.

[493] *Id.* at 2650.

[494] That only 455 rapists were executed for rape between 1930-1964 (*id.* at 2651) although many multiples of that number were convicted of rape, exemplifies this Country's restraint and lack of brutality, in carefully limiting the death penalty to those few who, like Kennedy, clearly deserve it.

[495] *Id.* at 2661.

[496] *Kennedy v. Louisiana,* 128 S.Ct. 2641, 2653 (2008).

[497] http://www.pollingreport.com/crime.htm (visited 9/17/10).

[498] *Kennedy v. Louisiana,* 128 S. Ct. 2641, 2651-52 (2008).

[499] See Statement By Justice Scalia, on denial of rehearing (Oct. 1, 2008).

[500] *Kennedy v. Louisiana,* 128 S.Ct. 2641, 2652 (2008).

[501] *Id.* at 2658.

[502] *Id.*

[503] *Id.* at 2659.

[504] *Id.* at 2660.

[505] *Id.* at 2669 n. 2 (dissenting opinion).

[506] *Id.* at 2661.

[507] *Id.*

[508] 492 U.S. 302 (1989).

[509] *Id.* at 307.

[510] *Id.* at 307-08.

[511] *Id.* at 310.

[512] *Jurek v. Texas,* 428 U.S. 262 (1976).

[513] 492 U.S. at 310.

[514] *Id.* at 326-27.

[515] *Id.* at 325.

[516] *Id.* at 323-24.

[517] *Id.* at 331.

[518] *Id.* at 323.

[519] www.thefreedictionary.com/ (visited on January 24, 2011)(emphasis added).

[520] *Atkins v. Virginia,* 536 U.S. 304, 338 (2002)(dissenting opinion).

[521] *Id.* at 339.

[522] *Id.* at 339.

[523] *Id.* at 338-39.

[524] Two juries were required because the first jury had been given a technically incorrect verdict form. *Id.* at 309.

[525] *Id.* at 339.

[526] *Id.* at 322.

[527] *Id.* at 312.

[528] *Id.* at 312-13.

[529] *Id.* at 319-20.

[530] *Atkins v. Virginia,* 536 U.S. 304, 319 (2002).

[531] *Gregg v. Georgia,* 428 U.S. 153, 183 n. 28 (1976), reaffirmed more recently in *Graham v. Florida,* 130 S. Ct. 2011, 2028-29 (2010).

[532] 477 U.S. 399 (1986).

[533] *Id.* at 401.

[534] *Id.* at 402-03.

[535] *Id.* at 403-04.

[536] *Id.* at 404.

[537] *Id.* at 405, citing *Solesbee v. Balkcom,* 339 U.S. 9 (1950).

[538] 477 U.S. at 405.

[539] *Id.* at 410.

[540] *Atkins v. Virginia,* 536 U.S. 304, 353 (2002)(dissenting opinion).

[541] *Ford v. Wainwright,* 477 U.S. 399, 431 (dissenting opinion).

[542] *Id.* at 416 (plurality opinion).

[543] *Id.* at 429 (O'Connor, J., concurring).

[544] *Panetti v. Quarterman,* 551 U.S. 930 (2007).

[545] *Id.* at 935-36.

[546] *Id.* at 936-37.

[547] *Id.* at 937.

[548] *Id.* at 937-38.

[549] *Id.* at 971 (dissenting opinion).

[550] *Id.* at 940.

[551] *Id.* at 954-55.

[552] *Id.* at 956 (quoting with approval from *Ford v. Wainright, supra,* at 409-10).

[553] *Id.* at 957 (emphasis added).

[554] *McGautha v. California,* 402 U.S. 183, 310 (1971).

[555] *Furman v. Georgia,* 408 U.S. 238, 258 (Brennan, J), and 315 (Marshall, J.) (1972).

[556] *Id.* at 305 (Brennan, J., concurring).

[557] *Id.* at 329 (Marshall, j., concurring).

558 *Id.* at 362-63, 369.

559 *Gregg v. Georgia,* 428 U.S. 153, 232 (1976)(Marshall, J., dissenting opinion).

560 *Id.*

561 *Ayers v. Belmontes,* 127 S. Ct. 469 (2006).

562 *Id.* at 472.

563 *Id.*

564 *Kansas v. Marsh,* 548 U.S. 163, 188 (2006)(Scalia, J., concurring).

565 *Coleman v. Thompson,* 504 U.S. 188, 189 (1992).

566 Kansas v. *Marsh,* 548 U.S. 163, 189 (2006)(Scalia, J., concurring).

567 *Id.*

568 Lanier & Acker, *Capital Punishment, The Moratorium Movement and Empirical Questions,* 10 Psychology, Public Policy & Law 577 (2004)

569 *Id.* at 191-92 (Scalia, J., concurring).

570 *Id.* at 192.

571 *Herrera v. Collins,* 506 U.S. 430 n. 1 (1993)(Blackmun, J., dissenting, joined by Stevens and Souter, JJ.).

572 Joshua Marquis, *The Innocent and The Shammed,* N.Y. Times (Jan. 26, 2006).

573 Gross, Jacoby, Matheson, Montgomery & Patil, *Exonerations In The United States 1989 Through 2003,* 95 J. Crim. L. & C. 523 (2006)(hereinafter "Gross"), cited and discussed in *Kansas v. Marsh,* 548 U.S. 163, 194-95 (2006)(Scalia, J., concurring).

574 *Kansas v. Marsh,* 548 U.S. 163, 195-96 (2006)(Scalia, J., concurring).

575 Gross at p. 524.

576 Joshua Marquis, *The Innocent and the Shammed,"* N.Y. Times, Jan. 26, 2006, p. A23, quoted in *Kansas v. Marsh,* 548 U.S. 163, 197-98 (2006)(Scalia, J., concurring).

577 http://www.deathpenaltyinfo.org/documents/FactSheet.pdf (visited January 26, 2011).

578 http://www.aolnews.com/crime/article/ariz-prison-escapees-linked-to-nm-killings/19585107 (visited on 8/9/10).

579 *Furman v. Georgia,* 408 U.S. 238, 252 (1972).

580 *Coker v. Georgia,* 433 U.S. 584, 607 n. 4 (1977).

581 *Zant v. Stephens,* 462 U.S. 862, 864-65 (1983).

582 *Tison v. Arizona,* 481 U.S. 137, 139-41 (1987).

583 http://www.cbsnews.com/8301-50483_162-20025838-504083.html (visited on 12/17/10).

584 *Enmund v. Florida,* 458 U.S. 782, 799 (1982).

585 Stevens, *Book Review.*

[586] http://www.sef-defender.net/extras/kidnap/htm (visited 9/17/10).

[587]http://www.trutv.com/library/crime/criminal_mind/psychology/child_abducti on/8.html (visited 9/17/10).

[588] *Gregg v. Georgia*, 428 U.S. 153 (1976)(2+ years from crime to Supreme Court decision); *Coker v. Georgia*, 433 U.S. 584 (1977)(same); *Godfrey v. Georgia*, 446 U.S. 420 (1980)(same).

[589] *E.g., Tennard v. Dretke*, 542 U.S. 274 (2004)(18+ years); *Ayers v. Belmontes*, 127 S.Ct. 469 (2006)(25 years); *Panetti v. Quarterman*, 551 U.S. 930 (2007)(15 years).

[590] Burger, *What's Wrong With The Courts: The Chief Justice Speaks Out*, U.S. News & World Report Vol. 69, No. 8, p. 68, 71 (Aug. 24, 1970).

[591] Stevens, *Book Review*.

Chapter XI.

[592] *Williams v. Oklahoma*, 353 U.S. 576, 586 (1959).

[593] Wall St. Journal, *"Norway Killer Deemed Sane, Jailed 21 Years," August 25-26, 2012, p. A9.*

[594] *Spencer v. Texas*, 385 U.S. 554, 559 (1967). Although two Justices there dissented on procedural grounds, the nine Justices were again unanimous in affirming the constitutionality of recidivist statutes.

[595] http://realcostofprisons.org/blog/archives/2009/08/prisons_not_the.html (visited 2/8/2011)

[596] *Id.*

[597] *Moore v. Missouri*, 159 U.S. 673, 678 (1895).

[598] *Graham v. West Virginia*, 224 U.S. 616 (1912).

[599] *Rummel v. Estelle*, 445 U.S. 263, 266 (1980).

[600] *Id.* at 281-82.

[601] *Id.* at 287-88 (dissenting opinion).

[602] *Id.* at 303, in part quoting from *Erie R. Co. v. Tompkins*, 304 U.S. 64, 78-79 (1938).

[603] *Id.* at 307.

[604] *Id.*

[605] *Solem v. Helm*, 483 U.S. 277, 305 (1983)(dissenting opinion).

[606] *Id.* at 280-81 (majority opinion).

[607] *Id.* at 296.

[608] *Id.* at 303. This new majority's attempt to distinguish the facts in the *Rummel* decision (upholding a life term for a recidivist who committed four fewer felonies) on the ground that the life sentence in *Rummel* allowed parole,

while this life sentence did not, is not the least bit persuasive; the Constitution does not make opportunity for parole a Constitutional right – it is a matter of legislative judgment.

[609] *Id.* at 317-18 (dissenting opinion), quoting from *Boddie v. Connecticut*, 401 U.S. 371, 393 (1971)(Black, J. dissenting).

[610] *Harmelin v. Michigan*, 501 U.S. 957 (1991).

[611] *Id.* at 965.

[612] *Id.* at 967.

[613] *Rummel v. Estelle*, 445 U.S. 263, 272 (1980)(emphasis added).

[614] *Kennedy v. Louisiana*, 128 S. Ct. 2641, 2661 (2008).

[615] *Rummel, supra*, 445 U.S. at 275-76.

[616] *Hutto v. Davis*, 454 U.S. 370, 373 (1982)(*per curiam*), quoting from *Rummel, supra*, 445 U.S. at 275 (emphasis added).

[617] *Roper v. Simmons*, 543 U.S. 551, 572 (2005).

[618] *Graham v. Florida*, 130 S. Ct. 2011 (2010). Chief Justice Roberts, concurring in the judgment but not in the opinion, expressly rejected the absolute-bar ruling of the five Justices.

[619] *Graham v. Florida*, 130 S. Ct. 2011, 2018 (2010).

[620] *Id.* at 2018-19.

[621] *Id.* at 2020.

[622] *Id.*

[623] *Id.* at 2029.

[624] *Id.*

[625] *Id.*

[626] *Id.* at 2029-30.

[627] *Graham v. Florida*, 130 S. Ct. 2011, 2048 (2010)(Thomas, J., dissenting).

[628] *Id.* at 2041 (Roberts, CJ., concurring).

[629] *Id.* at 2051, (Thomas, J., dissenting).

[630] *Id.* at 2029 (majority opinion).

[631] *Id.* at 2031.

[632] *Id.* at 2032 (emphasis added), quoting from *Roper v. Simmons*, 543 U.S. 551, 572-73 (2005).

[633] Wall St. Journal, Oct. 29, 2010, p. A3.

[634] *United States v. C.R.*, No. 09CR155 (E.D.N.Y. May 16, 2011)(Weinstein, J.)

[635] *Miller v. Alabama*, 132 S. Ct. 2455 (2012).

[636] *Id.* at 2462.

[637] *Id.* at 2475.

[638] *Id.* at 2461.

[639] *Id.* at 2462-63.

[640] *Id.* at 2461-62.

[641] *Id.* at 2470.

[642] *Id.* at 2473.

[643] N.Y. Times, *Juvenile Killers and Life Terms: A Case In Point,*" Oct. 14, 2012, p. A1.

[644] *Id.*

[645] *Id.*

[646] *E.g., Kennedy v. Louisiana,* 554 U.S. 407, 438 (2008).

[647] *Bell v. Wolfish,* 441 U.S. 520, 525-26 (1979).

[648] *Id.* at 548.

[649] *Id.* at 562.

[650] *Rhodes v. Chapman,* 452 U.S. 337, 350 (1981).

[651] *Lewis v. Casey,* 518 U.S. 343 (1996).

[652] *Id.* at 349.

[653] *Id.* at 350.

[654] *Brown v. Plata,* 131 S. Ct. 1910, 1923 (2011).

[655] *Id.*

[656] See p. [9] *supra.*

[657] *Brown, supra* at 1965-66 (Alito, J., dissenting).

[658] *Id.* at 1967.

[659] *Id.* at 1941.

[660] *Id.* at 1942 (emphasis added).

[661] *Id.* at 1966 & n. 11.

[662] *Id.* at 1923.

[663] *Id.* at 1926-27.

[664] See, *e.g., The Health System Is Broken Beyond Repair,* by Dr. Agon Fly (Sept. 11, 2008) at http://www.themoneyforlifeblog.com/the-health-care-system-isbrokenbeyond/repair/ visited 2/10/12.

[665] *Physicians and Rural America,*" by Roger A. Rosenblatt & L. Gary Hart (Nov. 2000) at http://www.ncbi.nlm.nih.gov/pmc/articles/PMC1071163/ visited 2/10/12.

[666] *Id.*

[667] *Brown,* at 1925.

[668] *Lewis v. Casey, supra,* 518 U.S. at 349.

Chapter XII.

[669]http://www.revolutionary-war-and-beyond.com/samuel-adams-quotes-2.html (visited 8/4/12), in a letter to John Scollay (April 30, 1776)

[670670] *Id.*, the first in a letter to John Trumbull (Oct. 16, 1778); the second in a letter to James Warren (Feb. 12, 1779)

[671] 1 Journals Of The Continental Congress 108 (1774), quoted in the appendix to *United States v. Roth*, 237 F.2d 796 (2d Cir. 1956).

[672] http://www.ohio.edu/foundersday/essay.cfm (visited Aug. 8, 2012).

[673] http://www.wallbuilders.com/libissuesarticles.asp?id=63 (visited Aug. 8, 2012): Letter to Zabdiel Adams (June 21, 1776).

[674] *Id.*, IX John Adams, *The Works Of John Adams*, Edited by Charles Francis Adams (Boston: Little Brown 1854) p. 229

[675] *Id.*, Letter to James McHenry (Nov. 4, 1800).

[676] *Id.*, X Benjamin Franklin, *The Writings Of Benjamin Franklin, Edited By Jared Sparks (Boston: Tappan, Whittemore and Mason (1840) p. 297.*

[677] *Id.*, Letter to Col. Mortin Pickett (March 5. 1786).

[678] *Id.*, Benjamin Rush, *Essays, Literary, moral and* Philosophical (Philadelphia: Thomas and William Bradford, 1806) p. 8.

[679] *Id.*, George Washington, *Address Of George Washington* (Baltimore: George and Henry S. Keatinge), pp. 22-23.

[680] http://www.wallbuilders.com/libissuesarticles.asp?id=63 (visited Aug. 8, 2012).

[681]

http:///www.famguardian.org/Subjects/Politics/ThomasJefferson/jeff0250.htm (visited 7/2/12): Jefferson to John Langdon (1810).

[682] *Id.* at Jefferson's Reply to Philadelphia Democratic Republicans (1808).

[683] *Ex Parte Jackson*, 96 U.S. 727, 736 (1877).

[684] *Mugler v. Kansas*, 123 U.S. 623, 660-61 (1887).

[685] *Near v. Minnesota*, 283 U.S. 697 (1931).

[686] *Swearingen v. United States*, 161 U.S. 446, 450 (1896).

[687] *Kovacs v. Cooper*, 336 U.S. 77, 83 (1949).

[688] *Olmstead v. United States*, 277 U.S. 438, 478 (1928)(Brandeis, J., dissenting).

[689] *Schiro v. Clark*, 963 F.2d 962, 965-66 (7th Cir. 1992).

[690] *Id.* at 973.

[691] *Id.* at 971.

[692] *Id.* at 972.

[693] *Id.*

[694] Eberstadt & Layden, *The Social Costs Of Pornography* 9 (Witherspoon Institute 2010)

[695] *Id.* at 9-10.

[696] *Id.* at 24.

[697] *Id.* at 30-36.

[698] *Ginzburg v. United States*, 383 U.S. 463, 467 (1966).

[699] *Id.* at 485 & n. 4 (Douglas, J., dissenting).

[700] *Id.* at 485.

[701] *Id.*

702

http://facebook.com/EndMegansLaw/posts/381239339476?comment_id=0&to
talcomments=6 (visited 8/1/12).

http://www.boomantribune.com/story/2007/4/15/162717/286 (visited 8/1/12).

[703] http://www.tc150.com/content/camp-sky-topcamp-summerlane (visited 8/1/12).

[704] http://www.boomantribune.com/story/2007/4/28/11322/8079 (visited 8/1/12).

[705] *American Booksellers Association, Inc., v. Hudnut,* 771 F.2d 323, 329 (7th Cir. 1985).

[706] *Id.* at 330.

[707] *Id.* at 324, quoting Indianapolis Code § 16-3(q).

[708] *Chaplinsky v. State Of New Hampshire,* 315 U.S. 568, 571-72 (1942).

[709] 771 F.2d at 330.

[710] Eberstadt & Layden, *supra,* at pp. 13-14.

[711] *Id.* at 27-29.

[712] *Id.* at 28-29.

[713] Joseph Tartakovsky, *Bookshelf,* Wall Street Journal, August 13, 2010, p. A15, reviewing *Sex And The University,* by Daniel Reimold.

[714] http://www.dailymail.co.uk/news/article-2297168/University-pulls-Sex-week-funding-outrage-state-paying-events (visited March 21, 2013).

[715] http://www.newsnet5.com/dpp/news/education/Vagina-billboard-controversy-Groups-post-12-vagina-photographs-on-University-of-Cincinnati-campus (visited March 24, 2013).

[716] http://www.time.com/time/nation/article/0,8599,1855842,00.html (visited 7/1/12)

[717] http://www.ncbi.nlm.nih.gov/pubmed/20805150 (visited 7/29/12).

[718] Chandra, *Does Watching Sex On Television Predict Teen Pregnancy? Findings From A National Longitudinal Survey Of Youth,* published in 122 *Pediatrics,* No.5 (Nov. 1, 2008)

[719] New York Times, *A Hush-Hush Topic No More,* Feb. 27, 2013.

[720] http://www.harvard.edu/academic-experience (visited March 24, 2013).

[721] New York Times, *A Hush-Hush Topic No More,* Feb. 27, 2013.

[722] http://www.harvard.edu/harvard-glance (visited Feb. 27, 2013)

[723] Eric Spitznagel, *Interview With Raquel Welch,* Men's Health Magazine, http://www.menshealth.com/print/33528 (visited March 12, 2012).

[724] *Miller v. California,* 413 U.S. 15, 35-36 (1973).

[725] *Ex Parte Jackson,* 96 U.S. at 736.

[726] Story, *Commentaries On The Constitution* § 1874 (1833).

[727] *Near v. Minnesota,* 283 U.S. 697, 708 (1931).

[728] *E.g.,* Securities Act Of 1933, section 5; Securities Exchange Act Of 1934,

section 10b.

[729] *Chaplinsky v. State Of New Hampshire*, 315 U.S. 568, 571-72 (1942)

[730] *Roth v. United States*, 354 U.S. 476, 481, 484 (1957).

[731] *Chaplinsky v. State Of New Hampshire*, 315 U.S. 568, 571-72 (1942).

[732] *Id.* at 512 (Douglas, J. and Black, J., dissenting).

[733] *Id.*

[734] *Id.* at 34.

[735] http://thesaurus.com/browse/obscenity (visited 8/9/12). Our courts generally employ the word "obscenity," rather than "pornography," likely because the latter word did not appear in the English language until 1857 (http://www.takeoutword.com/TOW142/page2.html), by which date our laws and courts had started to use "obscenity."

[736] *United States v. Roth*, 237 F.2d 796, 798 (2d Cir. 1956), *reversed on other grounds*, 354 U.S. 476 (1957); see also 237 F.2d at 804 (Frank, J., concurring).

[737] *Roth v. United States*, 354 U.S. 476, 482-83 (1957).

[738] *Id.*

[739] *Id.* at 484-85.

[740] http://treaties.un.org/pages/ViewDetails.aspx?src=TREATY&mtdsg_no=VIII-5&chapter=8&lang=en (visited on 6/30/12)

[741] 3 Q.B. 360 (Court of the Queen's Bench 1868).

[742] *Id.*

[743] *Ex Parte Jackson*, 96 U.S. 727, 736-37 (1877).

[744] *Rosen v. United States*, 161 U.S. 29 (1896).

[745] *Id.* at 31.

[746] *Id.* at 42.

[747] *Id.* at 43.

[748] *Regina v. Hicklin, supra.*

[749] *Jacobellis v. Ohio*, 378 U.S. 184, 195-96 (1064) (majority opinion).

[750] *A Book Named "John Cleland's Memoirs Of A Woman Of Pleasure" v. Attorney General of Massachusetts*, 383 U.S. 413 (1966) (hereinafter "Woman of Pleasure")

[751] *Id.* at 419.

[752] *Id.* at 423 (Douglas, J., concurring).

[753] *Id.* at 445-46 (Clark, J., dissenting).

[754] Psalm 82:4.

[755] *New York v. Ferber*, 458 U.S. 747, 776 (1982)(Brennan, J., & Marshall, J., concurring).

[756] 378 U.S. at 194.

[757] *Roth v. United States, supra*, 354 U.S. at 490.

[758] *Id.* at 191.

[759] *Regina v. Hicklin, supra.*

[760] *Id.*

[761] *Jacobellis v. Ohio, supra,* 378 U.S. at 191. Although the Court asserts in that opinion that it was quoting the "test for obscenity enunciated" in *Roth,* a reading of *Roth* shows that the Court was merely quoting, without evaluation, those words used by some lower courts.

[762] http://www.merriam-webster.com/dictionary/prurient (visited 8/7/12).

[763] http://www.merriam-webster.com/medical/erotic (visited 8/7/12).

[764] *Woman Of Pleasure, supra,* 383 U.S. at 419.

[765] *Rosen v. United States,* 161 U.S. 29, 43 (1896)

[766] *Jacobellis v. Ohio, supra,* 378 U.S. 184, 191, asserts that this test was "enunciated" in the 1957 *Roth* decision, although, in fact, the opinion merely mentioned it as the test used by some lower courts, without adopting it.

[767] *Woman Of Pleasure, supra,* 383 U.S. at 419 (emphasis in original).

[768] Peggy Noonan, *The Captain and the King,* Wall St. Journal, Jan. 8-9, 2011, p. 13.

[769] *Miller v. California,* 413 U.S. 15, 24 (1973).

[770] *Id.* at 18.

[771] *Id.* at 21-22.

[772] *Id.* at 19.

[773] *Id.* at 24.

[774] *Id.* at 30-31.

Chapter XIII.

[775] *Paris Adult Theater I v. Slaton,* 413 U.S. 49, 106-07 (1973)(dissent), quoting with approval from Yale Law School Professor Thomas Emerson in his book *The System Of Freedom Of Expression.*

[776] *Redrup v. New York,* 386 U.S. 767, 769 (1967).

[777] *Erznoznik v. City Of Jacksonville,* 422 U.S. 205, 206-07 (1975).

[778] *Kovacs v. Cooper,* 336 U.S. 77, 86-87 (1949).

[779] *Packer Corp. v. Utah,* 285 U.S. 105, 110 (1932).

[780] *Erznoznik v. City of Jacksonville, supra,* 422 U.S. at 212.

[781] *Id.*

[782] *Erznoznik v. City of Jacksonville, supra,* 422 U.S. at 209.

[783] *Id.* at 213.

[784] *Id.* at 223 (dissenting opinion).

[785] *Id.* 214-15 (majority opinion).

[786] *Kovacs v. Cooper,* 336 U.S. 77, 87 (1949).

[787] *New York v. Ferber,* 458 U.S. 747, 776 (1982)(Brennan, J. & Marshall, J., concurring).

[788] *Osborne v. Ohio,* 495 U.S. 103, 108 (1990).

[789] *Ashcroft v. Free Speech Coalition,* 535 U.S. 234, 241-42 (2002)

[790] 1 Attorney General's Commission on Pornography, Final Report 649 (1986), quoted in *Osborne v. Ohio,* 495 U.S. 103, 111n. 7 (1990).

[791] *Ashcroft v. Free Speech Coalition, supra,* 535 U.S. at 241.

[792] *Id.* at 242.

[793] *Munn v. State of Illinois,* 94 U.S. 113, 132-33 (1876).

[794] *Jacobson v. Commonwealth of Massachusetts,* 197 U.S. 11, 30 (1905).

[795] *Tanner v. Little,* 240 U.S. 369, 385 (1916).

[796] *Mugler v. Kansas,* 123 U.S. 623, 660-61 (1887).

[797] *Ashcroft v. Free Speech Coalition,* 535 U.S. at 419.

[798] *Id.* at 240.

[799] *Id.* at 247-48.

[800] *Id.* at 250.

[801] *Id.* at 251.

[802] *Id.* at 250.

[803] *Red Lion Broadcasting Co. v. FCC,* 395 U.S. 367, 390 (1969).

[804] *Id.* at 395, 400.

[805] *National Broadcasting Co. v. United States,* 319 U.S. 190, 205-06, 217 (1943).

[806] 18 U.S.C. § 1464.

[807] 56 F.C.C.2d at 98, quoted in *FCC v. Pacifica Foundation,* 438 U.S. 726, 731-32 (1978).

[808] *FCC v. Pacifica Foundation,* 438 U.S. 726, 748-49 (1978)(hereinafter "*Pacifica*").

[809] *Pacifica,* 438 U.S. at 749.

[810] *Pacifica,* at 729-30.

[811] *FCC v. Fox Television Stations, Inc.,* 129 S. Ct. 1800 (2009)("*Fox I*").

[812] *Id.* at 1808.

[813] *Id.*

[814] *Id.* at 1809.

[815] *Id.* at 1813.

[816] When the case was returned to the Supreme Court following the Court of Appeals' ruling, the Supreme Court did not consider its substantive constitutionality, but held only that it could not be enforced since the broadcasters had never been given fair notice of what the FCC expected of them. *FCC v Fox Television Stations, Inc. ("Fox II"),* 132 S. Ct. 2307 (2012).

[817] *Fox I* at 1819.

[818] *Id.* at 1829 (Ginsburg, J., dissenting).

[819] *Fox Television Studios, Inc. v. FCC,* 489 F.3d 444, 462 & 461 (2d Cir. 2007).

[820] *Fox I* at 1819 (majority opinion).

[821] *Id.* at 1827 (Stevens, J., dissenting).

[822] http://www.thefreedictionary.com/shit (visited August 4, 2012).

[823] *United States v. Stevens,* 130 S. Ct. 1577, 1598 (2010)(Alito, J., dissenting).

[824] *Id.* at 1583 (majority opinion).

[825] *Chaplinsky v. State Of New Hampshire,* 315 U.S. 568, 572 (1942).

[826] 18 U.S.C. §48.

[827] H.R. Rep. No. 106-397, pp. 2-3 (1999).

[828] *United States v. Stevens, supra,* at 1585.

[829] Quoted in *id.*

[830] *Id.* at 1583.

[831] *Id.*

[832] *Id.*

[833] *Id.* at 1586.

[834] *Id.* at 1584.

[835] *Id.* at 1589.

[836] *Brown v. Entertainment Merchants Association,* 131 S. Ct. 2729, 2749-50 (2011)(Alito, J. & Roberts, CJ., concurring). Justice Alito and Chief Justice Roberts concurred solely on the ground that the specific California statute was not drafted in a manner to avoid Constitutional problems, although they applauded future "legislative efforts to deal with ... a significant and developing social problem." 131 S. Ct. at 2751.

[837] *Id.* at 2742 (Alito, J. & Roberts, CJ, concurring).

[838] California Civil Code § 1746.1.(a), (c).

[839] *Id.* § 1746.1.(b).

[840] *Id.* § 1746.(d)(1)(B).

[841] In *Ginsberg v. New York,* 390 U.S. 629 (1968), discussed at pp. [ ] *supra.*

[842] California Civil Code § 1746.(d)(1)(A).

[843] *Brown v. Entertainment Merchants Association, supra,* at 2767(Breyer, J., dissenting).

[844] *Id.* at 2767-69.

[845] Quoted at *id.* at 2769.

[846] Quoted at *id.* at 2769-70.

[847] *New York v. Farber,* 458 U.S. 747, 756-57 (1982), quoting, in part, from *Globe Newspaper Co. v. Superior Court,* 457 U.S. 596, 607 (1982)

[848] *Brown, supra.* at 2736-37 (majority opinion).

[849] *Id.* at 2734.

[850] *Id.* at 2738.

[851] *Id.* at 2741.

[852] http://www.nydailynews.com/news/national/exclusive-mind-newtown-killer-article-1.1223612 (visited Dec. 23, 2012).

[853] http://www.youplaytime.com/playfreegame/1167/kindergarten-killer.html#top (visited Dec. 23, 2012)

[854] http://www.nydailynews.com/news/national/exclusive-mind-newtown-

killer-article-1.1223612 (visited Dec. 23, 2012).

[855] *Chaplinsky v. State Of New Hampshire*, 315 U.S. 568, 571-72 (1942).

[856] http://www.gallup.com/poll/1588/children-violence.aspx (visited Dec. 23, 2012).

Chapter XIV

[857] *Legal Services Corp. v. Velazquez*, 531 U.S. 533, 536 (2001).

[858] *Id.* at 538.

[859] 42 U.S.C. § 2996(5).

[860] *Id.*, quoting § 504(a)(16) of the Appropriations Act of 1996, 110 Stat. 1321-53.

[861] *Maher v. Roe*, 432 U.S. 464, 474 (1977).

[862] *Id.*

[863] *Regan v. Taxation With Representation Of Wash.*, 461 U.S. 540 (1983).

[864] *Id.* at 546.

[865] *Id.* at 548.

[866] *Lyng v. Automobile Workers*, 485 U.S. 360, 373 (1988).

[867] *National Endowment For The Arts v. Finley*, 524 U.S. 569 (1998), quoting 20 U.S.C. § 954(d)(1).

[868] *Id.* at 588.

[869] *Railroad Retirement Board v. Alton R. Co.*, 295 U.S. 330, 362 (1935).

[870] http://www.thefreedictionary.com/compromise (visited Oct. 21, 2012).

[871] http://www.fed-soc.org/publications/detail/speech-by-judge-dennis-g-jacobs (visited Nov. 8, 2012).

[872] *Maher v. Roe*, 432 U.S. 464, 479 (1977).

[873] *Id.* at 479-80.

[874] *Planned Parenthood Association of Hidalgo County Texas v. Suehs*, No. 12-50377 (5th Cir. Aug. 21, 2012), quoting § 1(h), 2005 Tex. Gen. Laws at 2818.

[875] *Planned Parenthood Of Indiana*, No. 11, 2464 (7th Cir. Oct. 23, 2012).

[876] *Id.*, *slip opinion at p. 6.*

[877] *Id.*, at 6-7.

[878] *Id.*, at 24, quoting 42 F.F.R. § 431.51(c)(2).

[879] *Id.*, at 28, quoting S. Rep. No. 100-109, at 20 (1987)(emphasis added by the Court).

[880] *Id.*, at 29.

[881] *Id.*, at 46, quoting *Maher v. Roe*, 432 U.S. 464, 473 (1977).

5212812R00177

Made in the USA
San Bernardino, CA
28 October 2013